Illinois Central College
Learning Resources Center

The Penguin Book
of Women Poets

Edited by

Carol Cosman · Joan Keefe · Kathleen Weaver

The Penguin Book
of Women Poets

Consulting editors

Joanna Bankier · Doris Earnshaw · Deirdre Lashgari

The Viking Press · New York

Copyright © Carol Cosman, Joan Keefe, and Kathleen Weaver, 1978

Published in 1979 by The Viking Press
625 Madison Avenue, New York, N.Y. 10022

LIBRARY OF CONGRESS CATALOGING IN PUBLICATION DATA
Main entry under title:
The Penguin book of women poets.
Includes index.
1. Poetry—Women authors.
I. Cosman, Carol.   II. Keefe, Joan.   III. Weaver, Kathleen.
PN6109.9.P4   808.81   78-15342
ISBN 0-670-77856-7

Printed in the United States of America
Second printing July 1979
Set in Monotype Bembo
Acknowledgements for all copyright material used
are given on pages 383-396, which constitute an
extension of this copyright page.

TABLE OF CONTENTS

THE MIDDLE PERIOD 600–1500

THE RENAISSANCE AND ITS CONTEMPORARIES 1500–1800

THE NINETEENTH CENTURY

THE TWENTIETH CENTURY:
MODERNS AND CONTEMPORARIES

PERSONAL ACKNOWLEDGEMENTS

We gratefully acknowledge the work of the many people who helped put this book together, contributing translations, providing information about poets, and assisting in every way.

We would like to acknowledge the following contributors:

Jaako A. Ahokas prepared many translations of Finnish women poets, with biographies and literary histories. The Finnish presentation here is based on Mr Ahokas's work.

Tâlat S. Halman provided translations of the women poets of Turkey, a broad selection, again with biographies and literary background, enabling us to make a choice.

We would like to acknowledge the assistance of Bonnie R. Crown, Andrea Miller and Zelda Bradburd of the Educational Resources, Asian Literature Program of the Asia Society, New York, in collecting material for this volume. The Program was assisted by a grant from the National Endowment for the Humanities. The Asian Literature Program is now a programme of the Conference on World Affairs.

Nadia Christensen translated from Swedish, Danish and Norwegian, providing information about the women poets in those countries.

Hiroaki Sato and Professor Thomas Rimer of Washington University, St Louis, helped us find Japanese poets.

Gerald M. Moser, Pennsylvania State University, sent material on the Portuguese African poets, and helped with translation. H. G. Jones of *Présence africaine* also provided valuable assistance.

Judith Gleason translated a selection of traditional women's poetry from Africa and presented information about the role of women singers in African cultures. Lacking space we could include only one song from this material.

Susan C. Strong, Judy Wilkinson, and Allan Francovich also provided important help.

Special thanks to McGraw-Hill for their generous permission to reprint a large selection from *The Orchid Boat*, poems by Chinese women translated by Kenneth Rexroth and Ling Chung.

We are grateful to a number of people who advised us in our selections: to Lawrence Schneider, Professor of Chinese History at the State University of New York at Buffalo, for his patient counsel; to Nick Germanacos, translator, for his preliminary presentation of modern Greek poets; to Lynne Lawner, translator and scholar of Italian literature, for her time and effort in assembling a large portion of the Italian poetry, particularly that of the Renaissance women who are the subject of her forthcoming book.

We all owe an enormous debt of gratitude to Florence Mayer, our typist and sometime copy-editor, for her generous spirit and patient, not to say heroic, efforts.

This anthology could not have been compiled without the assistance of many people. The editors alone, however, are responsible for the final selections.

Finally, this book is indebted to earlier work on women poets that began in association with the Department of Comparative Literature, University of California, Berkeley. The consulting editors – JOANNA BANKIER, DORIS EARNSHAW, and DEIRDRE LASHGARI – formed an anthology group in 1972, in which the editors also participated, to collect and publish poetry by women. The group's research, which established the existence of an important body of poetry from many periods and cultures, is the foundation of this book. In joint collaboration we have also published *The Other Voice: Twentieth-Century Women's Poetry and Translation*, W. W. Norton & Co., Inc., 1976.

PREFACE

In 1755 an enterprising English editor published an anthology of women's poetry entitled *Poems by Eminent Ladies*. The preface to the book is a model of its kind – an elaborate apologia for producing such a book, for its limitations, for its size, for its omissions, indeed for its very existence. Every sentence, every phrase is hedged with humble modifiers. And yet this book is a selective and thoughtful representation of the poets' work. It includes the remarkable sexual frankness of Aphra Behn, the wit and intelligence of Ann Finch, the macabre imagination of Margaret Cavendish, and the down-to-earth realism of lesser-known poets who often wrote in spite of the disapproval of family and society. It is almost surprising that the anonymous editor, faced with such a wealth of humour and honesty, should have felt the need to resort to such statements as:

It will not be thought partiality to say that the reader will here meet with many pieces on a variety of subjects excellent in their way; and that this collection is not inferior to any miscellany compiled from the works of men.

In the course of two centuries a great deal of social and cultural change has taken place, yet in 1977 it seems still necessary to offer explanation and justification for an anthology of work by women. Many women now live lives in which the development of talent is not blocked by such enormous obstacles. More women are encouraged and confirmed in their pursuit of education, and some have even achieved what Virginia Woolf deemed necessary for the flowering of art and intellect: economic independence and 'a room of one's own'. Nevertheless, very real barriers – economic, social, and psychological – still stand in the way of production of art by women and the full acceptance of the woman artist.

Whatever the complicated determinants favouring the emergence of art, it cannot be denied that women artists have always had a special place defined by the fact of their sex. As long ago as the sixth–fifth century B.C. the Greek poet Corinna wrote, surely with some irony:

> I blame Myrtis,
> gifted though she is,
> that she, a woman,
> dared take on Pindar.

In nineteenth-century Europe, when the literary market expanded to meet the rising popular demand for fiction, public attitudes towards women writers moved some of the more successful – George Eliot, the Brontës, George Sand – to adopt male pseudonyms. The title 'poet' in common usage has always had an implicit masculine gender, while the feminine form 'poetess' rapidly acquired connotations of sentimentality and dilettantism. The stereotype of the poetess lingers on into our own time. The frontispiece of the Bianchi-Hampson edition (1930) of the poems of Emily Dickinson shows an artist's drawing of the poet based on the only existing photograph. The plainness and honesty of the photograph have been replaced by a highly romantic portrait. This bold trenchant poet has become a poetess. It does not come as a surprise that even today some women poets will not allow their work to appear in anthologies devoted exclusively to women (and thus to our regret are not represented in this book).

The tendency to consign women poets in general to second-class status has characteristically been accompanied by a neglect of their work. Even now, when more women than ever before are writing and publishing poetry and have made major contributions to almost every literature, anthologies of national poetries in English translation tend to include very few of them. This book, then, in the first instance, is a contribution to redressing the balance and a response to the current interest in women as artists. When the rich achievement of women poets is placed in a historical and comparative perspective, the solid reputations of poets such as Sappho, Louise Labé, Li Ching-chao, and Anna Akhmatova can only be enhanced, while many fine poets largely unknown to English readers will begin to receive the attention and recognition they deserve.

It would be difficult in the space of a short preface to describe the entire historical context and background of so many women poets. Nevertheless it cannot be forgotten that each one existed in a complicated tradition of language and literary convention at a particular historical moment. The abbess Hroswitha of Gandesheim in the tenth century wrote for the edification of her nuns, composing plays in Latin after the classical manner of Terence. The Chinese poet Li Ching-chao (eleventh–twelfth century, Sung dynasty) wrote *t'zus* which, like the *tanka* of Ono no Komachi (ninth-century Japan) and the sonnets of Gaspara Stampa, depend for their effect upon the expression of intense feeling within the bounds of a conventional form. Christine de Pisan in the fourteenth century became one of the first women to write for a living, that is, for the favour and protection of dukes and princes. In addition to the *rondeleaux, chansons*, and other verse composed in the accepted lyric modes of her time, she wrote many important works referring to contemporary political and literary issues, among them a defence of women in reply to Jean de Meung's misogynistic *Roman de la Rose*, and a poem in vindication of Joan of Arc. The women poets, then, belonged very much to their respective histories and traditions. Their collection into a single anthology must inevitably remove them from their immediate contexts, but the comparative view to be gained by the presentation in English of poetry from so many different languages and cultures is illuminating.

In this connection, it is fortunate that this book is appearing at a time of growing interest in foreign literatures which has given increasing impetus to the practice of poetic translation. With the proliferation of translations in recent years, of course, has come a growing awareness of the problems of translating poetry. Indeed these problems have been closely discussed in print by the proponents of various approaches. It is our view that a good poetic translation gives a faithful rendering of the meaning of the original poem, that it conveys a sense of the poet's individual emotion and style, that it is at the same time readable verse in its new form. For the versions of the poems included here we have turned to a wide range of poets, scholars and professional translators. Necessarily the translations are of many kinds: free-verse translations in the contemporary idiom, metrical and rhymed verse, some versions from earlier periods employing diction which might not be used today and others preserving the formal pattern of the originals. Necessity, then, provided the opportunity to present diverse translations which, while conveying the sense of the originals, succeed as readable, often extremely fine poems in English.

Despite our desire to represent as many literatures as possible we have not been able to include poetry from a number of cultures, and we have not included material for which adequate translations were not available. We have been conscious of the difficulty of spanning 3,500 years and representing almost forty literary traditions in a single volume. Limitations of space, therefore, have forced us to restrict our selection. Three main considerations have governed our choice of material: first, the desire to present a cross-cultural panorama by representing as many literatures as possible; second, the desire to be representative with respect to each literature; third and most important, the concern for literary excellence, against which the other factors were weighed. In determining the scope of this book, it was felt that the great wealth of oral poetry from traditional cultures was largely outside our purview. Anonymous poems in the main literary and folk tradition have been generally excluded except in the case of a few poems written in a woman's voice or transmitted by women singers and whose authorship is unknown or a matter of dispute. Again, for reasons of space, most of the younger contemporary poets have been excluded in order to make room for the preceding generations who are in greater danger of being neglected. We have chosen very sparingly among the contemporary poets altogether, aware of the great quantity of important poetry being written today.

When an anthology is intended to correct a long neglect the question of choice and presentation rests on the editors even more heavily than usual. The materials we have collected are by necessity quite varied, but we have tried to provide the sort of structure that would bring out the significant lines of connection and distinction among the various poets and literatures. The organization of the book according to chronological development seemed to us the logical way to achieve a comparative perspective and to avoid creating merely inadequate anthologies of the various national literatures. When poets of the same periods are placed side by side, whatever the differences in their respective traditions, suggestive similarities of genre and motif emerge. The lament, whether a formal elegy or a cry of personal desolation, is a form common to many literatures and in certain cultures seems to have been the province of women singers. A striking parallel exists, for example, between the seventh-century Bedouin poet Al-Khansâ's 'Elegy for her Brother' and the anonymous ninth-century Welsh poem 'Eagle of Pengwern'. Religious movements from the twelfth to the sixteenth centuries in the East and West are reflected in the devotional lyrics of the Indian poets Mahādēviyakka and Mira Bai, the Dutch religious mystic-poet Hadewijch, and Spain's Saint Theresa. In some instances, the similarities to be observed result directly from the fact that different national literatures participated in the same international literary movement. Thus, the sonnet form highly developed and widely practised in the European Renaissance was adapted by Gaspara Stampa in Italy, Louise Labé in France, and Sor Juana de la Cruz in colonial Mexico.

Out of this wealth of material we sought to create a book which would allow the reader to view women poets in new and mutually enlivening perspectives. There are several contexts that condition the work of every writer: national history, cultural milieu, individual experience. We have tried to illuminate the additional context of sexual identity as it may affect the poetry of women across the lines of time and culture. Women poets over the centuries have struggled for acceptance as artists. We hope that this book is presented in a way that permits each poem to be appreciated for its particular merits and each poet to speak in her own voice.

THE ANCIENT WORLD

Anonymous: Love Poems

(1567–1085 B.C.)

EGYPT

These versions, translated by Ezra Pound and Noel Stock, are based on literal translations of the hieroglyphic texts into Italian by Boris de Rachewiltz. Most of the original Egyptian texts have survived only in incomplete form, dating from 1567 to 1085 B.C.

With you here at Mertu
Is like being at Heliopolis already.

We return to the tree-filled garden,
My arms full of flowers.

Looking at my reflection in the still pool —
My arms full of flowers —
I see you creeping on tip-toe
To kiss me from behind,
My hair heavy with perfume.

With your arms around me
I feel as if I belong to the Pharaoh.

*

So small are the flowers of Seamu
Whoever looks at them feels a giant.

I am first among your loves,
Like a freshly sprinkled garden of grass and
    perfumed flowers.

Pleasant is the channel you have dug
In the freshness of the north wind.

Tranquil our paths
When your hand rests on mine in joy.

Your voice gives life, like nectar.

To see you, is more than food or drink.

*

There are flowers of Zait in the garden.
I cut and bind flowers for you,

Making a garland,
And when you get drunk
And lie down to sleep it off,
I am the one who bathes the dust from your feet.

★

I find my love fishing
His feet in the shallows.

We have breakfast together,
And drink beer.

I offer him the magic of my thighs
He is caught in the spell.

(translated from Italian by Ezra Pound and Noel Stock)

Anonymous: Song of Deborah

(*c.* 11th century B.C.)

ANCIENT ISRAEL (HEBREW)

The 'Song of Deborah', a victory song recounting the events narrated in Judges 5, is thought to be possibly the oldest piece of extended Israelite poetry in the Hebrew Bible. The authorship of the poem is not known, and there is some confusion about the verb-ending usually translated 'I', which would make the singer the prophetess and charismatic leader Deborah – who led her people to victory against the Canaanites. Many scholars are of the opinion that the song may have been composed shortly after the battle described and sung at the victory celebration.

SONG OF DEBORAH

Then sang Deborah and Barak the son of Abinoam on that day, saying,

2 Praise ye the Lord for the avenging of Israel, when people willingly offered themselves.

3 Hear, O ye kings; give ear, O ye princes; I, *even* I, will sing unto the Lord; I will sing *praise* to the Lord God of Israel.

4 Lord, when thou wentest out of Seir, when thou marchest out of the field of Edom, the earth trembled, and the heavens dropped, the clouds also dropped water.

5 The mountains melted from before the Lord, *even* that Sinai from before the Lord God of Israel.

6 In the days of Shamgar the son of Anath, in the days of Jael, the highways were unoccupied and the travellers walked through the byways.

7 *The inhabitants of* the villages ceased, they ceased in Israel, until that I Deborah arose, that I arose a mother in Israel.

8 They chose new gods; then *was* war in the gates; was there a shield or spear seen among forty thousand in Israel?

9 My heart *is* toward the governors of Israel, that offered themselves willingly among the people. Bless ye the Lord.

10 Speak, ye that ride on white asses, ye that sit in judgement, and walk by the way.

11 *They that are delivered* from the noise of the archers in the places of drawing water, there shall they rehearse the righteous acts of the Lord, *even* the righteous acts *toward the inhabitants* of his villages in Israel: then shall the people of the Lord go down to the gates.

12 Awake, awake, Deborah: awake, awake, utter a song: arise, Barak, and lead thy captivity captive, thou son of Abinoam.

13 Then he made him that remaineth have dominion over the nobles among the people: the Lord made me have dominion over the mighty.

14 Out of Ephraim *was there* a root of them against Amalek; after thee, Benjamin, among thy people; out of Machir came down governors, and out of Zebulun they that handle the pen of the writer.

15 And the princes of Issachar *were* with Deborah; even Issachar, and also Barak: he was sent on foot into the valley. For the divisions of Reuben *there were* great thoughts of heart.

16 Why abodest thou among the sheepfolds, to hear the bleatings of the flocks? For the divisions of Reuben *there were* great searchings of heart.

17   Gilead abode beyond Jordan: and why did Dan remain in ships? Asher continued on the sea shore, and abode in his breaches.

18   Zebulun and Naphtali *were* a people *that* jeoparded their lives unto the death in the high places of the field.

19   The kings came *and* fought, then fought the kings of Canaan in Taanach by the waters of Megiddo; they took no gain of money.

20   They fought from heaven; the stars in their courses fought against Sisera.

21   The river of Kishon swept them away, that ancient river, the river of Kishon. O my soul, thou hast trodden down strength.

22   Then were the horsehoofs broken by the means of the pransings, the pransings of their mighty ones.

23   Curse ye Meroz, said the angel of the Lord, curse ye bitterly the inhabitants thereof; because they came not to the help of the Lord, to the help of the Lord against the mighty.

24   Blessed above women shall Jael the wife of Heber the Kenite be, blessed shall she be above women in the tent.

25   He asked water, *and* she gave him *milk*; she brought forth butter in a lordly dish.

26   She put her hand to the nail, and her right hand to the workmen's hammer; and with the hammer she smote Sisera, she smote off his head, when she had pierced and stricken through his temples.

27   At her feet he bowed, he fell, he lay down: at her feet he bowed, he fell: where he bowed, there he fell down dead.

28   The mother of Sisera looked out at a window, and cried through the lattice, Why is his chariot *so* long in coming? why tarry the wheels of his chariots?

29   Her wise ladies answered her, yea, she returned answer to herself,

30   Have they not sped? have they *not* divided the prey; to every man a damsel *or* two? to Sisera a prey of divers colours of needlework, of divers colours of needlework on both sides, *meet* for the necks of *them that take* the spoil?

31 So let all thine enemies perish, O Lord: but *let* them that love him *be* as the sun when he goeth forth in his might. And the land had rest forty years.

(King James version)

Sappho
(6th century B.C.)

GREECE

Much legendary gossip without historical basis surrounds the story of Sappho's life. It can be fairly stated that she was a poet of high reputation and that young girls of birth and education came to the island of Lesbos where they studied under her tutelage and perhaps took part in a form of service dedicated to the goddess Aphrodite. All that is known with certainty of Sappho is the small body of poetry that exists today, and this confirms her place among the great poets.

People do gossip

And they say about
Leda, that she

once found an egg
hidden under

wild hyacinths

★

You know the place: then

Leave Crete and come to us
waiting where the grove is
pleasantest, by precincts

sacred to you; incense
smokes on the altar, cold
streams murmur through the

apple branches, a young
rose thicket shades the ground
and quivering leaves pour

down deep sleep; in meadows
where horses have grown sleek
among spring flowers, dill

scents the air. Queen! Cyprian!
Fill our gold cups with love
stirred into clear nectar

*

He is more than a hero

He is a god in my eyes —
the man who is allowed
to sit beside you – he

who listens intimately
to the sweet murmur of
your voice, the enticing

laughter that makes my own
heart beat fast. If I meet
you suddenly, I can't

speak – my tongue is broken;
a thin flame runs under
my skin; seeing nothing,

hearing only my own ears
drumming, I drip with sweat;
trembling shakes my body

and I turn paler than
dry grass. At such times
death isn't far from me

*

We put the urn aboard ship
with this inscription:

This is the dust of little
Timas who unmarried was led
into Persephone's dark bedroom

And she being far from home, girls
her age took new-edged blades
to cut, in mourning for her,
these curls of their soft hair

*

Don't ask me what to wear

I have no embroidered
headband from Sardis to
give you, Cleis, such as
I wore
        and my mother
always said that in her
day a purple ribbon
looped in the hair was thought
to be high style indeed

but we were dark:
                    a girl
whose hair is yellower than
torchlight should wear no
headdress but fresh flowers

*

I hear that Andromeda —

That hayseed in her hay-
seed finery – has put
a torch to your heart

and she without even
the art of lifting her
skirt over her ankles

(translated from Greek by Mary Barnard)

Corinna

(5th century B.C.)

GREECE

Of Tanagra in Boeotia, she was an older contemporary of the famous poet Pindar. Much of her poetry, of which only fragments survive, concerns local legends and shows great command of her craft.

FRAGMENTS

I

Terpsichore looks kindly on me
as I sing noble, heroic things
to the white-robed women of Tanagra,
and the city rejoices mightily
at the keen melody of my voice.

2

Will you sleep forever?
You were not like that, Corinna,
in the old days.

3

I blame Myrtis,
gifted though she is,
that she, a woman,
dared take on Pindar.

(translated from Greek by John Dillon)

Praxilla

(c. 450 B.C.)

GREECE

Praxilla of Sicyon was a product of Dorian Greek society, where women had a freer life than at Athens. She wrote hymns, drinking-songs and songs for choruses. Only a few fragments of her work have been preserved. The first fragment was quoted only as an example of how *not* to write poetry – 'sillier than Praxilla's Adonis' became proverbial among literary men.

FRAGMENTS

1. ADONIS, DYING

Loveliest of what I leave
               is the sun himself
Next to that the bright stars
               and the face of mother moon
Oh yes, and cucumbers in season,
               and apples, and pears.

2. Watch out, my dear,
               there's a scorpion under every stone.

3. Lovely girl, you look at me through the window,
   Your face a virgin's, all beneath a bride.

(translated from Greek by John Dillon)

Anonymous: from *Song of Songs*

(3rd century B.C.)

ANCIENT ISRAEL (HEBREW)

The 'Song of Songs', or 'Song of Solomon' as it is also called, was probably included in the canon of the Hebrew Bible as an allegory of Yahweh's love for his people Israel. According to most recent Old Testament scholarship, the 'Song of Songs' is a group of songs, not a unified poem or drama, collected around the third century B.C. from Jerusalem and the surrounding region. Some seem to have been composed for wedding festivities, others are simply love poems,

possibly cultic in origin. The three included here are spoken in the
woman's voice.

> Yes, I am black! and radiant —
> O city women watching me —
> As black as Kedar's goathair tents
> Or Solomon's fine tapestries.
>
> Will you disrobe me with your stares?
> The eyes of many morning suns
> Have pierced my skin, and now I shine
> Black as the light before the dawn.
>
> And I have faced the angry glare
> Of others, even my mother's sons
> Who sent me out to watch their vines
> While I neglected all my own.

Turning to him, who meets me with desire —

Come, love, let us go out to the open fields
And spend our night lying where the henna blooms,
Rising early to leave for the near vineyards
Where the vines flower, opening tender buds,
And the pomegranate boughs unfold their blossoms.

There among blossom and vine I will give you my love,
Musk of the violet mandrakes spilled upon us . . .
And returning, finding our doorways piled with fruits,
The best of the new-picked and the long-stored,
My love, I will give you all I have saved for you.

> Under the quince tree
>   you woke
>   to my touch
> there
>   where she conceived
>   where she who carried
>   and bore you
> conceived

> (translated from Hebrew by Marcia Falk)

Sulpicia

(*c.* 20 B.C.)

ROME (LATIN)

She is the only known Latin woman poet. Her father was a distinguished lawyer who lived in the time of Augustus and was a friend of Cicero. After her father's death she became the ward of a prominent statesman and patron of the arts, Valerius Messalla, around whom a group of poets had gathered. The most notable of these was Tibullus. She became an accomplished love-poet, mastering a considerable expertise in the conventions, which is allied in her work with genuine poetic feeling. The only poems of hers extant are those contained in this short sequence which are found at the end of a manuscript of Tibullus.

Drat my hateful birthday
           to be spent in the boring old country.
It's going to be a day of mourning
           without Cerinthus to hug.
Oh the joys of *city* life!
           Is a musty old country house
Any fit place for a girl?
           And that freezing river at Arezzo!
Please, sweet Messalla, relax,
           too anxious, as ever, for my comfort!
Banish this grim expedition
           totally out of your mind.
If I'm to be snatched away
           I'll leave heart and soul behind here,
Since I'm not to be granted
           licence to run my life.

                    *

I'm grateful, really grateful
           for the favour you've just done me.
You've saved me from being a fool,
           and rushing into your arms,

Go chasing whores as you will
                    seducing maids from their sewing,
So much better prospects, I'm sure,
                    than the daughter of Servius Sulpicius!
The main thing prompting
                    the *kind* friend who told on you
Was the pain of seeing me lose out
                    to a love-couch of no standing.

*

Let your longing for me, my love,
                    lose the heat of a few days ago
If I have ever before committed
                    in the whole of my youthful life
As stupid a mistake as this
                    or one I've regretted more.
I left you yesterday night,
                    ran off and left you alone —
Honestly, love, it was only
                    that I didn't dare show my passion.

(translated from Latin by John Dillon)

Ts'ai Yen

(*c.* A.D. 200)

CHINA

Traditionally she is considered the first great woman poet of China.
Her father was a writer and friend of Ts'ao Ts'ao, warlord of the
Three Kingdoms period. As a widow she was captured by the Huns
and taken to the north, where she became the concubine of a chieftain
and bore him two sons. Later Ts'ao Ts'ao ransomed her and married
her to one of his officers. Her two sons were left behind. The 'Tartars'
referred to in this translation were probably Huns.

from EIGHTEEN VERSES SUNG TO A TARTAR REED WHISTLE

1

I was born in a time of peace,
But later the mandate of Heaven
Was withdrawn from the Han Dynasty.

Heaven was pitiless.
It sent down confusion and separation.
Earth was pitiless.
It brought me to birth in such a time.
War was everywhere. Every road was dangerous.
Soldiers and civilians everywhere
Fleeing death and suffering.
Smoke and dust obscured the land
Overrun by the ruthless Tartar bands.
Our people lost their will power and integrity.
I can never learn the ways of the barbarians.
I am daily subject to violence and insult.
I sing one stanza to my lute and a Tartar horn.
But no one knows my agony and grief.

2

A Tartar chief forced me to become his wife,
And took me far away to Heaven's edge.
Ten thousand clouds and mountains
Bar my road home.
And whirlwinds of dust and sand
Blow for a thousand miles.
Men here are as savage as giant vipers,
And strut about in armour, snapping their bows.
As I sing the second stanza I almost break the lutestrings,
Will broken, heart broken, I sing to myself.

(translated from Chinese by Kenneth Rexroth
and Ling Chung)

Classic Tamil Love Poems

(1st–3rd centuries A.D.)

INDIA

These poems are among those selected by A. K. Ramanujan (editor
and translator of *The Interior Landscape*) from the Kuṟuntokai, one of
the earliest of the eight anthologies of classic Tamil – one of the two
classic languages of India – ascribed to the first three centuries A.D.
An entire body of mythology, including a Great Flood myth, has
grown up around these love poems written in a kind of blank verse,
but very little is known of the poets themselves, many of whom were
women.

My lover capable of terrible lies
at night lay close to me
in a dream
that lied like truth.

I woke up, still deceived,
and caressed the bed
thinking it my lover.

It's terrible. I grow lean
in loneliness,
like a water lily
gnawed by a beetle.

Kaccipēṭṭu Naṉṉākaiyār

WHAT SHE SAID

The rains, already old,
have brought new leaf upon the fields.
The grass spears are trimmed and blunted
by the deer.

The jasmine creeper is showing its buds
through their delicate calyx
like the laugh of a wildcat.

In jasmine country, it is evening
for the hovering bees,
but look, he hasn't come back.

He left me and went in search
of wealth.

Okkūr Mācātti

WHAT HER GIRL-FRIEND SAID TO HER

Come, let's go climb on that jasmine-mantled rock

and look

if it is only the evening cowbells
of the grass-fed contented herds
returning with the bulls

or the bells of his chariot
driving back through the wet sand of the
forest ways,
his heart full of the triumph of a job
well done,
with young archers driving by his side.

Okkūr Mācātti

WHAT SHE SAID TO HER GIRL-FRIEND

On beaches washed by seas
older than the earth,
in the groves filled with bird-cries,
on the banks shaded by a *puṇṇai*
clustered with flowers,
when we made love
my eyes saw him
and my ears heard him;

my arms grow beautiful
in the coupling
and grow lean
as they come away.

What shall I make of this?

Veṇmaṇippūṭi

(translated from Tamil by A. K. Ramanujan)

THE MIDDLE PERIOD 600–1500

Líadan

(7th century)

IRELAND

Líadan is said to have been an early seventh-century poet who rejected her lover Cuirithir and became a nun. Repenting her decision later, she went to Cuirithir, but he meanwhile had become a monk and fled across the sea from her. The story, told in ninth-century Irish, is preserved in sixteenth-century manuscripts.

LÍADAN LAMENTS CUIRITHIR

Joyless
what I have done:
to torment my darling one?

But for fear
of the Lord of Heaven
he would lie with me here.

Not vain,
it seemed, our choice,
to seek Paradise through pain.

I am Líadan,
I loved Cuirithir
as truly as they say.

The short time
I passed with him
how sweet his company!

The forest trees
sighed music for us;
and the flaring blue of seas.

What folly
to turn him against me
who had treated me most gently

No whim
or scruple of mine
should have come between

Us, for above
all others, without shame
I declare him my heart's love.

A roaring flame
has consumed my heart:
I will not live without him.

(translated from Irish by John Montague)

Anonymous
(9th century)

IRELAND

The Old Woman of Beare laments her lost youth and her dead
lovers. Beare is an island off the south coast of Ireland and may have
been connected with the cult of a mythological goddess of fertility
who was mother of races and tribes.

from THE HAG OF BEARE

Ebb tide has come for me:
My life drifts downwards
Like a retreating sea
With no tidal turn.

I am the Hag of Beare,
Fine petticoats I used to wear,
Today, gaunt with poverty,
I hunt for rags to cover me.

Girls nowadays
Dream only of money —
When we were young
We cared more for our men.

Riding over their lands
We remember how, like gentlemen,
They treated us well;
Courted, but didn't tell.

Today every upstart
Is a master of graft;
Skinflint, yet sure to boast
Of being a lavish host.

But I bless my King who gave —
Balanced briefly on time's wave —
Largesse of speedy chariots
And champion thoroughbreds.

These arms, now bony, thin
And useless to younger men,
Once caressed with skill
The limbs of princes! . . .

. . .

Alas, I cannot
Again sail youth's sea;
The days of my beauty
Are departed, and desire spent.

I hear the fierce cry of the wave
Whipped by the wintry wind.
No one will visit me today,
Neither nobleman nor slave.

I hear their phantom oars
As ceaselessly they row
And row to the chill ford,
Or fall asleep by its side.

Flood tide
And the ebb dwindling on the sand!
What the flood rides ashore
The ebb snatches from your hand.

Flood tide
And the sucking ebb to follow!
Both I have come to know
Pouring over my body.

Flood tide
Has not yet rifled my pantry
But a chill hand has been laid
On many who in darkness visited me.

Well might the Son of Mary
Take their place under my roof-tree
For I lack other hospitality
I never say 'No' to anybody —

Man being of all
Creatures the most miserable —
His flooding pride always seen
But never his tidal turn.

Happy the island in mid-ocean
Washed by the returning flood
But my aging blood
Slows to final ebb.

I have hardly a dwelling
Today, on this earth.
Where once was life's flood
All is ebb.

(translated from Irish by John Montague)

Gormley

(10th century)

IRELAND

Queen Gormley lived during the tenth century. An account of this
famous woman is given in the *Annals of Clonmacnoise*:

> Neale Glunduffe was king three years and was married to the lady
> Gormphley, daughter to king Flann, who was a very faire, vertuous
> and learned damozell, was married first to Cormack mc O'Cuillennann,
> king of Munster, secondly to king Neale, by whome she had issue a
> sonn calle prince Donnell who was drowned, upon whose death she
> made many pittifull and learned dittyes in Irish, and lastly shee was
> married to Kervall mcMoregan king of Leinster, after all which royall
> marriages she begged from doore to doore, forsaken of all her friends
> and allies, and glad to be relieved by her inferiours.

This poem is part of a sequence of laments she composed for her
third and last husband Niall (not Carroll, the 'Kervall' of the *Annals*
above, who was actually her second husband).

from GORMLEY'S LAMENTS

I have loved thirty by three,
I have loved nine by nine,
though I have loved twenty men
this is not what women seek.

I left them all for Niall,
it was my wish to do his bidding,
had I not good reason
to be Niall's first queen?

Though heroes are many in Leath Conn
there was nothing he could not win,
better for me, the sadness of life,
to have been a poor man's wife.

His painted cloaks, his gold rings,
his strong horses that won their race,
his full tide of fortune ebbed,
each in its turn has fled.

I have nothing between ground and sky
but a white shift and black cloak,
in Cennanas ot a hundred kings
who cares if I am hungry?

One Sunday we were at the church,
my lord and I at the figured stone,
at Cennanas of the great cross
announcing the tax of Leath Conn.

My king said to me
with a gentle tap of his left hand,
'Go to church where people are
accustomed to adore God's Son.'

We went then, it is true,
twelve score young girls,
Mór came before me as her duty
and took from me my pointed shoes.

To her, woman of Abbot Colum,
I gave a globe wreathed in gold
and two score cows, and cattle
on the north side of the great chapel.

I gave her a foreign blue hood
and a horn stand for psalms,
and thirty ounces of gold,
she has them still in her hands.

To-night she gave me – poor
charity is not good —
two tenths of hard oats,
two hen's eggs from her store.

By the King who brightens the sun,
if Niall Glunduv lived,
Abbot's wife of Tulach Leis
I would not need your eggs.

I got a cup, I got a comb,
I got fine cloth from Mór,
From me she got a brown-red horse
and gold apples in a bowl.

Sorrow to one whose pride is gold,
sorrow, Mór, to one who's selfish,
I paid poets for their words
before God took my riches.

The man who pays for poems with horses
may God give him their worth —
if my words do Niall justice,
how much better the poets!

(translated from Irish by Joan Keefe)

Anonymous

(9th century)

WALES

Heledd, who makes this lament for her brother Cynddylan, is one of the central figures in a saga composed in the ninth century. She mourns for her brother and for the destruction of her home, Pengwern (the modern Shrewsbury), by the Mercians.

EAGLE OF PENGWERN

Eagle of Pengwern, grey-crested, tonight
   its shriek is high,
   eager for flesh I loved.

> Eagle of Pengwern, grey-crested, tonight
>   its call is high,
> eager for Cynddylan's flesh.

> Eagle of Pengwern, grey-crested, tonight
>   its claw is high,
> eager for flesh I love.

> Eagle of Pengwern, it called far tonight,
>   it kept watch on men's blood;
> Trenn shall be called a luckless town.

> Eagle of Pengwern, it calls far tonight,
>   it feasts on men's blood;
> Trenn shall be called a shining town.

(translated from Welsh by Gwyn Williams)

Anonymous

(*c.* 11th century)

ENGLAND (OLD ENGLISH)

These two poems are contained in the Exeter Book, an anthology of Anglo-Saxon poetry presented to Exeter cathedral by Leofric (bishop of Exeter from 1050 to 1071). It contains many famous poems including 'The Wanderer', numerous riddles, and the two poems given here. The modern English versions preserve the alliterative pattern of the originals.

EADWACER

> It is to my own as if the man made them a gift:
> if trouble comes on him, they will take him in;
> with us it is otherwise.

> Wulf is on an island, I on another.
> It is a fastness, that island, the fens ring it.

Lusty fighters live on the island:
if trouble comes on him, they will take him in;
with us it is otherwise.

I waited for my wanderer, my Wulf, hoping and fearing:
when it was rainy weather and I sat wretched, weeping;
when the doughty man drew me into his arms —
it was heaven, yes, but hateful too.

Wulf, my Wulf, waiting for thee
hath left me sick, so seldom hast thou come;
a starving mood, no stint of meat.

Hearest thou, Eadwacer? Our whelp is borne off,
a wolf bears him to the woods.

It takes little to loose a link never made,
our gladness together.

WIFE'S LAMENT

I sing of myself, a sorrowful woman,
of my own unhap. All I have felt,
since I grew up, of ill let me say,
be it new or old – never more than now:
I have borne the cross of my cares, always.

First my friend went far from home,
over the waves; I was awake at dawn,
I wondered where he was, day and night.
Then I went out, unhappy wife,
lonely and wretched, looking for fellowship.

The man's kindred, with minds of darkness,
began to plot to part us two,
that we might lead a life most hateful,
live most aloof, and I longed for him.

My lord bade me lodge in this hut.
Little I know of love-making here,
of sweet friendship. My soul is mournful
to find my man, my friend, my mate

heavy-hearted, happy not at all,
hiding his mood, harbouring ill
under a blithe bearing. We both made vow
that death alone should drive us asunder,
naught else in the world; that was, but is no more;
it is now as if it had never been,
that friendship of ours. Far and nigh now
I must bear the hate of my best beloved.

They drove me out to dwell in the woods
under an oak tree, in that old stone-heap.
Fallen is this house; I am filled with yearning.
The dales are dim, the downs are high,
the bitter yards with briars are grown,
the seats are sorrowful. I am sick at heart,
he is so far from me. There are friends on earth,
lovers living that lie together,
while I, early and all alone,
walk under the oak tree, wander through these halls.
There I must sit the summerlong day,
there I can rue my wretchedness,
bewail my many woes, my hardships
for I cannot rest from my cares ever,
nor from all the longing that in this life befell me.

It is the way of a young man to be woeful in mood,
hard in his heart's thought; to have, besides,
a blithe bearing and a breast full of care,
a throng of woes alike when his worldly bliss
belongs all to him and when he lives an outcast
in a far country. My friend is sitting,
a cliff for shelter, cold in the storm,
a friend weary in mood, flooded with water
in his dismal dwelling, doomed to sorrow.

That man, my friend, is mindful too often
of a happier house. Hard is the lot
of one that longs for love in vain.

(translated from Old English by Kemp Malone)

Al-Khansâ
(7th century)
PRE–ISLAMIC ARAB

Al-Khansâ, 'the snub-nosed one', is an epithet given to four Arabic women poets from the pre-Islamic period. The most famous was Tumâḍir bint 'Amr, of the Sulaym, born around A.D. 590. She probably died by 644 and left a daughter 'Amra, also a poet. Stories of her life include her refusal to marry an old man; her marriage with the warrior Mirdas; her grief at the death of her two brothers, which inspired her to write elegies; her presence as part of a deputation of the Sulaym to Mohammed. Al-Khansâ's role as a poet was primarily that of ritual mourner – a role traditionally belonging to women. Many elegies transmitted by oral tradition have been attributed to her.

FOR HER BROTHER

Weep! Weep! Weep!
These tears are for my brother,
Henceforth that veil which lies between us,
That recent earth,
Shall not be lifted again.
You have gone down to the bitter water
Which all must taste,
And you went pure, saying:
'Life is a buzz of hornets about a lance point.'

But my heart remembers, O son of my father and mother,
I wither like summer grass,
I shut myself in the tent of consternation.

He is dead, who was the buckler of our tribe
And the foundation of our house,
He has departed in calamity.

He is dead, who was the lighthouse of courageous men,
Who was for the brave
As fires lighted upon the mountains.

He is dead, who rode costly horses,
Shining in his garments.
The hero of the long shoulder belt is dead,
The young man of valiance and beauty breathes no more;
The right hand of generosity is withered,
And the beardless king of our tribe shall breathe no more.

He shall be cold beneath his rock.

Say to his mare Alwa
That she must weep
As she runs riderless for ever . . .

When the red millstone ground the flowers of youth,
You shattered a thousand horses against the squadrons;
High on the groaning flanks of Alwa
You lifted the bright skirts of your silver mail.

You made the lances live,
You shook their beams,
You quenched their beams in red,
O tiger of the double panoply.

White women wandered with disordered veils
And you saved them in the morning.
Your captives were as troops of antelopes
Whose beauty troubles the first drops of rain . . .

How effortless were your rhymes of combat
Chanted in tumult, O my brother!
They pierced like lances,
They live among our hearts for ever.

Let the stars go out,
Let the sun withdraw his rays,
He was our star and sun.

Who now will gather in the strangers at dusk
When the sad North whistles with her winds?
You have laid down and left in the dust, O wanderers,

Him who nourished you with his flocks
And bared his sword for your salvation.
You set him low in the terrible house
Among a few stakes planted,
You threw down boughs of salamah upon him.
He lies among the tombs of our fathers,
Where the days and the years shall pass over him
As they have passed over our fathers.
Your loss is a great distress to me,
Child of the Solamides,
I shall be glad no more . . .

While you have tears, O daughters of the Solamides,
Weep! Weep! Weep!

(translated from Arabic by E. Powys Mathers)

Sanskrit Poetry

(A.D. 700–1050)

INDIA

Selections from the *Treasury of Well-Turned Verse*, compiled around
A.D. 1100 by a Buddhist scholar, Vidyākara, who drew his material
from a large library in the monastery of Jagadda. This anthology of
Sanskrit court poetry contains verses by over two hundred poets,
including a good number of women, who lived mostly between the
eighth and the eleventh centuries. The original works of many of
these poets have been lost. According to Daniel Ingalls, Vidyākara's
collection gives a vivid picture of Indian attitudes in the centuries
preceding the Moslem conquest.

from THE SUN

I praise the disk of the rising sun
red as a parrot's beak, sharp-rayed,
friend of the lotus grove,
an earring for the goddess of the east.

Vidya

from THE WANTON

Say, friend, if all is well still with the bowers
that grow upon the Jumna bank,
companions to the dalliance of cowherd girls
and witnesses of Radha's love.

Now that there is no use to cut their fronds
to make them into beds for love,
I fear their greenness will have faded
and they grow old and hard.

Vidya

from SUBSTANTIATIONS

One born to hardship in his place and station
does well enough to keep himself alive.
If its roots are burned by desert sands
will the champak think to blossom?

Vidya

from THE WANTON

My husband is the same who took my maidenhead
and these the moondrenched nights we knew;
the very breeze is blowing from the Vindhya hills
heavy with scent of newly blossomed jasmine.
I too am still the same;
and yet with all my heart I yearn for the reedbeds
        by the stream
which knew our happy, graceful
unending bouts of love.

Śīlabhaṭṭārikā

(translated from Sanskrit by Daniel H. H. Ingalls)

Kassia

(9th century)

BYZANTINE GREECE

She is the only woman poet of distinction in Byzantine history. Tradition says she was to be chosen as a bride by the Emperor but was rejected when she answered him with the edged wit for which she is famous. She founded a convent and was its abbess for the remainder of her life. She wrote epigrams in iambics, and a substantial number of hymns – that on Mary Magdalen has remained popular in the Greek church to the present day.

SELECTED EPIGRAMS

You meet your friend, your face
Brightens – you have struck gold.

Wealth covers sin – the poor
Are naked as a pin.

Poverty? wealth? seek neither —
One causes swollen heads,
The other, swollen bellies.

A half-deaf, bald, one-handed,
Stuttering, pint-sized, pimply,
Pigeon-toed, cross-eyed man,
When mocked by a lying pimp,
A thieving murderous drunk,
Of his misfortune said:
'I'm not to blame – you think
I asked to be like this?
But you! . . . the credit's yours.
Your Maker gave you nothing.
Behold! a self-made man.'

A learned fool? God save us!
The pigs are wearing pearls.

Better unborn than fool.
If born, spare earth your tread.
Don't wait. Go straight to hell.

No remedy for fools,
No helping them, but death.
In office? puffed and strutting.
Acclaimed? beyond endurance.
Columns of stone will kneel
Before you change a fool.

The artful Armenian.
Emerod. Wooden nickel. Mad
Dog. Weathervane. Back-
Biter. Bladder. Bog.
A wise man put it well —
'Without a name, he's naught,
Less when he gets a name,
Least of all when rich,
And richer, holding office,
Honoured – less than least.'

Ask for a taste of luck
Before you ask for beauty.

A nun's life – free as a bird.

A nun – a door unopened.

> (translated from Byzantine Greek by
> Patrick Diehl)

Hroswitha

(c. 935–1005)

GERMANY

Hroswitha was a canoness of the monastery of Gandesheim in Saxony. Details of her life are lacking, but she seems to have been of noble birth and to have entered the monastery at an early age. She was a prolific poet in the Latin language, writing a series of short epics in hexameters on historical themes, and six plays, based in language on those of Terence and designed to give the nuns a chaste and godly alternative to pagan plays. The present short poem is found at the end of the manuscript of her plays, and is a praise of virginity which uses the epithalamion, or marriage-hymn form.

IN PRAISE OF VIRGINITY

Look now, bride of God,
> what splendour on earth awaits you,
> what glories, too, in Heaven —
>> Look now, bride of God!

Joyful gifts you'll get,
> festive, brilliant with torches.
> See there, the bridegroom comes!
>> Joyful gifts you'll get.

And you will play new songs,
> plucking sweet sounds from strings;
> hailing with hymns your wedding day,
>> you will play new songs.

No one will thrust away
> from the high-throned company of the Lamb
> you, whom he chose in love —
>> no one will thrust away.

(translated from Latin by John Dillon)

from the *Manyōshū*

(650–800)

JAPAN

The *Manyōshū*, or 'Collection of Ten Thousand Leaves', is the oldest and most revered of the Japanese anthologies. Compiled in the

middle of the eighth century, it includes about 4,500 poems, many
by members of the court aristocracy. Women are well represented
and among the most celebrated of the *Manyōshū* poets.

Princess Nukada (second half of 7th century)
As a favoured consort of the Emperor Temmu she bore him a
daughter and lived for some time in the Imperial Palace. She is con-
sidered the greatest woman poet of her time.

*When the Emperor Tenji commanded Fujiwara Kamatari, Prime Minister,
to judge between the luxuriance of the blossoms on the spring hills and the
glory of the tinted leaves on the autumn hills, Princess Nukada decided the
question with this poem.*

> When, loosened from the winter's bonds,
>   The spring appears,
> The birds that were silent
> Come out and sing,
> The flowers that were prisoned
> Come out and bloom;
> But the hills are so rank with trees
> We cannot seek the flowers,
> And the flowers are so tangled with weeds
> We cannot take them in our hands.
>
> But when on the autumn hill-side
> We see the foliage,
> We prize the yellow leaves,
> Taking them in our hands,
> We sigh over the green ones,
> Leaving them on the branches;
> And that is my only regret —
> For me, the autumn hills!

(the Nippon Gakujutsu Shinkōkai translation)

WAITING FOR THE EMPEROR TENJI

Sir – awaiting you
my longing more dwelt upon
as my chamber door's
*sudare** is agitated —
the autumn wind is blowing.

(translated from Japanese by Cid Corman and
Susumu Kamaike)

Empress Jito (7th century)

Spring is passing and
summer seems to be coming —
the fine white stuff of
apparel spread for drying —
heavenly Kaguyama.†

(translated from Japanese by Cid Corman
and Susumu Kamaike)

Lady Kasa (8th century)
Twenty-nine of her *tanka*, all addressed to the great Manyōshū poet,
Ōtomo Yakamochi, are included in the *Manyōshū.*

To love someone
Who does not return that love
Is like offering prayers
Back behind a starving god
Within a Buddhist temple.

(translated from Japanese by Harold P. Wright)

Lady Ōtomo of Sakanoé (fl. c. 728–46)
She was married to Ōtomo Sukunamaro and had several children.
Her daughter was also a poet, known only as 'Lady Ōtomo of

---

* *sudare:* a slat blind made of rush or bamboo.
† Kaguyama is regarded as a sacred female mountain.

Sakanoé's Elder Daughter'. The poet Ōtomo Yakamochi was her
nephew.

> Unknown love
> Is as bitter a thing
> As the maiden-lily
> Which grows in the thickets
> Of the summer moor.

★

> My heart, thinking
> 'How beautiful he is'
> Is like a swift river
> Which though one dams it and dams it
> Will still break through.

(translated from Japanese by Arthur Waley)

Ono no Komachi

(834–80)

JAPAN

She is the most famous of the 'Six Poetic Geniuses' of the *Kokinshū*,
the first of the Japanese anthologies to be compiled by Imperial order.
Renowned for her beauty and talent, she served at Court in the
middle of the ninth century. Stories of her life are part of the folklore
of Japan.

> A thing which fades
> With no outward sign —
> Is the flower
> Of the heart of man
> In this world!

(translated from Japanese by Arthur Waley)

When my love becomes
All-powerful,
I turn inside out
My garments of the night,
Night dark as leopard-flower.

> (translated from Japanese by Geoffrey Bownas
> and Anthony Thwaite)

This night of no moon
There is no way to meet him.
I rise in longing —
My breast pounds, a leaping flame,
My heart is consumed in fire.

> (translated from Japanese by Donald Keene)

So lonely am I
My body is a floating weed
Severed at the roots.
Were there water to entice me,
I would follow it, I think.

> (translated from Japanese by Donald Keene)

Izumi Shikibu
(late 10th century)
JAPAN

As lady-in-waiting to Empress Akiko, she was a member of the
Imperial Court at the height of its brilliance in the Heian era (784–
1186). With Lady Murasaki, author of *The Tale of Genji*, she was
part of a circle of gifted women who were to become major figures
in the classical literature of Japan. She was married to a provincial
governor and had one daughter, Koshikibu, who died in childbirth.

The scandal of her love affairs and her fame as a poet made her, like Ono no Komachi, a figure of Japanese legend.

> *After the death of her daughter in childbirth, looking at the child*

Leaving us behind,
Whom will she have pitied more —
Infant or mother?
My child it was for me:
Her child it must have been.

*

Recklessly
I cast myself away;
Perhaps
A heart in love
Becomes a deep ravine?

*

Never could I think
Our love a worldly commonplace
On this morning when
For the first time my heart
Is filled with many thoughts.

*

As the rains of spring
Fall, day after day, so I
Fare on through time
While by the fence the grasses grow
And green spreads everywhere.

*

From that first night,
Although I have not wept
Cold, rainy tears upon my bed,
Yet I have recklessly
Slept in strange places and strange ways.

*

From darkness
Into the path of darkness
Must I enter:
Shine upon me from afar,
O moon above the mountain crest.

(translated from Japanese by Edwin A. Cranston)

Princess Shikishi

(d. 1201)

JAPAN

She was the third daughter of Emperor Go-Shiragawa. In her early youth she was made a vestal and remained unmarried throughout her life. The poems below are from the *Shinkokinshū*, an Imperial anthology completed in 1205.

AUTUMN

There has been no change
but I am no longer young.
Autumn wind blows and
I am as disturbed as before.

WINTER

The wind is cold.
Leaves one by one
are cleared from the
night sky. The moon
bares the garden.

SPRING

The cherry blossoms
have lost their fragrance.
You should have come
before the wind.

(translated from Japanese by Hiroaki Sato)

The Nun Abutsu

(d. *c.* 1283)

JAPAN

She is the author of the last famous work by a woman writer before the modern era, *The Diary of the Waning Moon*, a travel account containing many *tanka*. It marks the end of an epoch in which women were the major figures in Japanese literature.

from THE DIARY OF THE WANING MOON

The shore wind is cold on my travel clothes.
In the drizzling sky of the Godless Moon, snow too
   is falling.

Your subdued voice is low, cuckoo,
When, high in the clouds, will you proclaim your
   name?

Between the pines of the shore hills on the
   eastern road,
Even the waves rise in the image of flowers.

(translated from Japanese by Edwin O. Reischauer)

Unknown Kisaeng

(*c.* 1275–1308)

KOREA

'The Turkish Bakery' is thought to be by a *kisaeng* (Korean woman entertainer) from a period when popular songs and music flourished, encouraged by the king, who gathered musicians and dancers from all over the country for his amusement. Critics consider it a city folk-song rather than a poem of definite authorship.

THE TURKISH BAKERY

I go to the Turkish shop, buy a bun,
An old Turk grasps me by the hand.
If this story is spread abroad,
You alone are to blame, little doll on the shelf.
I will go, yes, go to his bower;
A narrow place, sultry and dark.

I go to the Samjang Temple, light the lantern,
A chief priest grasps me by the hand.
If this story is spread abroad,
You alone are to blame, little altar boy.
I will go, yes, go to his bower;
A narrow place, sultry and dark.

I go to the village well, draw the water,
A dragon within grasps me by the hand.
If this story is spread abroad,
You alone are to blame, O pitcher.
I will go, yes, go to his bower;
A narrow place, sultry and dark.

I go to the tavern, buy the wine,
An innkeeper grasps me by the hand.
If this story is spread abroad,
You alone are to blame, O wine jug.
I will go, yes, go to his bower;
A narrow place, sultry and dark.

(translated from Korean by Peter H. Lee)

Yü Hsüan-chi

(mid 9th century)

CHINA

Yü Hsüan-chi was born in Ch'ang An and became the concubine of an official. His wife was jealous, tortured her and forced her out of the house. She became a Taoist priestess, travelled widely, and had many lovers. She was accused of murdering her maid and was executed about 870.

ADVICE TO A NEIGHBOUR GIRL

Afraid of the sunlight,
You cover your face with your silk sleeves.
Tired out with Spring melancholy,
You neglect your makeup.
It is easier to get priceless jewels
Than to find a man with a true heart.
Why wet your pillow with secret tears?
Why hide your heartbreak in the flowers?
Go, seek a handsome famous man like Sung Yü.
Don't long for someone who will never come back.

On a Visit to Ch'ung Chen Taoist Temple I See in the South Hall the List of Successful Candidates in the Imperial Examinations

Cloud capped peaks fill the eyes
In the Spring sunshine.
Their names are written in beautiful characters
And posted in order of merit.
How I hate this silk dress
That conceals a poet.
I lift my head and read their names
In powerless envy.

(translated from Chinese by Kenneth Rexroth
and Ling Chung)

Chu Shu-chên

(early 12th century)

CHINA

Almost nothing is known of Chu Shu-chên's life, though she is considered one of the finest women poets of China. Her poems were published in 1182 from a collection of copies made, it was claimed, from the originals before they were burned by her parents after her death.

PLUM BLOSSOMS

The snow dances and the frost flies.
Through the bamboo blinds I see vaguely
The sparse shadows of slanting plum branches.
Unexpectedly a cold perfume,
Borne with the sound of a Tartar flute,
Is blown to our bed curtains.
Enveloped in this puzzling scented wind,
Who can appreciate such a subtle joy?
I quickly get up
In my dishevelled cloud dark hair.
We taste the stamens
And adorn ourselves with the blossoms,
Frowning and smiling,
Still drowsy with wine.

(translated from Chinese by Kenneth Rexroth
and Ling Chung)

Li Ching-chao

(1084–1151)

CHINA

Li Ching-chao is universally considered to be China's greatest woman poet. She and her husband, Chao Ming-ch'eng, both from eminent families, were not only poets but also scholars and collectors of bronzes, manuscripts, calligraphy and paintings. When in 1127 the army of Chin Tartars invaded Sung China, they were driven from their home and lost most of their collection. In 1129 when Li was forty-six, her husband went alone to a new official post and was taken ill on the way. He died before Li could reach him. After her husband's death she lived alone, usually in flight, attempting to save what was left of their collection while the Chin were driving the Sung out of North China. Li Ching-chao was one of the finest poets of the *t'zu*, a lyric form composed to a particular tune which was developed during the Sung dynasty (960–1278).

TUNE: CRIMSON LIPS ADORNED

Ride in the swing
                         over
she stands up
                    languid
                    flexing delicate hands
Multitudinous dew
                         on thin flower
a mist of sweat
                    dampens
                    her light dress through
She looks
               A stranger coming
Her stockings down
                         Gold hairpin slipped
Shyly
          She runs
and
      leaning against the door jamb
looks back
lingering
               to sniff at a green plum

TUNE: MAGNOLIA BLOSSOM

Bought

             from the flower-peddler's tray

one spring branch

                  just open

                  in bloom

Droplets

             fleck it evenly

still clouded red

                  with a mist of dew

I'm afraid he'll

                  take it into his head

that my face is not

             so fair!

             so fair!

In high-

combed hair

             I fasten

                  a gold pin

                  aslant

There!

let him look

                  Let him compare the two

TUNE: THE BUTTERFLY WOOS THE BLOSSOMS

Long placid evening

                  my diversions few

I

             vacantly dreaming of Ch'ang-an

how the road

                goes up

                to the old capital

Please tell them:

                spring

                is fine

                this year

Flower glow
                        set each other off
moon shadow
                   wine
Pleasant to take
                   food
                   without picking and choosing
Excellent wine
                             a tart plum
— just right for my mood
Tipsy
          I put a flower in my hair
                   O flower! flower!
                   don't make fun of me
Have pity!
                   Spring
                   like all men living
                   will soon
                   grow old

TUNE: ENDLESS UNION

Sunset
                   molten bronze
evening clouds
                        marbled white jade
     Where is he?
A mist of light
                             stains the willows
Plum blowing
                        A flute's wail
     Spring reveries
     how much you know!
New Year's Eve
                        the merrymaking festival
Serene weather —
                        wind
               no   in its wake?
                        rain

Friends come
> to invite me out
>> horses
>>> travelling carts
>> wine-drinking friends

I thank these
> poem-making companions

At the capital
> joyful days

In my room
> much
> time to myself

I recall
> another New Year's Eve

how I put on
> the green-feather headdress

narrow snow-white sash
>> worked
>> with gold thread

Headdress and sash
>> to vie with any beauty

I
> haggard now
>> wind-tangled locks
>> hair
>>> frosted white
>>> at the temple

Too diffident
> to venture among flowers

I loiter
> under the window screen

eavesdropping
>> on the talk
>> and laughter
>> of others

(translated from Chinese by C. H. Kwôck and
Vincent McHugh)

Wallāda

(11th century)

SPAIN (ARABIC)

The Hispano-Arabic poet Wallāda lived in Cordova in the first half of the eleventh century. She was the daughter of the ruling khalif and her salon was the meeting-place for poets and men of letters. She was a highly independent woman who refused to wear the veil or to hide her literary ambitions, and she took for her lover Ibn Zaidūn, the finest writer of classical Arabic poetry in Andalusia. Those of Wallāda's poems which have been preserved are part of a verse correspondence she carried on with Zaidūn.

A reply to Zaidūn's complaint at the brief and infrequent nature of their meetings:

1. I wonder: is there no way for us to meet again
   After this separation, and tell again each other of our love?
2. Before, when you visited me during the wintry season
   I spurned the brazier, so great was my fire of passion!
3. How can I bear this being cut off from you, alone?
   Yes, Fate did hasten what I had been afraid of!
4. Time passes, yet I see no end to your long absence,
   Nor does patience free me from the bondage of yearning!
5. May God pour rain on the land where you're dwelling
   From every cloud, in mighty streams, to refresh it!

Angry at Zaidūn's interest in her maid, Wallāda wrote:

1. If you were just in keeping our pact of love,
   You would not love my slave-maid, preferring her,
2. Leaving aside the bough that produced beauty's fruit,
   Inclining toward a bough that no such fruit does show:

3. You know full well that I'm the heaven's full moon,
   Yet, to my grief, you let *al-mustarī** beguile you!

(translated from Arabic by A. R. Nykl)

Mahādēviyakka
(12th century)
INDIA (KANNADA)

Mahādēviyakka flourished in India in the twelfth century. She was
initiated to Śiva worship at the age of ten by an unknown guru.
Though she seems to have been married by her parents to an un-
believing chieftain, she left him to wander the world, worshipping
Śiva in the form of Mallikārjuna, 'the lord white as jasmine'. She is
one of the great poet saints of the medieval Hindu protestant move-
ment, Vīraśaivism, which defied the classical belief systems and social
customs of orthodox Hinduism. The vacanas of the Vīraśaiva saints
are free verse lyrics of intense personal devotion written in Kannada,
a Dravidian language whose literary tradition can be traced back
through fifteen centuries.

> Like a silkworm weaving
> her house with love
> from her marrow,
> > and dying
> in her body's threads
> winding tight, round
> and round,
> > I burn
> desiring what the heart desires.
>
> Cut through, O lord,
> my heart's greed,
> and show me
> your way out,
>
> O lord white as jasmine.

*

* A pun on *al-mustarī*, Jupiter, and *al-mustarā*, 'the purchased one'.

Till you've earned
knowledge of good and evil

it is
lust's body,
site of rage,
ambush of greed,
house of passion,
fence of pride,
mask of envy.

Till you know and lose this knowing
you've no way
of knowing
my lord white as jasmine.

*

Like an elephant
lost from his herd
suddenly captured,

remembering his mountains,
   his Vindhyas,
      I remember.

A parrot
come into a cage
remembering his mate,
   I remember.

O lord white as jasmine
show me
your ways.
   Call me: Child, come here,
      come this way.

*

Riding the blue sapphire mountains
wearing moonstone for slippers
blowing long horns
O Śiva
when shall I
crush you on my pitcher breasts

O lord white as jasmine
when do I join you
stripped of body's shame
and heart's modesty?

(translated from Kannada by A. K. Ramanujan)

Hadewijch
(13th century)
NETHERLANDS (DUTCH)

She was of noble birth but in her time could not find a milieu befitting her talents and disposition other than a 'beguinage' – a cloister of lay nuns in Antwerp. Her mystical writings have an intensity and passion which make her work outstanding in medieval literature. Her accounts of her visions in prose and much poetry are preserved in manuscripts, but little is known of the facts of her life. One poem included here, 'All Things Confine', is attributed to her as it is part of a manuscript which contains many poems bearing her signature.

ALL THINGS CONFINE

All things
Crowd me in!
I am so wide!

After the unshapen
Have I grasped
In everlasting time.

I have caught it.
It has cast me
Wider than wide!

Me is too narrow
All else!
You know this well
You that have been there too.

*

Ah yes, when love allows
Me to bewail my heart's duress,
I hear no longer of her vows:
My claims are small, she has prowess.
They say, the swan, when in distress
Of death, first sings, then bows.
Whatever still be love's requests
I would thus still complete them now.

*

What helps it if of love I sing
If now I too am suffering?
How tight and strong love's fettering
Within her might I am a thing.
  I suffer all love suffers me
  Love bridled me so forcefully
What good is now my reining in?

*

Had I been mindful of my high descent,
Mine had been thoughts to rise, and not descend
And, had I given me to love
Entire, for efforts lent and spent
I'd have received for what was spent what lent
A bond of life and love.
  Then might I dwell with all above
  And everything the dearth whereof
  My lowly deeds do so reveal.
  Now up to God goes our appeal.

(translated from Dutch by Frans van Rosevelt)

Marie de France

(late 12th century)

FRANCE

Marie de France is the earliest woman poet in French literary history. Little is known about her life. Born in France, she lived in England in the second half of the twelfth century, probably at the Court of Henry II. Her best-known poems are her Norman-French tales, or 'lays', short romantic narratives containing Celtic themes and images. Her other works include *Les Fables* and *L'Espurgatoire Seint Patriz*.

GOAT'S-LEAF

Well pleasing 'tis to me
The lay called *Goat's-leaf*,
And I wish the truth to say,
How and where it came to be.
From people I have heard,
And in books I have seen
The story of Tristan and the Queen,
Of their love so complete,
It brought them many a grief
And then, death, one day.

Wrathful was King Mark,
Angry with Tristan his nephew,
Banished him from the realm
For the love he bore the Queen.
To his country Tristan returned,
To Southwales where he was born,
There to bide a year's length,
Unfree to re-enter the realm.
Thence he laid his life
Open to death and destruction.
Marvel not at such conduct,
For he who loves most loyally,

Most wretched is and desolate
When prey to thwarted desires.
Anguish and sorrow move
Tristan his country to leave.
Straight to Cornwall he goes;
Thereat dwells the Queen.
Alone he enters the forest,
Fearful of being seen.
At vesper he comes forth
To seek a resting place.
With peasants, with poor people,
He finds refuge at night,
Inquires what tidings or news,
How the king is faring.
They tell him this they heard:
The barons have been summoned;
They will assemble in Tintagel,
Where, at Whitsuntide,
The king will hold festival;
The court will joy and revel,
And there shall be the Queen.

Tristan hears and exults:
Bound is she to pass by,
Sure is he to see her.
The day the king sets forth,
Tristan comes to the woods
Near the road which he knows
The cortege must travel.
A branch of hazel he cuts,
Squares it all nicely.
Upon the trimmed bough,
With his knife he carves his name.
Were the Queen to notice it,
Alert to these signals,
She will know, seeing it,
The branch is Tristan's envoy.
It happened in times past

They used a similar sign.
'Tis the sum and symbol
Of what he would write and say:
That long has he been there,
Waited long, remained
To watch, perchance discover
Possible means of seeing her,
For he cannot live without her.
It is with the two of them
As it is with the goat's-leaf
Which clings to the hazel-tree;
When it twines and takes hold,
And coils all round the bole,
Together, both survive;
But if they be severed
The hazel quickly dies,
And dies also the goat's-leaf.
'Dear heart, thus are we:
Together, we both live.
Asunder, we both die.'

The Queen rides onward,
Observant all the while.
On a slope she sees the branch,
Deciphers all the letters.
She bids the chevaliers,
Who guide and escort her,
To stop, for she wishes
To dismount and rest a while.
They obey the Queen's command.
Far from her entourage
She goes, and calls her maid,
The trusted Brenguein.
She walks off the road a little;
In the forest she finds the being
She loves above all beings.
Joyful is their intimacy.
He talks to her at leisure;

She tells him her delight,
And conveys to him the means
To a reconcilement with the king,
Who now greatly deplores
Having banished him thus
On one's accusation.
Then, she left her beloved,
But at the moment of parting
Both began to weep.
To Wales, Tristan returned
To await his uncle's pardon.

For the happiness he enjoyed
Of his love whom he had seen,
For the record he kept
Of speech the Queen had spoken,
Lest the words be forgotten,
Tristan, who played the harp,
Made a new lay of their tryst.
One word 'tis briefly called:
The English say *Goat's-leaf*;
The French, *Chèvrefeuille*.
To you the truth I reported
Of the lay here unfolded.

(translated from Old French by Aline Allard)

Comtesse de Die

(late 12th century)

PROVENCE

Nothing definite is known of the Comtesse de Die, the most famous
of the *trobairitz* (the women troubadors), save what is recorded in the
five lyrics which have been preserved. In the love poems of the
troubadors the woman typically appears as a cult object, an in-
different goddess worshipped with a blend of sensuality and mysti-

cism. In the following complaint, the Comtesse de Die turns conven-
tion on its head and addresses her own indifferent lover with a mixture
of scepticism and self-respect. The troubador lyrics were highly
refined poetry which depended for their effect primarily upon the
ingenuity of versification and musicality of their language.

I sing a song reluctantly,
A complaint about my friend; for
I love him more than all the world
Yet he cares not for me:
Not for my pity or gentility,
My worth, intellect or beauty.
I am deceived and betrayed
As I should be if I were ugly.

My acts have been above reproach to you,
My friend – this comforts me;
Greater than Sequis' love for Valenssa
Is mine for you. And I am pleased that
My love surpasses yours, friend,
For renown is your nobility.
Disdainful are your words and deeds to me,
While others reap your generosity.

Your coldness, friend, amazes me,
And my complaints are only just;
No other woman has the right
To steal you from my love
With words or coquetry.
Remember our love's blossoming!
May God forbid our parting through a fault of mine!

Your nobility and graciousness
Indeed cause me distress;
For no woman, far or near, who wished to love
Would resist you. But you, friend,
Who are so discerning, must recognize
The finest from among the rest
And remember, I beg of you, our promises.

I must find strength and solace
In my merits and my birth,
In my beauty and in my heart's devotion:
And so to you, wherever you may be,
I send this song bearing my pain
And ask you, my lovely friend, to explain
Your coldness and your cruelty —
I know not if it is pride or malice.

My go-between, you bear a second message too:
Excess of pride can bring the greatest misery.

(translated from Provençal by Carol Cosman
and Howard Bloch)

Anonymous: Motets

(13th Century)

FRANCE

Motets were musical compositions for two, three or four voices, each voice singing different words. A large number have been preserved, mostly anonymous and dating from the thirteenth century.

My love, how could your heart consider
I've neglected you
because I did not welcome you
as you desired?

If you but knew how fast must woman bind
the lover whom she dreads to lose,
you would find I chose
my actions with the hope
your love for me would sharpen as it grew.

Sweet heart, do not stop loving me,
for my heart heeds nothing, only loving you.

★

I am a young girl
graceful and gay,
not yet fifteen when
my sweet breasts may
begin to swell;

Love should be my contemplation,
I should learn its indication,

But I am put in prison.
God's curse be on my jailer!

Evil, villainy and sin
did he
to give up a girl like me
to a nunnery;

A wicked deed, by my faith,
the convent life will be my death
     My God! for I am far too young.

Beneath my sash I feel the sweet pain.
God's curse on him who made me a nun.

     (translated from Old French by Carol Cosman)

Christine de Pisan

(1364–c. 1430)

FRANCE

Christine de Pisan was born in Venice but moved at an early age to
Paris, where her father and later her husband were attached to the
Court of Charles V. When her husband died in 1389 she was left
with three children to provide for and turned to letters as a means of
livelihood. She first practised the various forms of short poems –
lais, virelais, rondeaux – but later turned to prose, and she herself states
that she wrote fifteen important works between 1399 and 1405.
After Agincourt, she retired to a convent, probably about 1415, and
her next work was a song in honour of Joan of Arc in 1429. She died
shortly after.

Lepistre Othea la deesse que elle envoya a Hector de Troye quant il estoit en laage de quinze ans was written at the end of the fourteenth century. The portrait of Hector as a fifteen-year-old youth may be modelled on her own son, who was fifteen when *Lepistre* was composed. It is in the form of a courtesy book consisting of a hundred stories illustrating spiritual and chivalric virtues. Each story begins with a stanza setting forth the theme, a prose explanation follows, and a moral is pointed in a short ending paragraph. In English translation 'A Lytil Bibell of Knyghthod' was almost instantly popular, appearing early in the fifteenth century and again in another version towards the middle of the century. The stanzas included here come from the latter translation.

from THE EPISTLE OF OTHEA TO HECTOR, *A 'Lytil Bibell of Knyghthod'*

X

Phoebus, the goddess variant and changeable,
naturally contrariaunt to steadfast stableness,
whose mutability maketh people variable,
lunatic to be, and putteth them in distress,
of her condition take neither more nor less;
But upon constance set thy mind and heart,
And then will nobleness to thee-ward start.

XXI

From the god Bacchus thy conceit withdraw,
in aventure lest that thou repent.
Through his engine and mighty law
many for his service sell both land and rent.
Wherefore beware, for his bow is bent.
Whom that he striketh hath soon lost his wit.
Keep well thy diet and he shall not hit.

XXII

If thou to wisdom list to give credence,
Dote not nor fonne in no manner wyse

upon Pygmalion's images presence,
But ay in heart look thou it despise;
for I thee tell, after mine advise,
that were thee better be delven in the ground
than with that image for to be confound.

XXVII

If thou have fellows in arms to thee true,
thou owest of right, go they never so far,
Ay to be diligent them to rescue
In their necessity where they have war.
If thou Hercules follow, thou shalt not err,
which for his fellows did his busy pain.
Where true love is, it showeth; it will not feign.

XLV

Although Pasyphe were foolishly disposed,
and to lust unnatural set her appetite,
yet in thy kindly reason be it not supposed
that every woman be of that delight;
for many be full virtuous, or else it were unright.
He is too unwise that, for default of one,
will therefore despise woman everyone.

LIX

If thou desire subject for to be
to god Cupid, beware in any wise
of the great giant that loved Galathea,
lest he thee make fail of thine enterprise
as he did Axis in a full cruel wyse.
Who to Cupid will his service knit
behoveth a watchful eye about him set.

LXVII

Attend not overmickle to the harmony
of Orpheus harp, whose joyful merry sound
maketh fowls of their flight stint suddenly,

and venomous serpents to come out of the ground,
for the pleasant melody that they therein have found.
Little need hath he to give attendance
to any such instruments, that will himself advance.

LXX

Labour not nor travel to the infernal port
for to seek Eurydice, as poets tell
that the poet Orpheus thither did resort
with his harp melodious to stop the pains so fell.
Yet for all his melody, thou mayest read and spell,
that he could not speed there of his intent,
so desolate of comfort, home again he went.

LXXI

To know good knights, if thou have desire,
whose courage natural is toward chivalry,
the proof of Achilles thee clearly will inspire
how thou shall them know both far and nigh.
Ulysses this matter can well testify.
It was an old saw ere than thou were born:
He beginneth soon to prick that will be a thorn.

LXXIV

Trust not on fortune, called the great goddess;
for oft she conveyeth many to haddy-wist.*
In her is no sure hold nor steadfastness.
She will thee please or love no longer than she list.
Before men's eyes she casteth a great mist.
When they find her favourable, they think they be well;
And yet is it feeble hold on a slipper eel.

(anonymous translation, adapted by Joan Keefe)

* *haddy-wist:* vain regret.

Anonymous

(15th century)

ENGLAND

The lyric is one of a small number of English songs found scattered among the Latin sermons and homilies in the Caius College, Cambridge, MSS.383.

I loved a child of this countrie,
And so I wend he had do me;
Now my-self the sooth I see,
That he is far.
> *Were it undo that is y-do*
> *I would be-war.*

He said to me he would be true,
And change me for none other new;
Now I sykke and am pale of hue,
For he is far.
> *Were it undo that is y-do*
> *I would be-war.*

He said his saws he would fulfil,
Therefore I let him have all his will;
Now I sykke and mourne still,
For he is far.
> *Were it undo that is y-do*
> *I would be-war.*

THE RENAISSANCE AND ITS CONTEMPORARIES
1500–1800

Marguerite de Navarre
(1492–1549)

FRANCE

Marguerite d'Angoulême became Duchess of Alençon by her first marriage in 1509, then Queen of Navarre by her second marriage in 1527. She was the sister of François I, king of France, and the grandmother of another French king, Henri IV. Michelet calls her the mother of the Renaissance in France because she encouraged and protected many Humanists and poets. Although she wrote several plays and numerous poems, she is even better known for her *Heptameron*, a collection of novellas. Her deep religious faith is reflected in the poem 'Autant en emporte le vent'. The rondeau, 'The smell of death', was composed in 1547 shortly after the death of her brother, François I, to whom she was devoted. Both poems were first published in 1547 in *Marguerites de la Marguerite des Princesses*.

AUTANT EN EMPORTE LE VENT*

If someone insults you,
Endure him lightheartedly;
And if all slander you,
Give no heed to them:
  'Tis nothing new
To hear such frequent talk:
Autant en emporte le vent.

If someone speaks of Faith,
Minimizing its value
Compared with the works of the Law,
Judging these worthier,
  'Tis strange dogma.
Pass him by, go forth:
Autant en emporte le vent.

* Something like: 'all this is idle talk' or 'it will all vanish into thin air'.

And if, to impair your Faith,
He lauds your noble deeds,
Declaring (to flatter you)
That he ranks you with the elect,
        Flee such talk
That leads to false pride:
Autant en emporte le vent.

If the world comes a-tempting
With riches, honours, pleasures,
And offers them all to you,
Deny it your heart and will,
    For temporal things
Return whence they came:
Autant en emporte le vent.

If you are told of a place
(Not God's) where can be found
Solace and true salvation,
It is to murder your soul.
    Be a rebel.
Belie the most learned:
Autant en emporte le vent.

★

The smell of death is so powerful
As to make most desired the liquor
Of that fare whose taste the ignorant man
Dreads, although he cannot reach
Heaven except by means of death.

The brother's death changed in the sister
Terror into a desire for death,
And makes her eager to consume with him
    The smell of death.

Her immense grief she deems a joy,
Knowing it the gate and sure path
One must travel fleeing to God.

Awaiting, she wishes to speak of death
Since her heart was resurrected by
  The smell of death.

                    (translated from French by Aline Allard)

Pernette du Guillet

(1520–45?)

FRANCE

She was born in Lyon probably about 1520. She was beautiful,
accomplished in music and languages, familiar with the classics. The
most momentous event in her life was her liaison with the famous
Maurice Scève. He wrote for her his sequence *Delie*. She died about
1545 and left behind her a body of work which shows her to have
been a conscious and polished literary artist.

CHANSON

If they say my furred cloak
drips with the gold rain
that wrapped Daphne in ecstasy:
                    how should I know?

If they say I love too many,
passing the time for joy,
taking my pleasure here and there:
                    how should I know?

If they say I showed you
the flame hidden deeply in me
to test its force in you:
                    how should I know?

If they say with the common passion
that churns in young people
I need you – and with no more:
                    how should I know?

But if they say that Virtue
which cloaks you richly
shines through to me in love:
>   this I do know!

And if they say that Holy Love
hits me cleanly in the heart,
never winging honour:
>   this I do know!

EPIGRAM

As the body denies the means to look
into the spirit or know its force,
likewise Error for me drew
around my eyes the blindfold of ignorance,
forbidding me the means to know
the one for whom I so widely searched
when by the gods' wish he approached;
but such Perfection could not be perceived,
therefore truly I can be reproached:
the closer Good, the less my chance to see.

>   (translated from French by Joan Keefe
>   with Richard Terdiman)

Louise Labé
(1525–66)
FRANCE

Louise Labé was born in Lyon and both her father and husband were
wealthy ropemakers. She herself was called '*la belle cordière*'. She
learned Greek, Latin, Spanish and Italian as a child and was re-
nowned for her wit and beauty. She was also a fine horsewoman and
is said to have enlisted in the Dauphin's army and to have fought at
the siege of Perpignan. She collected a distinguished library, held a

celebrated literary salon and was intimately acquainted with many important poets of her day, including Maurice Scève and Clemence de Bourges. She is considered one of the greatest poets of the French Renaissance. She died in Lyon in 1566.

SONNETS

X

When I catch sight of your fair head
garlanded with living laurel,
making your sad lute sound so well
that you compel to rise and be your followers
rocks and trees – when I see you adorned
in virtues legion, chief in honour among men,
then does my passionate heart suppose
that by such virtue as you are beloved,
esteemed by all, so could you love,
and to such worthy virtue could you amend
the virtue of taking pity,
and the virtue of being aroused
sweetly and slowly by my love.

    (translated from French by Judith Thurman)

XIII

As long as I continue weeping
Tears for our past happiness,
As long as, sounds of grief suppressed,
My voice comes clearly singing,
As long as tender hands in fingering
The gentle lute can ring your praise,
As long as peace my soul allays,
Contented truly with your understanding,
Then I do not wish to die.
But when I feel my eyes grow dry,

My voice grow hoarse, my hand grow slack,
And on this mortal earth my spirit lack
A sign of love's quick life,
Then, Death, please turn my day to night.

(translated from French by Joan Keefe
with Richard Terdiman)

XX

A seer foretold that I would love one day —
a certain man – and thus with words she drew him.
I had no other image, but I knew him,
recognized my lover straight away.

Then I saw him love me fatally,
and pitied his sad amorous mischance,
and urged my nature on relentlessly
till I loved with the same extravagance.

Who would suppose a passion wouldn't thrive
that fates and gods together did contrive?
But when I see such ominous preparation,

Cruel winds gathering to a violent storm,
I think, perhaps, hell sent the invitation,
long ago, to watch my bark go down.

(translated from French by Judith Thurman)

XXIV

Don't scold me, Ladies, if I have loved,
if I have felt a thousand burning fires,
a thousand pains, a thousand unfulfilled desires,
if, weeping, I have thus my time consumed.
Let not my name be blackened by your blame.
If I have failed, I have my punishment,
don't deepen wounds already violent.
Remember that Love, above all else,

could make you fall in love, if he but wished,
without a Vulcan's ardour to excuse,
without Adonis' beauty to accuse.
And with occasion less than mine
and yet a passion stranger and as deep,
take care: your eyes still more than mine may weep.

(translated from French by Carol Cosman)

Veronica Gambara

(1485–?)

ITALY

Veronica Gambara was born in 1485 in Pratalboino near Brescia. In 1509 she married the lord of Corregio, Gilberto X, who died nine years later leaving her the responsibility of governing their tiny state and bringing up their two children. She also maintained extensive literary relationships with important writers, including the illustrious Pietro Bembo, and entertained the Emperor Charles V twice at her court.

When I see the earth ornate and lovely
with a thousand beautiful and sweet flowers,
and as every star shines in the sky,
so shine in her the varied colours;
and every beast, lithe and solitary,
moved by natural instinct, comes
forth from wood and ancient grotto
searching his companion day and night;
    and when I see the plants
clothed too with lovely flowers and new shoots
and hear the varied voices of the birds
in sweet and cheerful notes;
and with welcome sound
every brook bathing its flowered shores

so that Nature, of herself enamoured,
joys in seeing how beautifully she's made,
   I say to myself, thinking:
How brief is this miserable mortal life!
Even this meadow now green and blossoming
before was full of snow,
a troubled heavy air obscured
the beauty of the sky,
and those wandering and loving beasts
were hidden alone among mountains and woods.
   Nor did one hear sweet harmonies sung
among the tender plants by lovely birds,
for blown by the most angry winds
plants were dry and birds mute,
and the swiftest streams and little brooks
were held firm by the ice,
and all that now is beautiful and joyful
was in that season languid and mournful.
   Thus time flees and with its fleeing
bears off the years together with our life!
For we, to flower anew as those,
Through heaven's will, lack all hope,
sure of nothing but our dying
whether of noble blood or humble birth;
nor can such happy fate be given us
as will make death pity us.

(translated from Italian by Brenda Webster)

Vittoria Colonna

(1490–1547)

ITALY

Vittoria Colonna was born near Rome to one of the greatest families
in Italy. In 1509 she married the Marchese di Pescara, who became a
captain of the imperial forces and died after the Battle of Pavia in

1525. Vittoria's poems are a record of her grief tempered by her Catholic faith and adherence to the neo-Platonism of her time. Michelangelo, with whom she corresponded, dedicated poems and drawings to her.

When the troubled sea swells and surrounds
a solid rock with force and rage,
and, finding it firm, the stormy pride
breaks and the wave falls back upon itself;
    So I, like the rock, when the world's
deep angry waters come against me,
raise my eyes to heaven, robbing them as much of force
as they with greater strength abound.
    And if, at times, desire's gale
attempts new war, I race to land
and with a knot of love intwined with faith
    I tie my bark to that in which I trust,
Jesus, live rock, so that whenever I wish
I can return to port.

                (translated from Italian by Brenda Webster)

O what transparent waves, what a tranquil sea
my speedy vessel travelled through,
laden, adorned with richest freight,
the clear air and breezes aiding it!

The sky that now hides its beautiful lamps
rayed soft light then, erased most shadows.
How must one fear who happily proceeds! —
for the end is not always like the beginning.

Regard how fickle and impious Fortune,
uncovering her wicked, angry face,
gives rise in her fury to a vast tempest.

But though she collects wind, rain, and arrows
and sends wild beasts to devour me,
the soul still catches sight of its faithful star.

                (translated from Italian by Lynne Lawner)

Like a hungry fledgeling that watches and hears
his mother beating her wings about her
as she brings back nourishment and, loving
the food and her, gladdens and rejoices

and, confined to his nest, chafes with the desire
to follow after her and fly himself
and thanks her by singing in such a way
that his tongue seems loosened beyond natural power,

thus do I, whenever the warm, vital ray
of the divine sun that nourishes my heart
shines forth more splendidly than usual,

write, my pen inspired by inner
love, and without even being aware myself
of what it is I say I compose his praises.

(translated from Italian by Lynne Lawner)

Gaspara Stampa

(*c.* 1520–54)

ITALY

Gaspara Stampa, born between 1520 and 1525 in Padua, is considered
one of the finest poets of the Italian Renaissance. She grew up in
Venice in an artistic family. It was discovered only in this century that
she had been an 'honest' (high-ranking) courtesan, and not simply
the tragic victim of betrayal by her lover Collaltino di Collalto as her
poetry would indicate. Her affair with him lasted in fact only three
years, during which time he was frequently away in France. Her
poetry is unusually personal within the bounds of sixteenth-century
Petrarchan convention.

Love made me such that I live in fire
like a new salamander on earth
or like that other rare creature, the Phoenix,
who expires and rises at the same time.

All the joys there are arc mine, my game's
to live burning but not to feel the pain
and not to care if he who causes this
has any compassion for me or not.

As soon as the first flame extinguished,
Love kindled another, as far as I can tell
a much stronger and more vital one.

Thus as long as he who stole my heart again
stays satisfied with my burning,
I'll not repent of burning as I love.

★

The stars have given me a hard fate
but nothing could be harder than my Count.
He flees. I follow after. Others seek me.
But I am blind to others' loveliness.

I hate who loves me, love who scorns me.
When someone's kind, I must be harsh,
harshness rewards my own humility:
I've taught my heart to feed upon such strangeness.

He always finds new ways to hurt me.
They try to comfort me and give me peace.
Despite all this, I turn from them to him.

Thus, Love, in your school one learns
to do the opposite of what seems right,
crushing the humble underfoot, indulging the cruel.

★

If I could believe that death
would put an end to all this suffering,
then certainly I'd seek it —
dying once consoles, not kills.
But, alas, I fear that, after death,
my loving pains might be much keener.
I should know this, for I die
many times and each time love augments.

Thus to undergo less torment I agree
to go on living in this martyrdom.

*

Often I compare my lord to heaven,
his lovely face the sun, his eyes the stars,
and in his voice there sounds the harmony
of the songs of Delian Apollo.

When he grows furious, everywhere around
there's thunder, raging storms, and freezing rain,
but when he wants to lift the mask of anger
his kindness is a sea becalmed, serene.

Sometimes he lets me realize my hopes
and promises that things will stay that way.
Life's then perpetual spring and springtime flowering.

But other times he changes moods and threatens
to leave me here deprived of richest glories:
a horrid winter overtakes my soul.

(translated from Italian by Lynne Lawner)

Veronica Franco
(1546–?)

ITALY

Veronica Franco was born in Venice. When quite young she married
a doctor, but soon after that launched her career as an 'honest
courtesan'. She frequented the famous salon of Domenico Venier in
Venice, was a friend of writers and artists like Tintoretto, and even
received Henry III of France at her home. Around 1580 she seems to
have abandoned her worldly activities in order to devote herself to
pious works and, specifically, to found a hospice for fallen women.

No more words! To the field, to arms!
I intend to rid myself of pain
even if I end up dying for it.

Should my complaints be read out? —
after all, it is you who provoked me.
But why quarrel about precedence?

I can consider myself challenged,
or I can challenge you – it's all the same;
I'm grateful for any chance to get even!

You choose the site or choose the weapons,
and leave the other choice to me
or, if you want to, you decide everything.

I'm certain that you'll soon perceive
how ungrateful and faithless you were
and what a mistake it was to betray me.

For unless love holds me back
I'll extract the live heart from your breast
bravely with my own hands

just as I'll rip out from its roots
the falsely lying tongue that wounds me —
you'll already have bitten it!

If none of all this saves me,
in desperation I'll attempt
to avenge myself through bloody murder;

then satisfied with having killed you
yet filled with regret, I'll turn and plunge
the knife into my very own heart.

Now that my mind is bent upon revenge,
my disrespectful, my rebellious lover,
step up and arm yourself with what you will.

What battlefield do you prefer? this place?
this secret hideaway where I have sampled —
unwarily – so many bitter sweets?

Let my bed be set up here before us! —
this is where I took you to my bosom,
the traces are still there of our mingled bodies.

Past is the time when I would sleep there,
past is the time when I enjoyed,
now weeping night and day I flood it with tears.

Nevertheless, elect this very space
once-precious nest of joy where I endure —
alone – all sorts of torture and distress

to be the site of our encounter,
so that the news of cruelty, deceit
will die out here, not spread to others' ears.

. . .

But what if you should sue for peace,
lay down your weapons, choose to use the bed
for love's own purposes and love's own wars? —

should I go on fighting you?
I hear that he's considered vile
who, begged forgiveness, fails to grant it.

If it should ever come to this,
I know that I would never swerve
from the course of honest and just behaviour.

Probably I'd follow you to bed,
then lying stretched out there and skirmishing,
I'd not give in to you even an inch;

instead, to punish you for your rotten ways,
I'd get on top and in the heat of battle,
as you grow hotter still defending yourself,

we'd die together shot down by one shot.

(translated from Italian by Lynne Lawner)

Saint Theresa of Avila

(1515–82)

SPAIN

She was born into a noble family of Avila, and as a child, under the influence of tales of knights and martyred saints, she ran away with her brother to seek martyrdom in the land of the Moors. In 1531 she entered the convent in Avila and in 1536 took the habit. After many years and long ordeals of sickness, she began to experience the ecstatic visions that continued throughout her life. She was thought to be possessed and was investigated, though never arrested, by the Inquisition. In the midst of the intrigues of the Counter-Reformation and under harsh physical conditions, she travelled all over Spain to establish the Discalced, or Barefoot, Order of Carmelites by founding convents and monasteries. Saint John of the Cross, whom she called her 'spiritual father', was one of the first Discalced friars. She wrote accounts of her life and religious experience and a small number of poems. In 1622 she was canonized and is now revered as one of the greatest mystic saints of the Catholic Church.

POEM

Nothing move thee;
Nothing terrify thee;
Everything passes;
God never changes.
Patience be all to thee.
Who trusts in God, he
Never shall be needy.
God alone suffices.

(translated from Spanish by Yvor Winters)

If, Lord, Thy love for me is strong
As this which binds me unto Thee,
What holds me from Thee, Lord, so long,
What holds Thee, Lord, so long from me?

O soul, what then desirest thou?
– Lord, I would see Thee, who thus choose Thee.
What fears can yet assail thee now?
– All that I fear is but to lose Thee.

Love's whole possession I entreat,
Lord, make my soul Thine own abode,
And I will build a nest so sweet
It may not be too poor for God.

O soul in God hidden from sin,
What more desires for thee remain,
Save but to love, and love again,
And, all on flame with love within,
Love on, and turn to love again?

(translated from Spanish by Arthur Symons)

Anonymous: Sephardic Ballad
(15th–16th centuries)
MEDITERRANEAN LITTORAL (LADINO)

Spanish narrative ballads of the fifteenth and sixteenth centuries have
survived, through oral transmission, for over four hundred years.
The Spanish Jews (Sephardim) in North Africa, Rhodes, Turkey,
Greece and now in the United States have preserved the Ladino
language and the Judeo-Spanish ballads – *romansas* – which were
customarily sung by women. 'The Lowly Peasant' is part of a field
collection compiled in the Sephardic communities of Los Angeles
and Seattle, 1972–3, by Rina Benmayor of Stanford University.

THE LOWLY PEASANT
An Anonymous Sephardic Ballad

In the city of Marseilles,   there lived a beautiful lady.
She adorned and combed herself,   and sat at her window.

A lovely shepherd passed by,   clothed in finery.
– Come up, lovely shepherd!   You will feast on my wealth.
You shall eat and drink your fill,   and do what you wish!
– I do not heed strange women! said Selví.
  With my beloved I will go!
– If you could see my braids,   ah, so beautiful and so long!
– Go hang yourself with them! said Selví.
  With my beloved I will go!
– If you could see my cheeks,   so beautiful and so white!
– In the fire may they burn! said Selví.
  With my beloved I will go!
– If you could see my hands,   so beautiful and so white!
My small, painted fingers,   laden with rings!
– In the fire may they burn! said Selví.
  With my beloved I will go!
– Off with you, then, lovely shepherd!
You will see your woman with another,   and your children at
    my table!*

> (version from Rhodes, sung by Mrs Regina Hanan;
> translated from Ladino by Rina Benmayor)

Mihri Hatun

(d. 1506)

TURKEY

She was the first major woman poet of the Ottoman Empire. Her
father, a judge, also wrote poetry. She acquired an excellent know-
ledge of Arabic and Persian. Her beauty was legendary. For many
years she was a member of the intellectual circle around Prince
Ahmed, son of Sultan Bayezid II. She had a number of love affairs
with others in this circle. Her collected poems were published in 1967
by the Academy of U.S.S.R.

* The final invective reveals that the seductress is the wife in disguise, testing
her husband's fidelity.

At one glance
I loved you
With a thousand hearts

They can hold against me
No sin except my love for you
Come to me
Don't go away

Let the zealots think
Loving is sinful
Never mind
Let me burn in the hellfire
Of that sin

(translated from Turkish by Tâlat S. Halman)

Mira Bai

(1498–1547)

INDIA (MEDIEVAL HINDI)

Soon after her death Mira Bai became the subject of popular legend. Her devotional lyrics – love songs and songs of entreaty to Krishna, each apparently meant to be sung in a special mode – were preserved through musical and oral traditions. She was probably born in Merta and raised by her grandfather, a warrior-king and devout worshipper of Vishnu. Legend has it that as a child she was given an idol of Krishna, Vishnu's most appealing incarnation worshipped by many followers of Bhakti, the Hindu protestant movement which arose at this time as a response to the threat of Moslem conquest. It is said that Mira took her treasured idol with her when she was married, at 18, to the Prince of Mewar, and offended his family by her refusal to worship his patron goddess Kali. After her husband's death, Mira spent her days singing her songs in the temple and receiving wandering mendicants. For this violation of class and family propriety, the king tried to kill her. Finally, tired of persecution, Mira Bai left

Mewar and lived in various places associated with Krishna. She died
in Dwarka.

O King, I know you gave me poison.
But I emerged
just as gold burned in fire
comes out bright as a dozen suns.
Family prestige, fear of the world's opinion
I threw away as water.
You should hide your own self, Rana,*
I am a powerless mad woman,
Krishna's arrow has pierced my heart
taking away my reason.
I dedicate body and soul to the holy men
I cling to their lotus feet.
Mira's Lord has acknowledged
her as his servant.

*

Keep me as your servant, O Girdhar,†
keep me as your slave.
While I am serving I shall plant gardens
arising every day I shall see you.
In the shaded lanes of Brindavan
I shall sing of Govinda's deeds.
In my servanthood I shall get his vision,
the remembrance would be my pay.
And my estate, the devotion and love,
all three are pleasing to me.
Adorned with the peacock feather crown,
the yellow scarf, the victory garland,
Mohan, the one with the flute,
grazes cows in Brindaban.
I shall build high palaces
having (latticed) windows throughout.

---

* *Rana:* King.
† *Girdhar:* an epithet of Krishna. The name refers to Krishna's lifting of
Mount Govardhan to protect the people of Braj from the wrath of Indra.

I shall see my Dark One,
wearing a yellow sari.
Mira says: Lord Girdhar Nagar,
the heart is extremely impatient.
At midnight on the banks of Jumna
give me your vision.

(translated from medieval Hindi by Usha Nilsson)

Huang O
(1498–1569)
CHINA

She was the daughter of the President of the Board of Works of the
Ming Court. In 1519 she married Yang Shen, a poet and dramatist.
The attitude of the Chinese government towards erotic literature was
unusually lenient during the early sixteenth century, when many
erotic novels were written and bawdy comedies performed in the
theatre. Nevertheless, openly erotic poetry was not considered
appropriate for women writers who were not courtesans.

To the Tune 'Soaring Clouds'

You held my lotus blossom
In your lips and played with the
Pistil. We took one piece of
Magic rhinoceros horn
And could not sleep all night long.
All night the cock's gorgeous crest
stood erect. All night the bee
Clung trembling to the flower
Stamens. Oh my sweet perfumed
Jewel! I will allow only
My lord to possess my sacred
Lotus pond, and every night
You can make blossom in me
Flowers of fire.

To the Tune 'Red Embroidered Shoes'

If you don't know how, why pretend?
Maybe you can fool some girls,
But you can't fool Heaven.
I dreamed you'd play with the
Locust blossom under my green jacket,
Like a eunuch with a courtesan.
But lo and behold
All you can do is mumble.
You've made me all wet and slippery,
But no matter how hard you try
Nothing happens. So stop.
Go and make somebody else
Unsatisfied.

(translated from Chinese by Kenneth Rexroth
and Ling Chung)

Hwang Chin-i
(c. 1506–44)

KOREA

The most famous and most talented of the Korean women poets,
Hwang Chin-i lived in Songdo and had a great many admirers. Her
fame reached its height during the reign of King Chungjong. Her
achievement is most evident in her somewhat philosophical love
poems.

I cut in two
A long November night, and
Place half under the coverlet,
Sweet-scented as a spring breeze.
And when he comes, I shall take it out,
Unroll it inch by inch, to stretch the night.

(translated from Korean by Peter H. Lee)

Mountains are steadfast but the mountain streams
Go by, go by,
And yesterdays are like the rushing streams,
They fly, they fly,
And the great heroes, famous for a day,
They die, they die.

(translated from Korean by Peter H. Lee)

The blue hill is my desire,
    the green stream my beloved's love.
Even if the stream flows away,
    how can the hill ever change?
Never forgetting the hill, I wonder,
    does the stream cry as it leaves?

(translated from Korean by Ko Won)

Hŏ Nansŏrhŏn

(1563–89)

KOREA

The finest woman poet of the *kasa*, a form of narrative verse. She was the daughter of a minister, and her brother Hŏ Kyun wrote the first Korean novel. She died young but left a number of lovely poems in both Korean and Chinese. The following are excerpts from one of her most famous poems.

from A WOMAN'S SORROW

Yesterday I fancied I was young;
But already, alas, I am aging.
What use is there in recalling
The joyful days of my youth?
Now I am old, recollections are vain.
Sorrow chokes me; words fail me.

When Father begot me, Mother reared me,
When they took pains to bring me up,
They dreamed, not of a duchess or marchioness,
But at least of a bride fit for a gentleman.
The turning of destiny of the three lives
And the tie chanced by a matchmaker
Brought me a careless knight,
And careful as in a dream I trod on ice.
Or was it a dream, those innocent days?
When I reached fifteen, counted sixteen,
The inborn beauty in me blossomed, and
With this face and this body
I vowed a union of a hundred years.

The flow of time and tide was sudden;
The Gods too were jealous of my beauty.
Spring breezes and autumn rains,
Alas, they flew like a shuttle.
And my face that once was beautiful,
Where did it go? Who disgraced it so?

. . .

Lighting the blue lantern, I play
A Song of Blue Lotus on the green lute,
And play it as my sorrow commands me,
As though the rain on the Hsiao and Hsiang
Beat confusedly over the bamboo leaves,
As though the crane returned whooping
After a span of a thousand years.
Fingers may pluck the familiar tune,
But who will listen? The room
Is empty except for the lotus-brocaded curtains.

. . .

The Weaver and Herdboy in the sky
Meet once on the seventh day of the seventh moon,
However hard it is to cross the Milky Way,
And never miss this yearly encounter.

But since he left me, left me alone,
What magic water separates him from me
And what makes him silent across the water?
Leaning on the balustrade, I gaze at the path he took —
Dewdrops glitter on the young grass,
Evening clouds pass by; birds sing sadly
In the thickets of green bamboos.
Numberless are the sorrowful;
But none can be as wretched as I.
Think, love, you caused me this grief;
I know not whether I shall live or die.

(translated from Korean by Peter H. Lee)

Queen Elizabeth I
(1533–1603)
ENGLAND

One of the most famous monarchs of history, she headed a Court
brilliant both politically and culturally. Great poets were her friends
and it is no surprise that she herself should have practised the art of
poetry, just one of her many accomplishments. Only a very few
poems survive that are known indisputably to be written by her.

Written with a Diamond on Her Window at Woodstock

Much suspected by me,
Nothing proved can be,
    Quoth Elizabeth prisoner.

Written on a Wall at Woodstock

Oh fortune, thy wresting wavering state
Hath fraught with cares my troubled wit,
Whose witness this present prison late
Could bear, where once was joy's loan quit.

Thou caused the guilty to be loosed
From bands where innocents were inclosed,
And caused the guiltless to be reserved,
And freed those that death had well deserved.
But all herein can be nothing wrought,
So God send to my foes all they have thought.

Written in Her French Psalter

No crooked leg, no bleared eye,
  No part deformed out of kind,
Nor yet so ugly half can be
  As is the inward suspicious mind.

THE DOUBT OF FUTURE FOES

The doubt of future foes exiles my present joy,
And wit me warns to shun such snares as threaten mine annoy;
For falsehood now doth flow, and subjects' faith doth ebb,
Which should not be if reason ruled or wisdom weaved the web.
But clouds of joys untried do cloak aspiring minds,
Which turn to rain of late repent by changed course of winds.
The top of hope supposed the root upreared shall be,
And fruitless all their grafted guile, as shortly ye shall see.
The dazzled eyes with pride, which great ambition blinds,
Shall be unsealed by worthy wights whose foresight
    falsehood finds.
The daughter of debate that discord aye doth sow
Shall reap no gain where former rule still peace hath taught
    to know.
No foreign banished wight shall anchor in this port;
Our realm brooks not seditious sects, let them elsewhere resort.
My rusty sword through rest shall first his edge employ
To poll their tops that seek such change or gape for future joy.

ON FORTUNE

Never think you fortune can bear the sway
Where virtue's force can cause her to obey.

Mary Sidney, Countess of Pembroke
(1562–1621)

ENGLAND

After her marriage at the age of fifteen to Henry Herbert, second Earl of Pembroke, she reigned as patron of letters at the family seat of Wilton. Her brother, Sir Philip Sidney, wrote for her his 'Arcadia'; Spenser dedicated his 'Ruines of Time' to her. She and her brother started their joint versification of the Psalms some time before his death and subsequently she continued the work and improved and polished the work of her brother. Her versions of the Psalms are considered superior examples of all that was strong and excellent in Elizabethan poetry.

PSALM 62.   *Nonne Deo*

Yet shall my soule in silence still
  On God, my help, attentive stay:
Yet he my fort, my health, my hill,
  Remove I may not, move I may.
How long then shall your fruitlesse will
  An enimy soe farr from fall,
With weake endevor strive to kill,
  You rotten hedg, you broken wall?

Forsooth, that hee no more may rise,
  Advaunced eft to throne and crown:
To headlong him their thoughtes devise,
  And, past reliefe, to tread him downe.
Their love is only love of lies:
  Their wordes and deedes dissenting soe,
When from their lippes most blessing flyes,
  Then deepest curse in hart doth grow.

Yet shall my soule in silence still
  On God, my hope, attentive stay:
Yet hee my fort, my health, my hill,
  Remove? O no: not move I may.

My God doth me with glory fill,
  Not only shield me safe from harme:
To shun distresse, to conquer ill,
  To him I clime, in him I arme.

O then, on God, our certaine stay,
  All people in all times rely,
Your hartes before him naked lay:
  To Adams sonnes tis vain to fly,
Soe vain soe false, soe fraile are they;
  Ev'n he that seemeth most of might
With lightnesse self if him you waigh,
  Then lightnesse self will waigh more light.

In fraud, and force, noe trust repose:
  Such idle hopes from thoughtes expell,
And take good heed, when riches growes
  Let not your hart on riches dwell.
All powre is Gods, his own word showes,
  Once said by him, twice heard by me:
Yet from thee, Lord, all mercy flowes,
  And each manns work is paid by thee.

Máiri MacLeod

(1569–1674?)

SCOTLAND (GAELIC)

She was a daughter of Red Alastair and through him connected with
the chiefs of the MacLeods. She spent most of her life in Dunvegan
in Skye but was exiled briefly to Mull when she composed songs too
favourable to the relatives of her chief. Her position in the household
was apparently as nurse or foster-mother to the young heirs. She was
honoured as the clan's poet but only a few of her poems survive.

A COMPLAINT ABOUT EXILE

H-óran ó a vee-ó
Ro h-óran ó a vee-ó

I am troubled
for more than a week now

On a bare island
without grass or shelter.

If I am able
I will go to my home

Making my way
as best I can

To Ullinish
with its white-hoofed herds,

Where once in childhood
I was nourished

On breast-milk
of smooth-skinned women,

Across to the house of
Brown Fionngal, Lachann's daughter

Who gives sustenance
to strong men,

To Rory More
of the cloaks,

There in his big house
I have known indulgence

Danced with abandon
on spreading floors

Fiddle music
putting me to sleep

Pipes stirring
me in the morning

To there, this message ó hó-ó,
To Dunvegan hi-ó

Ro h-óran ó a hó-ó.

(translated from Gaelic by Joan Keefe)

Margaret, Duchess of Newcastle
(1625–73)

ENGLAND

An early critic wrote of her: 'It is plain, from the uncommon turn of her compositions, that she possessed a wild native genius, which, if duly cultivated, might probably have shewn itself to advantage in the higher sorts of poetry.' She was considered eccentric, if not mad, by her contemporaries. Her biography of her husband was described by Pepys as 'the ridiculous history of my Lord Newcastle writ by his wife, which shows her to be a mad, conceited, ridiculous woman, and he an ass to suffer her to write what she writes to him and of him'. But Charles Lamb described it as 'a jewel'.

NATURE'S COOK

Death is the cook of nature, and we find
Creatures drest several ways to please her mind;
Some Death doth roast with fevers burning hot,
And some he boils with dropsies in a pot;
Some are consumed for jelly by degrees,
And some with ulcers, gravy out to squeeze;
Some, as with herbs, he stuffs with gouts and pains,
Others for tender meat he hangs in chains;
Some in the sea he pickles up to keep,
Others he, as soused brawn, in wine doth steep;
Some flesh and bones he with the Pox chops small,
And doth a French fricassee make withall;
Some on grid-irons of calentures are broiled,
And some are trodden down, and so quite spoiled:
But some are baked, when smothered they do die,
Some meat he doth by hectick fevers fry;
In sweat sometimes he stews with savory smell,
An hodge-podge of diseases he likes well;
Some brains he dresseth with apoplexy,
Or fawce of megrims, swimming plenteously;

And tongues he dries with smoak from stomachs ill,
Which, as the second course he sends up still;
Throats he doth cut, blood puddings for to make,
And puts them in the guts, which cholicks rack;
Some hunted are by him for deer, that's red,
And some as stall-fed oxen knocked o'th' head;
Some singed and scald for bacon, seem most rare,
When with salt rheum and phlegm they powdered are.

Katherine Philips (Orinda)

(1631–64)

ENGLAND

She was born in London and 'educated in the presbyterian principles,
which her better judgment occasioned her to desert'. She married
James Philips in 1647. She was well known during her lifetime for
her writings. She translated Corneille's *Pompey* and *Horace*, which
were performed with some success. She died of smallpox when she
was 33.

UPON ABSENCE

1

'Tis now since I began to dy
    Foure moneths, and more yet gasping live.
Wrapp'd up in sorrows, doe I ly
    Hoping, yet doubting a reprieve.
Adam from Paradise expell'd
Just such a wretched being held.

2

'Tis not thy love I feare to loose
    That will in spight of absence hold;
But 'tis the benefit and use
    Is lost, as in imprison'd Gold:
Which though the summe be ne're so great,
Enriche's nothing but conceipt.

3

What angry star then govern's me
   That I must feele a double smart?
Pris'ner to fate as well as thee,
   Kept from thy face, link'd to thy heart
Because my Love, all Love excell's
Must my griefs have no parallells.

4

Hapless and dead as winter here
   I now remaine and all I see
Coppys of my wild 'state appeare,
   But I am their epitomy.
Love me no more! for I am grown
Too dead and dull for thee to own.

Aphra Behn
(1640–89)

ENGLAND

Aphra Behn seems to have been as witty, disreputable and intelligent as any Restoration heroine. She led an adventurous life, acting for a time as a spy in Amsterdam. She is the first English woman to have made her living by writing. She wrote many comedies, for which she is chiefly remembered.

from *A Voyage to the Isle of Love* (a lengthy exercise in titillation)

THE DREAM

All trembling in my arms Aminta lay,
Defending of the bliss I strove to take;
Raising my rapture by her kind delay,
Her force so charming was and weak.
The soft resistance did betray the grant,

While I pressed on the heaven of my desires;
Her rising breasts with nimbler motions pant;
Her dying eyes assume new fires.
Now to the height of languishment she grows,
And still her looks new charms put on;
– Now the last mystery of Love she knows,
We sigh, and kiss: I waked, and all was done.

'Twas but a dream, yet by my heart I knew,
Which still was panting, part of it was true:
Oh how I strove the rest to have believed;
Ashamed and angry to be undeceived!

Madame Deshoulières

(1637–94)

FRANCE

She was born Antoinette du Ligier de la Garde into a wealthy
Parisian family and received an excellent education in Latin and
several European languages. She married at fourteen and joined her
husband, a partisan of Condé, in exile in the Spanish Netherlands.
She was later prominent in Court circles in France and Austria.

REFLECTIONS

I

Why rejoice in beauty? What
In all the world is half so vain?
    Nay, there is naught
    Gives so much pain.
I know that over hearts her rule is sore,
    While one is beautiful that she
May have of passion and of lovers store:
    But that has little time to be
    And a long time to be no more.

2

Pathetic plaything of a witless chance,
  Victim of evils and of laws,
  Man, who in whatever cause,
  Must suffer life's impertinence,
    Still, after all that's past,
Whence comes it that you fear the power of death?
Coward! regard it with unhurried breath,
  And know this outrage for the last.

(translated from French by Yvor Winters)

Sor Juana Ines de la Cruz
(1652–95)
MEXICO (SPANISH)

Sor Juana is one of the great figures in Latin American literature. She became a lady-in-waiting to the Vicereine when she was about eighteen but shortly afterwards became a nun. She continued to study, write, and entertain her friends. Her fame grew. When the Bishop of Puebla reprimanded her for her love of worldly learning she replied with her famous 'Reply to Sor Filotea de la Cruz', which is a vindication of the right of women to intellectual emancipation. She then renounced all her personal pursuits and died two years later while looking after the sick in a fever epidemic.

This coloured counterfeit that thou beholdest,
vainglorious with the excellencies of art,
is, in fallacious syllogisms of colour,
nought but a cunning dupery of sense;

this in which flattery has undertaken
to extenuate the hideousness of years,
and, vanquishing the outrages of time,
to triumph o'er oblivion and old age,

is an empty artifice of care,
is a fragile flower in the wind,
is a paltry sanctuary from fate,
is a foolish sorry labour lost,
is conquest doomed to perish and, well taken,
is corpse and dust, shadow and nothingness.

(translated from Spanish by Samuel Beckett)

VERSES FROM 'A SATIRICAL ROMANCE'

Ignorant men, who disclaim
women with no reason,
you do not see you are the reason
for what you blame.
Importuning her disdain
with such pressing desire,
why is it goodness you then require,
who have caused her shame?

What humour can be so rare
that carelessly will blur
a mirror, and then aver
that it's not clear?

Critics: in your sight
no woman can win:
keep you out, and she's too tight;
she's too loose if you get in.

*

I can't hold you and I can't leave you,
and sorting the reasons to leave you
    or hold you,
I find an intangible one to love you,
and many tangible ones to forgo you.

As you won't change, nor let me
    forgo you,
I shall give my heart a defence against
    you,
so that half shall always be armed to
    abhor you,
though the other half be ready to
    adore you.

Then, if our love, by loving flourish,
let it not in endless feuding perish;
let us speak no more in jealousy and
    suspicion.

He offers not part, who would all
    receive —
so know that when it is your intention
mine shall be to make believe.

★

This evening, my love, even as I spoke vainly
to you, beholding how your gestures strayed,
and how the words I spoke failed to persuade,
so I desired you to see my heart plainly.

And to my aid came Love, who took my part,
and willed what by my will had futile seemed:
that from the torrent where my grief streamed
I might, by drops, distil my streaming heart.

Enough harshness, my love, cease and resist
jealousy, even as to a tyrant's torture;
to shadows, rumour, doubt do not give over;
weigh not your peace against such proof as this;

    for even as water could you touch and behold
    my heart, as through your hands it flowed.

    (translated from Spanish by Judith Thurman)

Catharina Regina von Greiffenberg
(1633–94)

GERMANY

Catharina von Greiffenberg was born in Vach (upper Austria) and died in Nuremberg, where she had been exiled because of her Protestant beliefs. Considered to be the major woman poet of the German Baroque, her central work is the *Geistliche Sonette* collection of 1662.

ON THE INEFFABLE INSPIRATION
OF THE HOLY SPIRIT

You unseen lightning flash, you darkly radiant light,
you power that's heart-infused, incomprehensible being!
Something divine within my spirit had its being
That stirs and spurs me: I sense a curious light.

Never by its own power the soul is thus alight.
It was a miracle-wind, a spirit, a creative being,
The eternal power of breath, prime origin of being
That in me kindled for himself this heaven-flaring light.

You mirror-spectrum-glance, you many-coloured gleam!
You glitter to and fro, are incomprehensibly clear;
in truth's own sunlight the spirit-dove-flights gleam.

The God-stirred pool has also been troubled clear!
First on the spirit-sun reflecting it casts its gleam,
The moon; then turns about, and earthward, too, is clear.

(translated from German by Michael Hamburger)

WHY THE RESURRECTION WAS
REVEALED TO WOMEN

Not he who holds the sceptre high atop the eagle's throne
Nor students of the stars, nor brawny heroes bold,
Were first to whom the Resurrection was made known.

To weak women you appeared, O mighty Christ!
To us alone did Heaven grant this greatest good
So that the miracle grew all it could
In pure praise of faith and fame, not in sly power of the wise.

Our simplicity pleased you, O Wellspring of wise minds:
So let your victory song reverberate in mine.
God, man, light, life, salvation, all good things arise.

The heavenly Kingdom lies in life's demise.
God finds united being in the beingless death he dies,
And lifts it up to secret majesty of skies.

(translated from German by Bill Crisman)

Anne Bradstreet

(1612–72)

COLONIAL AMERICA

An early poet of the American colonies, she was born and educated
in England on her father's estate. At the age of sixteen she married
Simon Bradstreet, and in 1630 her entire family sailed with the
founding party of the Massachusetts Bay Colony. Both her father
and her husband were to serve as Governor of Massachusetts.
Though life in New England was harsh and her health extremely
poor, she lived to be sixty, bore eight children, and left behind a
large body of poems. During her lifetime she was published anony-
mously in London and for long after her death was considered the
finest woman poet in English. She is remembered today not for her
long allegories, but for her short poems not intended for publication
– elegies for the deaths of her infant grandchildren, personal reflec-
tions, love poems, and her masterpiece, *Contemplations*, a sequence of
thirty-three stanzas in praise of God and the natural world. Her
Meditations, left to her children after her death, is one of the finest
prose works of the era.

from CONTEMPLATIONS

2

I wist not what to wish, yet sure thought I,
If so much excellence abide below;
How excellent is he that dwells on high?
Whose power and beauty by his works we know.
Sure he is goodness, wisdome, glory, light,
That hath this under world so richly dight:
More Heaven than Earth was here no winter and no
    night.

8

Silent alone, where none or saw, or heard,
In pathless paths I lead my wandring feet,
My humble Eyes to lofty Skyes I rear'd
To sing some Song, my mazed Muse thought meet.
My great Creator I would magnifie,
That nature had, thus decked liberally:
But Ah, and Ah, again, my imbecility!

18

When I behold the heavens as in their prime,
And then the earth (though old) stil clad in green,
The stones and trees, insensible of time,
Nor age nor wrinkle on their front are seen;
If winter come, and greeness then do fade,
A Spring returns, and they more youthfull made;
But Man grows old, lies down, remains where once he's
    laid.

20

Shall I then praise the heavens, the trees, the earth
Because their beauty and their strength last longer
Shall I wish there, or never to had birth,
Because they're bigger, and their bodyes stronger?

Nay, they shall darken, perish, fade and dye,
And when unmade, so ever shall they lye,
But man was made for endless immortality.

35

O Time the fatal wrack of mortal things,
That draws oblivions curtains over kings,
Their sumptuous monuments, men know them not,
Their names without a Record are forgot,
Their parts, their ports, their pomp's all laid in th' dust
Nor wit nor gold, nor buildings scape times rust;
But he whose name is grav'd in the white stone
Shall last and shine when all of these are gone.

Anne Finch, Countess of Winchilsea

(1661–1720)

ENGLAND

Born near Southampton, she became a maid of honour to Mary of
Modena, duchess of York. She married in 1684 Heneage Finch, later
fifth Earl of Winchilsea, and published during her lifetime a poem,
'The Spleen' (1701), and a volume of *Poems* (1713).

A NOCTURNAL REVERIE

In such a *Night*, when every louder Wind
Is to its distant Cavern safe confin'd;
And only gentle *Zephyr* fans his Wings,
And lonely *Philomel*, still waking, sings;
Or from some Tree, fam'd for the *Owl's* delight,
She, hollowing clear, directs the Wand'rer right:
In such a *Night*, when passing Clouds give place,
Or thinly vail the Heav'ns mysterious Face;
When in some River, overhung with Green,
The waving Moon and trembling Leaves are seen;
When freshen'd Grass now bears itself upright,
And makes cool Banks to pleasing Rest invite,

Whence springs the *Woodbind*, and the *Bramble*-Rose,
And where the sleepy *Cowslip* shelter'd grows;
Whilst now a paler Hue the *Foxglove* takes,
Yet checquers still with Red the dusky brakes
When scatter'd *Glow-worms*, but in Twilight fine,
Shew trivial Beauties watch their Hour to shine;
Whilst *Salisb'ry* stands the Test of every Light,
In perfect Charms, and perfect Virtue bright:
When Odours, which declin'd repelling Day,
Thro' temp'rate Air uninterrupted stray;
When darken'd Groves their softest Shadows wear,
And falling Waters we distinctly hear;
When thro' the Gloom more venerable shows
Some ancient Fabrick, awful in Repose,
While Sunburnt Hills their swarthy Looks conceal,
And swelling Haycocks thicken up the Vale:
When the loos'd *Horse* now, as his Pasture leads,
Comes slowly grazing thro' th' adjoining Meads,
Whose stealing Pace, and lengthen'd Shade we fear,
Till torn up Forage in his Teeth we hear:
When nibbling *Sheep* at large pursue their Food,
And unmolested Kine rechew the Cud;
When *Curlews* cry beneath the Village-walls,
And to her straggling Brood the *Partridge* calls;
Their shortliv'd Jubilee the Creatures keep,
Which but endures, whilst Tyrant-*Man* do's sleep;
When a sedate Content the Spirit feels,
And no fierce Light disturb, whilst it reveals;
But silent Musings urge the Mind to seek
Something, too high for Syllables to speak;
Till the free Soul to a compos'dness charm'd,
Finding the Elements of Rage disarm'd,
O'er all below a solemn Quiet grown,
Joys in th' inferior World, and thinks it like her Own:
In such a *Night* let Me abroad remain,
Till Morning breaks, and All's confus'd again;
Our Cares, our Toils, our Clamours are renew'd,
Or Pleasures, seldom reach'd, again pursu'd.

Lady Mary Wortley Montagu
(1689–1762)

ENGLAND

Lady Mary Wortley Montagu led an adventurous and eccentric life. She eloped in 1712 with Edward Wortley Montagu. They travelled in Turkey, from where she brought back to England the method of inoculation against smallpox. She was greatly criticized for having her own children so inoculated. While she was in the East, Pope addressed to her many extravagant letters of admiration, but after her return they quarrelled and thereafter he attacked her frequently in his compositions. She left her husband in 1739 and travelled in Europe, making another enemy, Horace Walpole. Her health failed and she returned to England to die in 1762. Her most famous writings are her *Letters*, some of which appeared in print in 1763. During her lifetime her 'Town Eclogues' were published in a pirated edition as *Court Poems* in 1716.

RECEIPT FOR THE VAPOURS
Written to Lady J——————n

Why will *Delia* thus retire,
And languish life away?
While the sighing croud admire,
'Tis too soon for hartshorn tea.

All those dismal looks and fretting
Cannot *Damon*'s life restore;
Long ago the worms have eat him,
You can never see him more.

Once again consult your toilet,
In the glass your face review:
So much weeping soon will spoil it,
And no spring your charms renew.

I, like you, was born a woman,
Well I know what vapours mean:
The disease, alas! is common,
Single, we have all the spleen.

All the morals that they tell us
Never cur'd the sorrow yet:
Choose, among the pretty fellows,
One of humour, youth, and wit.

Prythee hear him every morning,
At the least an hour or two;
Once again at night returning,
I believe the dose will do.

Anonymous

(18th century)

IRELAND

Lady Gregory published her *Kiltartan Poetry Book*, from which this poem is taken, in 1919. In her introduction she writes: 'In translating these poems I have chosen to do so in the speech of the thatched houses where I have heard and gathered them . . . using the Gaelic construction and Elizabethan phrases, as I have used them in my creative work.'

GRIEF OF A GIRL'S HEART

O Donal Oge, if you go across the sea,
Bring myself with you and do not forget it;
And you will have a sweetheart for fair days and market days,
And the daughter of the King of Greece beside you at night.

It is late last night the dog was speaking of you;
The snipe was speaking of you in her deep marsh.
It is you are the lonely bird through the woods;
And that you may be without a mate until you find me.

You promised me, and you said a lie to me,
That you would be before me where the sheep are flocked;
I gave a whistle and three hundred cries to you,
And I found nothing there but a bleating lamb.

You promised me a thing that was hard for you,
A ship of gold under a silver mast;
Twelve towns with a market in all of them,
And a fine white court by the side of the sea.

You promised me a thing that is not possible,
That you would give me gloves of the skin of a fish;
That you would give me shoes of the skin of a bird;
And a suit of the dearest silk in Ireland.

O Donal Oge, it is I would be better to you
Than a high, proud, spendthrift lady:
I would milk the cow; I would bring help to you;
And if you were hard pressed, I would strike a blow for you.

You have taken the east from me; you have taken the west
    from me,
You have taken what is before me and what is behind me;
You have taken the moon, you have taken the sun from me,
And my fear is great that you have taken God from me!

(translated from Irish by Lady Augusta Gregory)

Eibhlín Dhubh Ní Chonaill

(1743–?)

IRELAND

Eibhlín Dhubh married Arthur O'Leary in 1768. He was a dashing
young Captain in the Hungarian army, whose great pleasure it was
to bait Protestants in his native Cork. One, Morris, in a fit of anger
demanded that O'Leary sell him his horse for five pounds (no
Catholic was allowed to own a horse worth more than that, by law).

O'Leary refused, and late the same night he was waylaid and shot by Morris. Eibhlín Dhubh composed this, one of the most famous Laments in the language.

from THE LAMENT FOR ARTHUR O'LEARY

I

My love forever!
The day I first saw you
At the end of the market-house,
My eye observed you,
My heart approved you,
I fled from my father with you,
Far from my home with you.

II

I never repented it:
You whitened a parlour for me,
Painted rooms for me,
Reddened ovens for me,
Baked fine bread for me,
Basted meat for me,
Slaughtered beasts for me;
I slept in ducks' feathers
Till midday milking-time,
Or more if it pleased me.

III

My friend forever!
My mind remembers
That fine spring day
How well your hat suited you,
Bright gold banded,
Sword silver-hilted —
Right hand steady —
Threatening aspect —
Trembling terror

On treacherous enemy —
You poised for a canter
On your slender bay horse.
The Saxons bowed to you,
Down to the ground to you,
Not for love of you
But for deadly fear of you,
Though you lost your life to them,
Oh my soul's darling.

VII

My friend you were forever!
I knew nothing of your murder
Till your horse came to the stable
With the reins beneath her trailing,
And your heart's blood on her shoulders
Staining the tooled saddle
Where you used to sit and stand.
My first leap reached the threshold,
My second reached the gateway,
My third leap reached the saddle.

VIII

I struck my hands together
And I made the bay horse gallop
As fast as I was able,
Till I found you dead before me
Beside a little furze-bush.
Without Pope or bishop,
Without priest or cleric
To read the death-psalms for you,
But a spent old woman only
Who spread her cloak to shroud you —
Your heart's blood was still flowing;
I did not stay to wipe it
But filled my hands and drank it.

XVII

My friend and my treasure!
It's bad treatment for a hero
To lie hooded in a coffin,
The warm-hearted rider
That fished in bright rivers,
That drank in great houses
With white-breasted women.
My thousand sorrows
That I've lost my companion.

XXXV

My love and my dear!
Your stooks are standing,
Your yellow cows milking;
On my heart is such sorrow
That all Munster could not cure it,
Nor the wisdom of the sages.
Till Art O'Leary returns
There will be no end to the grief
That presses down on my heart,
Closed up tight and firm
Like a trunk that is locked
And the key is mislaid.

XXXVI

All you women out there weeping,
Wait a little longer;
We'll drink to Art son of Connor
And the souls of all the dead,
Before he enters the school —
Not learning wisdom or music
But weighed down by earth and stones.

(translated from Irish by Eilís Dillon)

Anna Maria Lenngren
(1754–1819)
SWEDEN

The daughter of a professor at Uppsala University, she received a classical education and was distinguished as a translator of Latin poetry and drama. She married in 1780 and moved to Stockholm where her husband edited the *Stockholms Posten*, in which most of her poems first appeared. She was also a gifted singer and composed some songs. Extremely modest about her writing, she refused to allow her collected poems to be published until after her death and then only under the title *A Poetry Attempt* (*Skaldeförsök*). In 1800, she became the first woman to be honoured by the Swedish Academy with a yearly pension. She is the most famous woman poet in Swedish before the twentieth century.

OTHER FABRICS, OTHER MORES!

'When I was young,' said Aunt to me,
'Women then, about the year
Seventeen-thirty, Betty dear,
Dressed in decent linsey-woolsey!
No painted faces would one find,
Nor flimsy gowns on womenfolk.
The fairer sex possessed a mind
Of sturdy fabric, like her cloak.
Now all is different in our lives —
Other fabrics, other mores!
Taffetas, indecent stories
Of young girls as well as wives!
The path of lust they boldly walk;
Shameless manners, daring ways,
Make-up, muslins, brazen talk
Go hand-in-hand with modern days.'

(translated from Swedish by Nadia Christensen
and Mariann Tiblin)

Kaga no Chiyo

(1701–75)

JAPAN

The most famous woman writer of *haiku*, she was born seven years after the death of Bashō.

> Spring rain:
> Everything just grows
> More beautiful.

> The dew of the rouge-flower
> When it is spilled
> Is simply water.

> Autumn's bright moon,
> However far I walked, still afar off
> In an unknown sky.

> (translated from Japanese by R. H. Blyth)

Ho Xuan Huong

(late 18th century)

VIETNAM

The dates of her birth and death are unknown, but she lived during a time of great political intrigue in the history of Vietnam. Her poems were extremely controversial because they dealt with sex, a taboo subject in a Confucian society. She also spoke out for the rights of women and against the prevailing custom of polygamy. She is very famous; her poems appear in high-school textbooks and are considered an integral part of the national tradition of Vietnam.

THE JACKFRUIT

I am like a jackfruit on the tree.
To taste you must plug me quick, while fresh:
the skin rough, the pulp thick, yes,
but oh, I warn you against touching —
the rich juice will gush and stain your hands.

(translated from Vietnamese by Nguyen Ngoc Bich)

Carved on an Areca Nut, To Be Presented to a Guest

A tiny nut, a bit of tasteless betel,
But still, your Xuan Huong rolled it.
If we come together let it turn red,
Not leaf-flat, lime-insipid.

(translated from Vietnamese by Nguyen Ngoc Bich
and Burton Raffel)

A BUDDHIST PRIEST

He's neither Chinese
Nor one of us:
Bald, his clothes unstitched,
He sits behind rows of rice-cake offerings
And in front of six or seven nuns.
Now and then he touches a gong,
A bell, cymbals;
He hums, drawls, incants.
Pray hard: you too can be a Superior
And squat, proud, on a lotus.

(translated from Vietnamese by Nguyen Ngoc Bich
and Burton Raffel)

THE NINETEENTH CENTURY

Sun Yün-feng
(1764–1814)

CHINA

She was a native of Chekiang, the daughter of an official. She married
the scholar Ch'en and was one of the favourites of the thirteen women
students of the Ch'ing Dynasty poet Yüan Mei.

STARTING AT DAWN

Under the waning moon
In the dawn —
A frosty bell.
My horse's hooves
Tramp through the yellow leaves.
As the sun rises
Not a human being is visible,
Only the sound of a stream
Through the misty trees.

THE TRAIL UP WU GORGE

The trail climbs in zig-zags
High above spiralling whirlpools.
Swift waters break against sheer rocks.
On the evening breeze comes the sound
Of a boy playing his flute,
Riding home on the back of an ox.
The last drops of rain mingle
With the cloud of my horse's breath.
New grass grows on the ancient ramparts.
On the abandoned monuments
The old inscriptions are lost in time.
I am bound on a journey without end,
And cannot bear the song of the cuckoo.

(translated from Chinese by Kenneth Rexroth
and Ling Chung)

Karolina Pavlova

(1807–93)

RUSSIA

Her youthful love affair with the great Polish poet Mickiewicz was
the most lasting emotional influence on her life. Her marriage to the
novelist Nicholas Pavlov was an unhappy one. She was an aristocrat
and rich, and for a time led a literary salon in Moscow. When critics
refused to take her work seriously, she retired to live on the Baltic.
A later generation, that of the Symbolist school, rediscovered her
work and gave it the consideration it deserved. The main subject of
her poetry is the courage of suppressed suffering.

TO MADAME A. V. PLETNEFF

You ask me

> Earnest, intelligent, charming,
> young (you want counsel
> from those the world has made old)
> Loving mother, happy wife —

You ask me
(lowering your voice):
Why?

Your cruel scorn,
sometimes.
Why?

I know you want only
to trust, to believe —
but you trust only partly.
Why?

Pitiless dissection,
harsh discourse.
Why?

Frozen observations
of the heart's happiness, always.
Why?

I cannot admire
this in you, cannot
love it.
Why?

And I answer
(perhaps):

I have only half lived.
I found only a master
when I needed
a friend.

I doubt?
And I want so much
to affirm!

*But I know the cost
of hope and trust and love.*

I observe? I dissect?
Renounce your fervent
flights?
But I've battled the flood!

I've never been afraid!
I've always pursued
one distant dream —
Justice, and Truth.

Am I scornful?
I have shut up
a burnt-out heart.
Paid for my passionate
longing with my life.

And within me
I know:
even that terrible price
was a waste.

I have learned,
un-learned,
nothing.

(translated from French by Paul Schmidt)

Larin Paraske

(1833–1904)

FINLAND

She is the most famous among the women singers and one of the last great singers of the traditional folk poetry of Finland. She knew by heart 1,343 poems, songs, and magic formulas. She was born, married, had children, and lived most of her life in the prosperous rural area north of St Petersburg (Leningrad), where in 1877 she was 'discovered' by a Finnish folklorist and taken to Helsinki; her portrait was painted by two of the best-known painters of the day, and in 1949 a statue to her was erected in Helsinki by national subscription.

SAD IS THE SEAGULL

Sad is the seagull
When swimming in wintry waters
sadder still the homeless
wandering in the wide world
unhappy the heart of the dove
when picking a foreign pittance
throbbing the throat of the sparrow
when drinking icy droplets
colder am I and wretched
colder still than that.

MY LITTLE LOVE LIES ON THE GROUND
A mother's imprecation at the loss
of her daughter's virginity

My little love lies on the ground
My bird has a broken wing
Should I know who left
Who left my love lying
He would writhe like a worm
Slither like a snake
Walk through a forest fire
Crawl through muddy marshes
Wallow in foul waters.

A WOMAN GROWS SOON OLD

Fair is not my face
Cherry-red are not my cheeks
White is not my weary skin;
Age has reached me early
Youth has left me soon.
Once a year I have a lamb
Once a month a calf.
   Did the great God make me
Did the Lord create me
Once a year to have a lamb
Once a month to have a calf.
Often am I by my husband
Always in the arms of man.

(translated from Finnish by Jaakko A Ahokas)

Annette von Droste-Hülshoff

(1797–1848)

GERMANY

Born in an ancestral castle near Münster, Annette von Droste-Hülshoff lived most of her life in retirement except for a brief affair with a young novelist, seventeen years her junior, who rejected her for another woman. Although in contact with some of the eminent writers of her day, such as the Grimm brothers, she lived very much in her own world of moral inhibition and Catholic faith. She is considered the most important German woman poet of the nineteenth century.

ON THE TOWER

I stand high in the belfry tower,
Where starlings scream and swirl in air;
As though I were a maenad, Storm,
You run your fingers through my hair.
O spirit free, entrancing youth,
Here at the very railing, I
would wrestle, hip to hip, against
Your hold; become alive – or die.

Below, along the sandy beach,
I see the whitecaps leap in play
Like frisky hounds tumbling the surf,
Darting in hissing, sparkling spray.
Oh, I would join them in their game,
Pursuing walrus, sportive prey,
Leading the romping pack through glades
Of coral, hunting dolphins gay.

Far off I see a pennant stream,
Bold as an admiral's banner;
I watch the masts bob in the sea,
From safe in my high-towered manor.
Oh, I would rule that tossing ship

And hold helm firm and guide her true,
Skim lightly over foaming reefs
As brushing wings of seagulls do.

If I could hunt the open fields,
Or march to war, a soldier tall,
If heaven listened to my plea,
Made me a man, even though small!
Instead, I sit here – delicate,
Polite, precise, well-mannered child.
Dreams shake my loosened hair – the wind
Lone listener to my spirit wild.

IN THE GRASS

Refreshing rest, ecstatic dream,
Sweet scent of herbs suffusing grass,
Deep, deep, wild-rushing stream;
When sky absorbs the clouds that pass,
When dancing laughter reels around
Your head like fluttering Mayflowers,
When gay notes drift across the ground,
Lime blossoms falling on a grave in showers —

Then all the ghosts within your breast
(Dead love, dead pleasure, and dead time)
Stir gently, gently, as in quest
of breath, stiffly, as a masked mime
Gropes sight beyond closed eyelashes;
Then all this wealth, abandoned, binned
As rubbish, sings hidden splashes
Of timid sound, like bells fingered by wind.

Hours, you are briefer than the kiss
Of sunbeam lips on saddened sea,
Than the cry of autumn birds is,
Dropped like pearls of melody,
Than sun-bright sparkle on the shell
The scuttling beetle wears for shield,
Than hand clasp broken by farewell,
A thinning warmth its lonely, final yield.

Despite this, Heaven, grant to me
One gift: for every bird's bright voice
A spirit matching the blue, free,
Limitless sky which is its choice;
For every weakened ray of light
My hem line's iridescent gleam;
For every hand my clasp, warm, tight;
For every joy the seedling of a dream.

(translated from German by James Edward Tobin)

Rahel Morpurgo

(1790–1871)

ITALY (HEBREW)

Rahel Morpurgo was born in Trieste, a daughter of the Luzatto family illustrious through several generations of Italian Jewry for its poets, scholars, and philosophers. Unlike most girls in Jewish society of the time, she was given a thorough training in Hebrew, the Bible, the Talmud, and later mystical and pietistic writings. She rejected an arranged marriage that her family had planned for her and married a man of her own choice. She became the only prominent woman poet in the Hebrew renaissance that flourished in Italy from the fourteenth century to the nineteenth; there were to be no others until the cultural emancipation of women in the modern Hebraist revival of the early twentieth century.

Woe is me, my soul says, how bitter is my fate,
My spirit overweening aspired to be great.
I heard a voice pronounce: your song deserves high state.
What peer have you, Rachel, mistress of song?

My spirit rebukes me: my virtue's held a sin,
Exile after exile has withered my skin,
My pungence is gone, my vineyard's cropped thin,
Fearing disgrace, I can no longer sing.

To the north I have turned, to south, east and west.
'Woman's mind is frail,' how can this one be best?
After years if her memory's put to the test,

Will it surpass a dead dog knowing province or town?
Wherever you go, you will hear all around:
The wisdom of woman to the distaff is bound.

(translated from Hebrew by Robert Alter)

Vittoria Aganoor Pompili

(1855–1910)

ITALY

Vittoria Aganoor Pompili was born in Padua in 1855 to a wealthy
Armenian family already established in Italy. She began writing very
early but did not publish her first book, *La Legend eterna*, until she was
forty-five. She seems to have had a tragic love affair, of which nothing
is known. She died in Rome.

FINALLY

Well then, *tomorrow*! the wood exalts under the mild
sun. I have so many things to tell you, so many
things! I will lead you under the tall
trees, with me, *alone with me*! Come!

Perhaps – who knows – I won't be able to speak
at first. Perhaps, finally alone
with you, I'll look for words in vain.
Ah, well! We'll listen.

We'll listen to the murmuring
branches, afraid of intoxication,
without a glance, without a touch,
our faces pale as dying men.

FEAR

All right, I'll die, my spirit is strong.
But, to confess the sacred truth,
there's something I fear: I fear that death, too,
        letting me off on the other side,

wants to play me a dirty trick:
burning tears fall over
my icy corpse, and someone
        covers the bier with flowers

through vain zeal, and in loving crowd
friends are drawn behind my coffin.
I fear – no sooner in the earth
        of the burying ground – to change

into a dear shadow, prized object of love,
and on my stone will pour fully
what alive my hungry heart asked
        always in vain.

(translated from Italian by Brenda Webster)

Gertrudis Gomez de Avellaneda

(1814–73)

CUBA (SPANISH)

She was born in Puerto Principe and lived in Cuba until she was twenty-two. At that time her family moved to Spain and she wrote her famous sonnet, 'On Leaving'. She always felt a deep commitment to Cuba and expressed her love for her fatherland in much of her writing. Her literary fame grew from the time she published the first edition of her poetry in Madrid in 1841. In 1859 she returned to Cuba, where on arrival she was proclaimed national poet. As well as poetry, she wrote plays and novels.

ON LEAVING

Sea pearl, western star,
shining Cuba, night hides
your bright sky in its thick veil
as grief clouds my sad brow.

Time to leave. The eager crew,
to wrench me from my earth,
hoists sails, and ready winds
rush from your fiery ground.

Fare well, my happy land, my Eden.
Wherever angry chance may force my path
your sweet name will soothe my ear.

Fare well. The huge sail crackles,
the anchor lifts, the anxious ship
cuts the waves and flies in silence.

(translated from Spanish by Frederick Sweet)

Rosalía de Castro

(1837–85)

SPAIN (GALICIAN)

The poetry of Rosalía de Castro has received high praise. That she is little known may be due to the fact that she wrote her best work in her native Galician rather than in Castilian. She was born in Compostela and was given her mother's name. Her father was not known. She married and lived her later life in Castile, unhappy to be exiled from her home. In her writing, her language is simple and direct; her themes are her love of nature and her own unhappiness.

LONG MAY

Long May . . . long May,
All covered with roses,
For some, winding sheets,
For others, wedding gowns.

Long May . . . long May,
You were short for me,
My happiness came with you,
It fled again with you.

*

How placidly shine
The river, the spring, and the sun;
How brightly they shine . . . but they do not shine
For me, no.

How the grasses and the bushes thrive,
How the flower buds on the tree;
But they do not thrive or bloom
For me, no.

How the birds sing
Songs of love;
But though they sing, they do not sing
For me, no.

How beautiful nature
Smiles to May, which gladdens it;
But for me it does not smile,
For me, no.

Yes . . . for everyone a bit
Of air, of light, or warmth . . .
But if there is some for everyone,
For me, no.

Well! . . . since here I find
No air, light, earth, or sun,
Will there not be a tomb for me?
For me, no.

*

In the sky, clearest blue;
On the ground, intense green;
At the bottom of my soul
Everything dark and black.

What a happy pilgrimage!
What laughter and joy!...
And my eyes meanwhile
Are full of tears.

Covered with green
The fields gleam freshly,
While the bitter bile
Overflows in my breast.

*

Crickets and locusts, cicadas,
Toads and insects of all kinds,
While in the distance the wagons creak,
It is a charming serenade
They always give us in our fields!
Just to remember their song,
I don't know what it does to me:
  I don't know whether it's balm,
  I don't know whether it's pain.

(translated from Galician by
Benjamin M. Woodbridge, Jr)

Leylâ Hanim

(d. 1847)

TURKEY

She received instruction in classical Ottoman poetry from the prominent poet Keçecizade Izzet Molla. Her marriage lasted less than a week. Later she became a member of the Mawlawi congregation, known in the West as 'The Whirling Dervishes'. She was reputed to have a remarkable capacity for composing poems ex-temporaneously. Some of her verses, including the one below, caused the displeasure of the moralists of her day.

> Let's get going,
> Start the festivities,
> Never mind what they say.
>
> Drink wine
> With your loved one,
> Never mind what they say.
>
> What do I care
> If people approve or disapprove?
> God bless my friends,
> Never mind what they say.
>
> Leylâ, indulge in pleasure
> With your lovely friend:
> Enjoy yourself in this world,
> Never mind what they say.

(translated from Turkish by Tâlat S. Halman)

Irihapeti Rangi te Apakura

(19th century)

NEW ZEALAND (MAORI)

This 'Reply to a Marriage Proposal' was composed by Irihapeti Rangi te Apakura, a high-born woman of a sub-tribe of Ngati Porou. She lived in the mid-nineteenth century. Te Keepa was Toihau's son; the proposal was carried by an intermediary. The song is in the Maori form of *Waiata*, sung to a melody perhaps composed by the author or to one taken from older songs.

REPLY TO A MARRIAGE PROPOSAL

Don't hand me over with a word, Toihau,
don't give me to Te Keepa!
Isn't it enough that people are talking
as far as the quicksands of Karewa?
I am a canoe cast up and broken in the big surf,
I am getting old, my love play days are done,
it will not be long before I dig my grave.

That is my path as it was yours, Paoa,
my ancestral path across Te Whakaurunga,
unbroken view of the burning island
Whaakari, the demon's flames.
Here on the mainland, Hinehore's lover —
She can forget her jealousy!
She shall have her husband,
I embrace him only for a while.

The lips are made to taste with
but the body is firmly held.

(translated from Maori by Roger Oppenheim
and Allen Curnow)

Elizabeth Barrett Browning
(1806–61)

ENGLAND

Devotion to poetry, to Robert Browning, and to Italy were the
formative passions of Elizabeth Barrett Browning. She spent her
youth in the Malvern Hills, Devon, and London. A spinal injury
made her an invalid for some years. Her father had forbidden his
daughters to marry, and when Elizabeth and Robert Browning fell
in love, she eloped and was never forgiven. After her marriage she
spent most of the rest of her life in Italy. Her most ambitious work is
Aurora Leigh. It is a novel-poem in which the chief character, Aurora

Leigh, is a heroine embodying the author's personality as woman, poet, and thinker. The section quoted is a statement on the duty of poetry to portray the everyday life of the present.

from AURORA LEIGH:
Fifth Book, ll. 139–222

The critics say that epics have died out
With Agamemnon and the goat-nursed gods;
I'll not believe it. I could never deem,
As Payne Knight did (the mythic mountaineer
Who travelled higher than he was born to live,
And showed sometimes the goitre in his throat
Discoursing of an image seen through fog),
That Homer's heroes measured twelve feet high.
They were but men: – his Helen's hair turned grey
Like any plain Miss Smith's who wears a front;
And Hector's infant whimpered at a plume
As yours last Friday at a turkey-cock.
All actual heroes are essential men,
And all men possible heroes: every age,
Heroic in proportions, double-faced,
Looks backward and before, expects a morn
And claims an epos.
     Ay, but every age
Appears to souls who live in't (ask Carlyle)
Most unheroic. Ours, for instance, ours:
The thinkers scout it, and the poets abound
Who scorn to touch it with a finger-tip:
A pewter age, – mixed metal, silverwashed;
An age of scum, spooned off the richer past,
An age of patches for old gaberdines,
An age of mere transition, meaning nought
Except that what succeeds must shame it quite
If God please. That's wrong thinking, to my mind,
And wrong thoughts make poor poems.
     Every age,
Through being beheld too close, is ill-discerned

By those who have not lived past it.
        We'll suppose
Mount Athos carved, as Alexander schemed,
To some colossal statue of a man.   •
The peasants, gathering brushwood in his ear,
Had guessed as little as the browsing goats
Of form or feature of humanity
Up there, – in fact, had travelled five miles off
Or ere the giant image broke on them,
Full human profile, nose and chin distinct,
Mouth, muttering rhythms of silence up the sky
And fed at evening with the blood of suns;
Grand torso, – hand, that flung perpetually
The largesse of a silver river down
To all the country pastures. 'Tis even thus
With times we live in, – evermore too great
To be apprehended near.
                    But poets should
Exert a double vision; should have eyes
To see near things as comprehensively
As if afar they took their point of sight,
And distant things as intimately deep
As if they touched them. Let us strive for this.
I do distrust the poet who discerns
No character or glory in his times,
And trundles back his soul five hundred years,
Past moat and drawbridge, into a castle-court,
To sing – oh, not of lizard or of toad
Alive i' the ditch there, – 't were excusable
But of some black chief, half knight, half sheep-lifter,
Some beauteous dame, half chattel and half queen,
As dead as must be, for the greater part,
The poems made on their chivalric bones;
And that's no wonder: death inherits death.

Nay, if there's room for poets in this world
A little overgrown (I think there is),
Their sole work is to represent the age,

Their age, not Charlemagne's, – this live, throbbing age,
That brawls, cheats, maddens, calculates, aspires,
And spends more passion, more heroic heat,
Betwixt the mirrors of its drawing-rooms,
Than Roland with his knights at Roncesvalles.
To flinch from modern varnish, coat or flounce,
Cry out for togas and the picturesque,
Is fatal, – foolish too. King Arthur's self
Was commonplace to Lady Guenever;
And Camelot to minstrels seemed as flat
As Fleet Street to our poets.

                               Never flinch,
But still, unscrupulously epic, catch
Upon the burning lava of a song
The full-veined, heaving, double-breasted Age:
That, when the next shall come, the men of that
May touch the impress with reverent hand, and say
'Behold, – behold the paps we all have sucked!
This bosom seems to beat still, or at least
It sets ours beating: this is living art,
Which thus presents and thus records true life.'

Emily Brontë
(1818–48)

ENGLAND

Emily Brontë lived an uneventful life, mostly in Haworth Parsonage on the Yorkshire Moors. The wild loneliness of the nearby graveyard and the surrounding countryside worked in her imagination to produce her mystical poems, and her masterpiece, *Wuthering Heights*.

THE VISIONARY

Silent is the house: all are laid asleep:
One alone looks out o'er the snow-wreaths deep,

Watching every cloud, dreading every breeze
That whirls the 'wildering drift, and bends the
    groaning trees.

Cheerful is the hearth, soft the matted floor;
Not one shivering gust creeps through pane or door;
The little lamp burns straight, its rays shoot
    strong and far:
I trim it well, to be the wanderer's guiding-star.

Frown, my haughty sire! chide, my angry dame!
Set your slaves to spy; threaten me with shame:
But neither sire nor dame, nor prying serf shall know
What angel nightly tracks that waste of frozen snow.

What I love shall come like visitant of air,
Safe in secret power from lurking human snare;
Who loves me, no word of mine shall e'er betray,
Though for faith unstained my life must forfeit pay.

Burn then, little lamp; glimmer straight and clear —
Hush! a rustling wing stirs, methinks, the air:
He for whom I wait thus ever comes to me;
Strange Power! I trust thy might; trust thou
    my constancy.

STANZAS

Often rebuked, yet always back returning
    To those first feelings that were born with me,
And leaving busy chase of wealth and learning
    For idle dreams of things which cannot be:

To-day, I will seek not the shadowy region:
    Its unsustaining vastness waxes drear;
And visions rising, legion after legion,
    Bring the unreal world too strangely near.

I'll walk, but not in old heroic traces,
    And not in paths of high morality,
And not among the half-distinguished faces,
    The clouded forms of long-past history.

I'll walk where my own nature would be leading:
    It vexes me to choose another guide:
Where the grey flocks in ferny glens are feeding;
    Where the wild wind blows on the mountain-side.

What have those lonely mountains worth revealing?
    More glory and more grief than I can tell:
The earth that wakes *one* human heart to feeling
    Can centre both the worlds of Heaven and Hell.

COLD IN THE EARTH

Cold in the earth – and the deep snow piled above thee,
Far, far removed, cold in the dreary grave!
Have I forgot, my only Love, to love thee,
Severed at last by Time's all-severing wave?

Now, when alone, do my thoughts no longer hover
Over the mountains, on that northern shore,
Resting their wings where heath and fern-leaves cover
Thy noble heart for ever, ever more?

Cold in the earth – and fifteen wild Decembers,
From those brown hills, have melted into spring:
Faithful, indeed, is the spirit that remembers
After such years of change and suffering!

Sweet Love of youth, forgive, if I forget thee,
While the world's tide is bearing me along;
Other desires and other hopes beset me,
Hopes which obscure, but cannot do thee wrong!

No later light has lightened up my heaven,
No second morn has ever shone for me;
All my life's bliss from thy dear life was given,
All my life's bliss is in the grave with thee.

But, when the days of golden dreams had perished,
And even Despair was powerless to destroy;
Then did I learn how existence could be cherished,
Strengthened, and fed without the aid of joy.

Then did I check the tears of useless passion —
Weaned my young soul from yearning after thine;
Sternly denied its burning wish to hasten
Down to that tomb already more than mine.

And, even yet, I dare not let it languish,
Dare not indulge in memory's rapturous pain;
Once drinking deep of that divinest anguish,
How could I seek the empty world again?

Christina Rossetti

(1830–94)

ENGLAND

Sister of Dante Gabriel Rossetti, she drew attention to the pre-Raphaelite movement with the publication of 'Goblin Market' in 1862. This is a long poem (too long for inclusion here, unfortunately), strangely mixing the sinister and the sensual; it is open to varying interpretations. She led a life of religious simplicity, refusing to marry the man she loved because of differences of faith. She wrote much religious poetry.

A TRIAD
Sonnet

Three sang of love together: one with lips
   Crimson, with cheeks and bosom in a glow,
Flushed to the yellow hair and finger-tips;
   And one there sang who soft and smooth as snow
   Bloomed like a tinted hyacinth at a show;
And one was blue with famine after love,
   Who like a harpstring snapped rang harsh and low
The burden of what those were singing of.
One shamed herself in love; one temperately
   Grew gross in soulless love, a sluggish wife;

One famished died for love. Thus two of three
  Took death for love and won him after strife;
One droned in sweetness like a fattened bee:
  All on the threshold, yet all short of life.

LONG BARREN

Thou who didst hang upon a barren tree,
My God, for me;
  Though I till now be barren, now at length,
  Lord, give me strength
To bring forth fruit to Thee.

Thou who didst bear for me the crown of thorn,
Spitting and scorn;
  Though I till now have put forth thorns, yet now
  Strengthen me Thou
That better fruit be borne.

Thou Rose of Sharon, Cedar of broad roots,
Vine of sweet fruits,
  Thou Lily of the vale with fadeless leaf,
  Of thousands Chief,
Feed Thou my feeble shoots.

Emily Dickinson
(1830–86)

UNITED STATES

She was born into a distinguished Amherst family, attended Amherst
Academy and Mount Holyoke Female Seminary and, except for
brief trips, lived all her life in her father's house, for many years in
deliberate and drastic seclusion. In spite of encouragement and
opportunity, she refused to publish more than a few poems during
her lifetime. After her death her sister Lavinia discovered a box con-
taining hundreds of poems, some carefully copied in hand-stitched
booklets, others scrawled on scraps of paper, envelopes, shopping

lists, even candy wrappers. The first edition appeared in 1890, to be followed by new editions and new poems throughout the 1930s. A complete and scholarly edition containing 1,775 poems was published in 1955.

Wild Nights – Wild Nights!
Were I with thee
Wild Nights should be
Our luxury!

Futile – the Winds —
To a Heart in port —
Done with the Compass —
Done with the Chart!

Rowing in Eden —
Ah, the Sea!
Might I but moor – Tonight —
In Thee!

*

I felt a Funeral, in my Brain,
And Mourners to and fro
Kept treading – treading – till it seemed
That Sense was breaking through —

And when they all were seated,
A Service, like a Drum —
Kept beating – beating – till I thought
My Mind was going numb —

And then I heard them lift a Box
And creak across my Soul
With those same Boots of Lead, again,
Then Space – began to toll,

As all the Heavens were a Bell,
And Being, but an Ear,
And I, and Silence, some strange Race
Wrecked, solitary, here —

And then a Plank in Reason, broke,
And I dropped down, and down —
And hit a World, at every plunge,
And Finished knowing – then —

*

Because I could not stop for Death —
He kindly stopped for me —
The Carriage held but just Ourselves —
And Immortality.

We slowly drove – He knew no haste
And I had put away
My labor and my leisure too,
For His Civility —

We passed the School, where Children strove
At Recess – in the Ring —
We passed the Fields of Gazing Grain —
We passed the Setting Sun —

Or rather – He passed Us —
The Dews drew quivering and chill —
For only Gossamer, my Gown —
My Tippet – only Tulle —

We paused before a House that seemed
A Swelling of the Ground —
The Roof was scarcely visible —
The Cornice – in the Ground —

Since then – 'tis Centuries – and yet
Feels shorter than the Day
I first surmised the Horses' Heads
Were toward Eternity —

*

Behind Me – dips Eternity —
Before Me – Immortality —
Myself – the Term between —

Death but the Drift of Eastern Gray,
Dissolving into Dawn away,
Before the West begin —

'Tis Kingdoms – afterward – they say —
In perfect – pauseless Monarchy —
Whose Prince – is Son of None —
Himself – His Dateless Dynasty —
Himself – Himself diversify —
In Duplicate divine —

'Tis Miracle before Me – then —
'Tis Miracle behind – between —
A Crescent in the Sea —
With Midnight to the North of Her —
And Midnight to the South of Her —
And Maelstrom – in the Sky —

*

It sounded as if the Streets were running
And then – the Streets stood still —
Eclipse – was all we could see at the Window
And Awe – was all we could feel.

By and by – the boldest stole out of his Covert
To see if Time was there —
Nature was in an Opal Apron,
Mixing fresher Air.

*

As imperceptibly as Grief
The Summer lapsed away —
Too imperceptible at last
To seem like Perfidy —
A Quietness distilled
As Twilight long begun,
Or Nature spending with herself
Sequestered Afternoon —
The Dusk drew earlier in —
The Morning foreign shone —

A courteous, yet harrowing Grace,
As Guest, that would be gone —
And thus, without a Wing
Or service of a Keel
Our Summer made her light escape
Into the Beautiful.

Owl Woman
(*fl.* 1880?)

PAPAGO INDIAN – AMERICAN SOUTHWEST

Owl Woman, also known by the Spanish name Juana Manwell, was a medicine woman of the Papago Indians. A number of her medicine songs were collected by Frances Densmore in 1920. These songs were taught Owl Woman by spirits of the dead, and in the thirty or forty years prior to 1920 she received hundreds of songs. The following are part of a longer sequence to be sung over a sick person at four intervals throughout the night.

SONGS FOR THE FOUR PARTS OF THE NIGHT

IN THE BLUE NIGHT

How shall I begin my song
In the blue night that is settling?
I will sit here and begin my song.

IN THE DARK I ENTER

I can not make out what I see.
In the dark I enter.
I can not make out what I see.

I SEE SPIRIT-TUFTS OF WHITE FEATHERS

Ahead of me some owl feathers are lying,
I hear something running toward me,
They pass by me, and farther ahead
I see spirit-tufts of downy white feathers.

IN THE GREAT NIGHT

In the great night my heart will go out,
Toward me the darkness comes rattling,
In the great night my heart will go out.

I AM GOING TO SEE THE LAND

I am going far to see the land,
I am running far to see the land,
While back in my house the songs are intermingling.

THE DAWN APPROACHES

I am afraid it will be daylight before I reach the place to see.
I feel that the rays of the sun are striking me.

THE OWL FEATHER IS LOOKING
FOR THE DAWN

The owl feather is likely to find the daylight.
He is looking for it.
He is looking to see the dawn shine red in the east.

THE MORNING STAR

The morning star is up.
I cross the mountains into the light of the sea.

(translated from Papago by Frances Densmore)

THE TWENTIETH CENTURY:
MODERNS AND CONTEMPORARIES

Zinaida Hippius (Gippius)

(1869–1945)

RUSSIA

One of the great religious and Symbolist poets, Hippius began pub-
lishing poetry in the 1890s. Married to the writer Merezhkovsky at
the age of twenty, she lived with him in companionate-marriage. She
was uncomfortable with the role of women in the sexual relationship
and explored alternatives in her life and in her work. She and her
husband were of the band of Russian intellectuals who supported the
idea of the Revolution, believing it would bring freedom to pursue
religious experience and sexual fulfilment. When this was proven
wrong, they left Russia for Paris. Hippius became a bitter opponent of
the Soviet regime. She died in Paris. Her poetry had a strong influence
on the later poets Blok, Akhmatova and Mandelstam. Unfortu-
nately, little of her poetry has been translated into English.

L'IMPRÉVISIBILITÉ

According to the word of the Eternal Being,
The stream of time is continuous;
>   I only sense an oncoming breeze,
>   The chime of a new moment.

Does it lead to a downfall? To a victory?
Does it bear glory, or a sword?
>   I do not see its face;
>   I only know the breeze of encounters.

Moments with obscured faces fly,
Fly like birds from another world,
>   Forward, into the circle of life;
>   How am I to freeze them in their flight?

And so in their density, in their interlacing web,
Whether I desire it or not,
>   My vessel slices
>   Through the black shadow of uncertainty.

A GREY FROCK

Girl in a grey frock . . .

Your braids seem cotton-spun . . .
Girl, girl, to whom do you belong?

To my mother . . . Or to nobody.
If you wish – I shall be yours.

Girl in a grey frock . . .

Do you believe, dear, in a caress?
Sweet one, where are your eyes?

Here they are, my eyes. Empty ones,
Exactly the same as my mother's.

Girl in a grey frock,

What are you playing with?
What do you conceal from me?

Come now, do I have time to play?
There is much urgent work to do.

Now I spill a string of beads,
Now I wither the first sprout,
Now I cut pages out of books,
Or break the wings of a little bird . . .

Girl in a grey frock,

Girl with empty eyes,
Tell me, what is your name?

Everyone has his own name for me:
Call me whatever you like.

One calls me division,
Another – hostility,
Others call me doubt,
Or anguish.

Another calls me boredom,
Still another – pain . . .
And Mother-Death calls me Separation,

The girl in a grey frock . . .

(translated from Russian by Temira Pachmuss)

Anna Akhmatova

(1889–1966)

RUSSIA

Anna Akhmatova, one of the finest Russian poets of the twentieth century, was born near Odessa and grew up in St Petersburg, where she spent most of her subsequent life (save three years in Tashkent, to which she was evacuated during the war). She and Nikolai Gumilev, whom she married in 1910, were the founders of the Acmeist movement, demanding a poetry of concrete images and clarity of meaning free of Symbolist metaphysics. Her first book, *Evening*, was published in 1912. In 1921, three years after their divorce, Gumilev was shot for anti-Bolshevist activities; their son Lev was later detained for many years in Stalinist prison camps. Akhmatova herself was denounced and expelled from the Writers' Union and was unable to publish her poetry again in Soviet Russia until the thaw under Khrushchev, when she was officially rehabilitated along with a number of other writers, living and dead, who had been persecuted during the Stalinist years. In 1964 she was awarded an honorary doctorate by Oxford University.

> I taught myself to live simply and wisely,
> to look at the sky and pray to God,
> and to wander long before evening
> to tire my useless sadness.
>
> When the burdocks rustle in the ravine
> and the yellow-red rowanberry cluster droops

I write down happy verses
about life's decay, decay and beauty.

I come back. The fluffy cat
licks my palm, purrs so sweetly,
and the fire flares bright
on the saw-mill turret by the lake.

Only the cry of a stork landing on the roof
occasionally breaks the silence.
If you knock on my door
I may not even hear.

(translated from Russian by Richard McKane)

THE GREY-EYED KING

Glory to you, oh pain, sorrow unending!
Yesterday he died, the grey-eyed king.

A stifling autumn night, the sky red,
When my husband, returning home, calmly said,

'He was hunting, you know. They've brought the body back.
He lay by an old oak, on a forest track.

So sad for the queen. Her hair's gone white.
So young for death . . . turned old overnight.'

He found his pipe on the chimney, and then a light,
And went away, off to his work for the night.

Now I will go and awaken my daughter from sleep,
My grey-eyed daughter, into her eyes look deep.

And hear the poplars beside the window, sighing,
'He walks on the earth no longer, your grey-eyed king . . .'

(translated from Russian by Robert Tracy)

Hands clenched under my shawl . . .
'You are pale today, I think?'
– He was drunk, for I had poured him
A bitter grief to drink.

No forgetting his stagger away,
His mouth twisted in pain . . .
I ran after, but couldn't catch up,
I ran to the gate on the lane.

I panted, 'Only a joke,
That's all. Leave and you'll kill
Me.' His smile terrible, calm.
He said, 'Don't stand in the chill.'

(translated from Russian by Robert Tracy)

LOT'S WIFE

The just man followed then his angel guide
Where he strode on the black highway, hulking and bright;
But a wild grief in his wife's bosom cried,
Look back, it is not too late for a last sight

Of the red towers of your native Sodom, the square
Where once you sang, the gardens you shall mourn,
And the tall house with empty windows where
You loved your husband and your babes were born.

She turned, and looking on the bitter view
Her eyes were welded shut by mortal pain;
Into transparent salt her body grew,
And her quick feet were rooted in the plain.

Who would waste tears upon her? Is she not
The least of our losses, this unhappy wife?
Yet in my heart she will not be forgot
Who, for a single glance, gave up her life.

(translated from Russian by Richard Wilbur)

Marina Tsvetayeva

(1892–1941)

RUSSIA

Marina Tsvetayeva spent most of her adult life in exile from her country and, as she felt, from her language. Hostile to the excesses of the Revolution, she spent the years from 1917 to 1922 with her children in a near-starving Moscow and then followed her husband, Sergei Efron, to Prague and later Paris, where they lived for the next eighteen years the impoverished life of *émigrés*. In 1939 she again followed Efron, who had been exposed as a Soviet agent, back to Russia, only to find he had been shot in his attempt to enter the country. Alone, unable to work, evacuated to a distant province during the war, Tsvetayeva hanged herself in 1941.

We are keeping an eye on the girls, so that the *kvass*
doesn't go sour in the jug, or the pancakes cold,
counting over the rings, and pouring Anis
into the long bottles with their narrow throats,

straightening tow thread for the peasant woman:
filling the house with the fresh smoke of
incense and we are sailing over Cathedral square
arm in arm with our godfather, silks thundering.

The wet nurse has a screeching cockerel
in her apron – her clothes are like the night.
She announces in an ancient whisper that
a dead young man lies in the chapel.

And an incense cloud wraps the corners
under its own saddened chasuble.
The apple trees are white, like angels – and
the pigeons on them – grey – like incense itself.

And the pilgrim woman sipping *kvass* from the ladle
on the edge of the couch, is telling
to the very end a tale about Razin
and his most beautiful Persian girl.

from INSOMNIA

Black as the centre of an eye, the centre, a blackness
that sucks at light. I love your vigilance.

Night, first mother of songs, give me the voice to sing of you
in those fingers lies the bridle of the four winds.

Crying out, offering words of homage to you, I am
only a shell where the ocean is still sounding.

But I have looked too long into human eyes
Reduce me now to ashes Night, like a black sun.

from POEM OF THE END

Blatant as factory buildings,
    as alert to a call
here is the sacred and sublingual
    secret wives keep from husbands and

widows from friends, here is the full
    story that Eve took from the tree:
I am no more than an animal that
    someone has stabbed in the stomach.

Burning. As if the soul had been
    torn away with the skin. Vanished like steam
through a hole is that well-known foolish
    heresy called a soul.

That Christian leprosy:
    steam: save that with your poultices.
There never was such a thing.
    There was a body once, wanted to

live no longer wants to live.

Forgive me! I didn't mean it!
    The shriek of torn entrails.
So prisoners sentenced to death wait
    for the 4 a.m. firing squad.

At chess perhaps with a grin
    they mock the corridor's eye.
Pawns in the game of chess:
    someone is playing with us.

Who? Kind gods or Thieves?
    The peephole is filled with an
eye and the red corridor
clanks. Listen the latch lifts.

One drag on tobacco, then
    spit, it's all over, spit,
along this paving of chess squares
    is a direct path to the ditch

to blood. And the secret eye
    the dormer eye of the moon.

And now, squinting sideways, how
    far away you are already.

(translated from Russian by Elaine Feinstein and
Angela Livingstone)

Natalya Gorbanyevskaya
(1936–)

RUSSIA

Natalya Gorbanyevskaya graduated from the Philological Faculty
of Leningrad University in 1963 and has worked as an engineer and a
translator. Most of her poetry has circulated privately within the
Soviet Union and one collection has been published abroad. She has
been a leading civil rights activist and was arrested in 1969 because of
her participation in a demonstration against the Soviet invasion of
Czechoslovakia. She was declared schizophrenic and confined for
some months to a psychiatric hospital prison where drug treatment

was administered. She is considered one of the best poets of her
generation.

> Here, as in a painting, noon burns yellow,
> and the very air, like grief, is disembodied,
> and in the utter silence, like a winged army,
> the crows in Crow Park hang overhead.
>
> But the mouldering leaves of years past
> cling to my elbows, to my hands reeking
> of cigarette smoke, and the bare shrubbery thrusts
> its arms among my tangled curls.
>
> I have left home so far behind me,
> like a plane that in dense fog wanders
> from the aerodrome into the darkness . . .
> Am I living or dead, am I leaves or grass?

★

> In my own twentieth century
> where there are more dead than graves
> to put them in, my miserable
> forever unshared love
>
> among these Goya images
> is nervous, faint, absurd,
> as, after the screaming of jets,
> the trump of Jericho.

(translated from Russian by Daniel Weissbort)

Bella Akhmadulina
(1937–)
RUSSIA

A popular poet in Russia and abroad, Bella Akhmadulina was born in
Moscow. She has been married to Evgeny Yevtushenko and is now

married to the well-known Russian critic and writer Yuri Nagibin.
She is in demand throughout her country as a reader of her poetry
and is a member of the Writers' Union in her capacity as translator.

VOLCANOES

Extinct volcanoes are silent:
Ash chokes craters and vent.
There giants hide from the sun
After the evil they have done.

Realms ever denser and colder
Weigh on each brutal shoulder,
But the old wicked visions keep
Visiting them in their sleep.

They behold a city, sure
Here summer will endure,
Though columns carved from congealed
Lava frame garden and field.

It is long ago: in sunlit hours
Girls gather armfuls of flowers
And Bacchantes give a meaning sign
To men as they sip their wine.

A feast is in progress: louder
The diners grow, more heated and lewder ...
O my Pompei in your cindery grave,
Child of a princess and a slave!

What future did you assume,
What were you thinking of and whom
When you leaned your elbow thus
Thoughtlessly on Vesuvius?

Were you carried away by his stories?
Did you gaze with astonished eyes?
Didn't you guess – were you *that* innocent? –
Passion can be violent?

And then, when that day ended,
Did he lay a knowing forehead
At your dead feet? Did he, didn't he,
Bellow: 'Forgive me!'?

(translated from Russian by W. H. Auden)

THE BRIDE

Oh to be a bride
Brilliant in my curls
Under the white canopy
Of a modest veil!

How my hands tremble,
Bound by my icy rings!
The glasses gather, brimming
With red compliments.

At last the world says yes;
It wishes me roses and sons.
My friends stand shyly at the door,
Carrying love gifts.

Chemises in cellophane,
Plates, flowers, lace . . .
They kiss my cheeks, they marvel
I'm to be a wife.

Soon my white gown
Is stained with wine like blood;
I feel both lucky and poor
As I sit, listening, at the table.

Terror and desire
Loom in the forward hours.
My mother, the darling, weeps —
Mama is like the weather.

. . . My rich, royal attire
I lay aside on the bed.
I find I am afraid
To look at you, to kiss you.

Loudly the chairs are set
Against the wall, eternity . . .
My love, what more can happen
To you and to me?

(translated from Russian by Stephan Stepanchev)

Wislawa Szymborska

(1923–)

POLAND

She is considered one of the best of the post-war Polish women poets.
She exemplifies in her work the Polish poetic attraction for the
baroque allied with a modern sharpness and frankness. Her qualities
are most significantly portrayed in her volume *Salt*.

I am too near to be dreamt of by him.
I do not fly over him, do not escape from him
under the roots of a tree. I am too near.
Not in my voice sings the fish in the net,
not from my finger rolls the ring.
I am too near. A big house is on fire
without me, calling for help. Too near
for a bell dangling from my hair to chime.
Too near to enter as a guest
before whom walls glide apart by themselves.
Never again will I die so lightly,
so much beyond my flesh, so inadvertently
as once in his dream. Too near.
I taste the sound, I see the glittering husk of this word
as I lie immobile in his embrace. He sleeps,
more accessible now to her, seen but once,
a cashier of a wandering circus with one lion,
than to me, who am at his side.
For her now in him a valley grows,
rusty-leaved, closed by a snowy mountain

in the dark blue air. I am too near
to fall to him from the sky. My scream
could wake him up. Poor thing
I am, limited to my shape,
I who was a birch, who was a lizard,
who would come out of my cocoons
shimmering the colours of my skins. Who possessed
the grace of disappearing from astonished eyes,
which is a wealth of wealths. I am near,
too near for him to dream of me.
I slide my arm from under the sleeper's head
and it is numb, full of swarming pins,
on the tip of each, waiting to be counted,
the fallen angels sit.

(translated from Polish by Czeslaw Milosz)

Nina Cassian

(1924–)

ROMANIA

She studied at the Faculty of Letters and the Conservatory of Music in Bucharest and has published fifteen volumes of poetry, a number of prize-winning children's books, and translations from French and German. She received the Romanian State-Prize Laureate for her poems. She also is a distinguished musician and composer.

ORDEAL

I promise to make you more alive than you've ever been.
For the first time you'll see your pores opening
like the gills of fish and you'll hear
the noise of blood in galleries
and feel light gliding on your corneas
like the dragging of a dress across the floor.
For the first time, you'll note gravity's prick

like a thorn in your heel,
and your shoulder blades will hurt from the imperative of wings.
I promise to make you so alive that
the fall of dust on furniture will deafen you,
and you'll feel your eyebrows like two wounds forming
and your memories will seem to begin
with the creation of the world.

VEGETABLE DESTINY

Foolish impatient apricot trees,
gave off flowers in too great a hurry.

Look at them, as in years past,
wind-frozen, thin and vain,

on the branches, with transparent blood
I don't know how to staunch —

for the frost, cruel though it seems,
pays no heed to apricots.

The other trees, far-sighted,
await the floral hour quietly,
with dutiful branches and closed buds,

oblivious to apricot-tree death.

(translated from Romanian by Michael Impey
and Brian Swann)

Maria Banus
(1914–)

ROMANIA

She is a native of Bucharest, where she studied at the Faculty of
Letters and Law. She has published ten volumes of poetry, four plays,
and translations from five languages including works by Goethe,

Rilke, Rimbaud, and Neruda. She is a recipient of the Romanian
State-Prize Laureate.

THE NEW NOTEBOOK

Full of superstition
I begin a new notebook,
white leaves – sea foam.
I close my eyes and wait
for the first day of the world,
for Aphrodite with wet lips,
red curls of flame,
an open shell,
shy and sure,
to rise from the salt foam,
out of the primordial algae.
I wait under closed eyelids.
One can hear the grey rustle of sea gulls
under the low sky
and the monotonous thunder of waves
only of waves
which come and go.

(translated from Romanian by Laura Schiff
and Dana Beldiman)

Margit Kaffka
(1880–1918)
HUNGARY

She was born in Nagykároly into a family of the impoverished
Hungarian gentry. Her father died when she was six. She attended
convent school and graduated from the Erzsébet Girls' College in
Budapest. Her first book of poems appeared in 1903, her most
famous novel in 1912. She was married twice. In 1918 both she and
her son died in an epidemic of Spanish flu. She is generally regarded
as the most outstanding woman writer of Hungary.

FATHER

They say, his strange, large eyes,
Opal-like, odd, Nordic eyes,
Always looked far-off. He could
Fuss half a day with a flower's root.
He'd lean over it – and its fragile
Refined petal's belligerent fragrance.
In women too, he sought the soul.
He collected pictures, books, old embroidery
He also grappled with men.
The table glittered at his opulent feasts.
Servants moved silently, and the wines'
Crystal fire shimmered deep, flaming.
He savoured it, as long as the tablecloth
And flowers were unsplotched. But later
When the word became more and more shrill,
Heated, the smoke more stifling,
The county elite railed at the government.
Ten spoke at once – and roared bent over
Gross, crude jokes – and slumping,
They stammered in brotherly kisses, while
Some started snoring, thick-lipped.
Then he became upset, pensive,
He stared at them with clouded, sad eyes,
And felt that just he was the lonely one there.
Then he whistled for his dog.
The vizsla came padding, nuzzled against him,
And put his smart, pedigreed head in his lap.
In the greying wine-vapour morning
Petting him, they looked at each other.

They say: later I became the light of his eye.
For me, he forgot his celebrated flowers,
He leaned over my lacy, ribboned cradle,
And guarded me like a costly porcelain,
How often he kept watch at my small sickbed!
And when one day, untutored,

I could draw my first two letters, he drew me close,
And whispered; 'That's the way, little one!
When you grow up the world will be different!'
And then came the disease, and he lingered,
For a long time, knowing his end.
And he wasn't much older than I am today!...
They say, he suffered nights because of me,
If he looked at me he clenched his hands in his lap.
'You'll be a beggar!' – he said, and his words choked.
'Why couldn't I have been stingy, for your sake!'
Oh, my father, if you could know, how that's nothing!
If only I had never had a greater worry!
But you see, the world hasn't changed since then;
You were so wrong, father.
Now I hear the news – your grave is so grassy.
The marble bows and the gold letters
Are all washed away, I was there so long ago,
And every year there are downpours.
How many storms! How many have I survived,
And life, father, what chaos.

... If you could see, now you have a grandchild,
Bright-eyed, loud, lively small thing,
But his eyes are different from yours or mine!
Good. Because storms will come! – But maybe
The world will be different when he grows up?
It's been so long that you've slept below!
You weren't much older than I am today,
And time has washed away your golden letters,
And I hear the news, your grave is grassy.
Can I bring my flowers once more?
Who knows? Life is such chaos,
And I am so tired – father.

(translated from Hungarian by Laura Schiff)

Ágnes Nemes Nagy
(1922–)

HUNGARY

She was born in Budapest and graduated in Humanities from the University of Budapest. Her first book of poems appeared in 1946. She has continued to publish poetry and is a well-known translator of European writers into Hungarian.

STORM

A shirt races in the meadow.
In an equinoctial storm
it escaped from the clothes line
and now dips above the June-green grass
a wounded soldier's bodiless
choreography.

They race, the linens.
Under the lightning's muzzle fire
the last assault of an army of flags
and sheets, they speed, a strange hiss,
a torn sail, a rag,
in the endless green meadow,
falling and rising
their billows mark
a mass grave of linens.

Though motionless, I step out,
I run out of my contour
after, between them,
a runner slightly more transparent
with extended arms
like a half-wit calling back
a dead tree calling back
its flown bird —

Now they fall on their faces.
And with a white-winged sweep
suddenly the whole army soars
soars like a still etching
soars like the body's resurrection
from a seaborn eternity to a pistol crack.

Behind on the meadow remains
only a pleading gesture
and the dark green of grass. A lake.

(translated from Hungarian by Laura Schiff)

Anna Hajnal
(1907–)
HUNGARY

She has published twelve volumes of poetry, including her collected works, *That's All*, in 1971. She is also a translator and writes poems and stories for children. Her work has appeared in Bulgarian, Romanian, Chinese, and German.

THAT'S ALL?

Shearing, as the gardener
snips the sucker,
controlling wild growth
with shaping hands,
looking and choosing —
which bud's to be the branch —
rooting out, cutting or pardoning
by design and scheme:
trimming pyramids, tall arches,
scissoring bowers for gods —
how I'd love doing that —
taking hold of the passionate growth
in my unmastered heart.

Slicing through wild, winding
trailers, charming
with a bright, sharp blade —
to but loosen its hold on me!

release its hold?
and must the clasper wither?
trailers, leaves, tendrils droop?
A French park, my loving?
moderation, cautious suffering?
precise forms, narrow blossoms,
the reign of geometry,
is my calmness to be a tight calmness?

(translated from Hungarian by Jascha Kessler)

Vesna Parun

(1922–)

YUGOSLAVIA (CROATIAN)

She was born on the island of Zlarin, near Šibenik, and is the author
of many volumes of poetry and an important member of the post-war
generation of Croatian poets.

MOTHER OF MAN

Better it were had you borne black earth, o mother, rather
      than me
Had you borne a bear in a den, a snake in a nest
Or had you kissed a stone, rather than my face
That a beast had given me suck, rather than a woman.

Had you borne a bird, o mother, still you'd be a mother
You'd have been happy, warming the bird in your bosom
Had you borne a tree, the tree would have burgeoned
      in spring
The lime would have blossomed, the sedges turned green at
      your song

A lamb could have lain at your feet, were you mother to
    a lamb
If you crooned, and if you wept, a sweet small beast would
    heed you
This way you stand alone, and alone you share your grief
    with graves
It's bitter to be a man, while the knife is the brother of man.

(translated from Croatian by Mary Coote)

Malka Heifetz Tussman
(1896–)

YIDDISH

Malka Heifetz Tussman was born in a small village in the Ukraine. In 1912 she and her family left Russia under the threat of rising anti-Semitism and settled in Chicago, where she married soon after. She began writing poetry as a child and published several poems in English after she came to America. However, at a friend's suggestion that the Jews needed more poets of their own, she returned to Yiddish, her first language. Since 1949 she has published five books of poetry and has translated into Yiddish such poets as Dylan Thomas and Tagore. Mrs Tussman has lived most of her life in the Midwest and Los Angeles and is now settled in Berkeley.

MOUNT GILBOA

I lie here beside you,
like Ruth at the feet of Boaz,
but no Naomi has sent me.
I hurried to you on my own,
Gilboa, my man.

See, I am barren and fruitless,
but you will provide my help,
Gilboa, my man.

They say, in your open palm,
in the heights
where the eye barely sees,
there is a cure —
black irises,
Gilboa, my man.

Throw down a black iris
and I'll eat its fire
and swallow its poison,
Gilboa, my man.

You are so large, so good —
Cover me up
and cradle the cry
of my blood,
for you are merciful,
Gilboa, my man.

Then spread out your stars
over me —
I'll bear you white lambs
and I'll know that God is,
Gilboa, my man.

Whole flocks,
and I, too,
will play on your belly.
It will be
as it was
in the Garden of Eden,
Gilboa, my man.

And I'll keep on bearing,
bearing
until I'm a speck of dust
that you'll bear on your shoulder
forever.
And silenced,
I'll have no more to say —
For such joy

there are no words,
Gilboa, my man.

Throw down a black iris
and I'll eat its fire
and swallow its poison,
Gilboa, my man.

(translated from Yiddish by Marcia Falk)

Kadia Molodowsky
(1893–)
YIDDISH

Born in Lithuania, Kadia Molodowsky published her first poems in
1920. She taught and worked on left-wing newspapers in Warsaw,
where she was persecuted by the police for her socialist activities.
She came to New York in 1935, and her subsequent poetry reflects
the influence of America and of Israel, where she has made long
visits. She has written poems, novels, and plays and is particularly
known for her children's poetry.

SONG OF THE SABBATH

I quarrelled with kings till the Sabbath,
I fought with the six kings
of the six days of the week.

Sunday they took away my sleep.
Monday they scattered my salt.
And on the third day, my God,
they threw out my bread: whips flashed
across my face. The fourth day
they caught my dove, my flying dove,
and slaughtered it.
It was like that till Friday morning.

This is my whole week,
the dove's flight dying.

At nightfall Friday
I lit four candles,
and the queen of the Sabbath came to me.
Her face lit up the whole world,
and made it all a Sabbath.
My scattered salt
shone in its little bowl,
and my dove, my flying dove,
clapped its wings together,
and licked its throat.
The Sabbath queen blessed my candles,
and they burned with a pure, clean flame.
The light put out the days of the week
and my quarrelling with the six kings.

The greenness of the mountains
is the greenness of the Sabbath.
The silver of the lake
is the silver of the Sabbath.
The singing of the wind
is the singing of the Sabbath.

And my heart's song
is an eternal Sabbath.

(translated from Yiddish by Jean Valentine)

Rachel Korn

(1898–)

YIDDISH

She was born in Galicia, and her first literary efforts were written in Polish. It was not until 1919 that she began to write and publish in Yiddish. When the Nazis invaded Poland she escaped to Sweden and to Russia. Since the war she has been living in Montreal.

KEEP HIDDEN FROM ME

Keep from me all that I might comprehend!
O God, I ripen toward you in my unknowing.

The barely burgeoning leaf on the roadside tree
Limns innocence: here endeth the first lesson.

Keep from me, God, all forms of certainty:
The steady tread that paces off the self

And forms it, seamless, ignorant of doubt
Or failure, hell-bent for fulfilment.

To know myself: is not that the supreme disaster?
To know Thee, one must sink on trembling knees.

To hear Thee, only the terrified heart may truly listen;
To see Thee, only the gaze half-blind with dread.

Though the day darken, preserve my memory
From Your bright oblivion. Erase not my faulty traces.

If I aspire again to make four poor walls my house,
Let me pillow myself on the book of my peregrinations.

God, grant me strength to give over false happiness,
And the sense that suffering has earned us Your regard.

Elohim! Though sorrow fill me to the brim,
Let me carefully bear the cup of myself to Thee.

(translated from Yiddish by Carolyn Kizer)

Ricarda Huch

(1864–1947)

GERMANY

She was born in Brunswick and graduated with a degree in history
from the University of Zurich. She married twice, divorcing her
first husband to marry her cousin, Richard Huch, from whom she
later separated. Generally regarded as the most important woman

writer of the early twentieth century in Germany, she wrote poetry,
novels, literary criticism, history, and unorthodox essays on the
Bible and Martin Luther's Creed. She was also a student of Italian
and German popular movements and devoted one novel to the
depiction of life in a working-class district of Trieste. She lived in
several German and Italian cities before settling in Munich.

Music stirs me, for you
Sea and
Cloud
Mountain and Star
touch me for you.
Alien things only turn
the whole prayer of my heart
to you
All noble paintings
wake the dream of you
All singing lines
lead home to your memory —
Beauty is everywhere kin.

DEATH SEED

In a field of swaying grain
I saw a man moving.
From his free hand slid seeds
which he sowed again.
Strange to me seemed a reaper
who blessed with new seed the same field.
Then I saw his stern face:
Behold, it was Death I had met.

ARRIVAL IN HELL

Into Hell's cave stepped a new guest:
'Welcome, comrade.
Say, what name had you
on the fair earth?

Speak to us of the lovely sun
And of rose red cheeks.
Say whether the little gnats
soar gaily in swift dance.

Did you see lovers, hand in hand,
beneath the moon?
Did you see that happy host,
who live in the light,
over our gravestones
mourning us?

Tears gush to your eyes, the
kind drops unlocking pain
like March ice
in the soft spring wind.'

'Spring was there, when I was
forced to come here.
With me to your vault
I bring the scent of violets:
these perfect wreaths upon
my breast.'

Behold, the Danaides pause.
Tantalus turns from his agony.
Suddenly, away from slack hands
the stone of Sisyphus rushes
down.

(translated from German by Susan C. Strong)

Else Lasker-Schüler

(1869–1945)

GERMANY

Else Lasker-Schüler was born in Elberfeld, Germany, to a middle-
class Jewish family. At the age of eleven she contracted St Vitus
Dance and thereafter was educated by a governess. At twenty-five

she married a Berlin doctor, Jonathan Lasker; their son Paul, an artist, died of tuberculosis at the age of twenty-eight. Although her first book of poems, *Styx*, appeared as early as 1902, she was a leading figure in the Expressionist movement of the teens and twenties. In 1920 a ten-volume edition of her work was published and she later received the Kleist Prize. In 1933, fleeing from the Nazis, she emigrated to Switzerland and then to Palestine, where her last book of poems, *My Blue Piano*, was published in 1943. She died in Jerusalem.

RECONCILIATION

A great star has fallen into my lap . . .
We want to wake through the night,

To pray in languages
Notched like harps.

We want to be reconciled with the night —
God overflows so much.

Our hearts are children,
They may rest tiredsweet.

And our lips want to kiss,
Why do you hesitate?

Do not join my heart to yours —
Always your blood reddens my cheeks.

We want to be reconciled with the night,
When we embrace, we do not die.

A great star has fallen into my lap.

(translated from German by Robert Alter)

HOMESICK

I don't know the language
Of this cool country
And its pace is not mine.

Nor can I interpret
The clouds that pass.

The night is a step-queen.

Always I have to think of the Pharaoh forests
And kiss the images of my stars.

Already my lips are luminous
And speak far things,

And I am a gaudy picture book
On your lap.

But your face weaves
A veil made of weeping.

My glittering birds
Have had their corals ripped out,

In the garden hedges
Their soft nests turn to stone.

Who anoints my dead palaces —
They bore the crowns of my forefathers,
Their prayers have gone down in the holy river.

(translated from German by Michael Hamburger)

Nelly Sachs
(1891–1969)
GERMANY

Nelly Sachs was born in Berlin, and her early work, rooted in the Romantic tradition, underwent a transformation as the Nazis rose to power. When she fled to Sweden in 1940 she began to come to terms with the holocaust, and this became a major theme of her poetry. Nelly Sachs was co-winner, with the Israeli writer S. Y. Agnon, of the Nobel Prize for literature in 1966.

Oblivion! Skin
out of which what is newborn is wound
and sheets for the dying

that the white sleepers
who bring it home
lend out again.

At times on the blood's
last spit of land
the foghorn resounds
and the drowned sailor sings

or on a sandy country path
trails of footsteps run
from labyrinths of longing
like broken snail shells
bearing emptiness on their back —

Behind the dusk
music of blackbirds

The dead dance
flower stalks of the wind —

(translated from German by Michael Roloff)

Above the rocking heads of the mothers
the blossom branches of the shepherds' stars
open again at night
singing in the warm sleep of children
the eternal transformations up to God.
The homeless millennia
which since the burning of the temple roamed about
unloved in the hourglass of dust
break forth in new glory
in the children's beds
fresh branches of the trees surviving winter.

(translated from German by Ruth and Matthew Mead)

Awakening —
Voices of birds
from the well of night
time counting with water —

evening–morning star
pale seed
sharp with thorn
strews death into life.
Cow and calf
in the warm stall
smoking in the sweat of parting —
the gold-set terror
of creation's beginning
rooting
backwards
in their eyes.

(translated from German by Ruth and
Matthew Mead)

Gertrud Kolmar
(1894–1943?)
GERMANY

She was born Gertrud Chodziesner to Jewish parents in Berlin. As a
girl she studied foreign languages and during the First World War
served as an interpreter at the prison camp Döberitz. Following a
brief stay in France she returned to Berlin, where she worked as a
teacher of deaf-mute children. In 1930 her mother died and she was
left alone to care for her aging father. Under the Nazi regime their
situation grew more and more precarious until, in 1941, her father
was deported, and in 1943 she disappeared. The majority of her
poems were not published until 1955. Since then, her work has
grown steadily in reputation.

PARIS

A gloomy cathedral
Flickers gothically amidst double towers,
Flings up steep spires,
Hoary hair, at autumn clouds and storms;
Grotesque masks

Stare from still, rippling crevices,
A dragon brood clutches
With brutal claws at its sharp-pointed breasts.

Beneath a shrine
The ancient death-dance clatters scornfully.
From a pale, world-weary aunt
A child's garland hangs, youthful and blooming;
Streets dart about, venture
Lightly and lively towards ever-near ends,
Their markets revolve,
As round and as merry as a carousel.

Houses rise and embellish
The festivals with their stony music,
Across massive bridges
The teeming crowds push a colourful mosaic,
Branches laugh on the banks,
Nestling down deeper into early spring arms
Above silent small boats,
Rocked to and fro by a gentle, grey whisper.

White-powdered locks
Tumble in waves from delicate temples.
On a green, silken skirt
A loosely bound, rose-red ribbon flares,
Fleeting smiles fasten,
Silvery smooth, to an unspoken *tu*,
Dark lashes bounce
To the tapping of bright, high-heeled shoes.

Filthy gates loiter.
Windows gaze, wept-out and blind,
Scrawny bodies hunger
For the scraps to which they are enslaved.
The heavens flutter —
In evilest hell swells and shudders,
Like the head of an adder,
Black with veins, a fist . . .

(translated from German by David Kipp)

Ingeborg Bachmann
(1926–73)
AUSTRIA

She grew up in Carinthia and studied philosophy at Innsbruck, Graz and Vienna. Her doctoral subject was the Existential Philosophy of Martin Heidegger. She lived, at various times, in Rome, America, Munich, Zurich and Berlin and published her first volume of poems in 1953. She wrote much poetry and prose, including plays and libretti, and was awarded the Büchner Prize in 1964.

THE GREAT FREIGHT

The great freight of the summer has been loaded.
The sun-ship in the harbour waits the tide,
if behind you the seagull dives and cries.
The great freight of the summer has been loaded.

The sun-ship in the harbour waits the tide.
The unmasked smile of the lemurs treads
on the lips of the figureheads.
The sun-ship in the harbour waits the tide.

If behind you the seagull dives and cries,
from the west comes the order to sink from sight.
You will drown with open eyes in light,
if behind you the seagull dives and cries.

    (translated from German by Bill Crisman)

EVERY DAY

War is no longer declared
but continued. The unheard-of thing
is the every-day. The hero
keeps away from the fighters. The weak man
has moved up to the battle zones.
The uniform of the day is patience,
its decoration the humble star
of hope worn over the heart.

It is awarded
when nothing goes on,
when the drumbeat subsides,
when the enemy has grown invisible
and the shadow of everlasting arms
covers the sky.

It is awarded
for desertion of the flag,
for courage in the face of the friend,
for the betrayal of unworthy secrets
and for the non-observance
of every order.

(translated from German by Michael Hamburger)

Sarah Kirsch

(1935–)

EAST GERMANY

Sarah Kirsch lives in East Germany. After graduating in biology, she
worked as a research assistant and a freelance writer and participated
in an agricultural cooperative. She undertook further studies at the
Literaturinstitut Johannes R. Becher and then returned to freelance
writing. She has published translations of Russian poets, and a
volume of her poems, *Landaufenthalt*, was published by Aufbau-
Verlag in 1967.

SAD DAY IN BERLIN

I'm a tiger in the rain
water parts my fur
drops drip into my eyes

I shuffle on slowly, drag my paws
along the Friedrichstrasse
and am burnt out in the rain

When the lights turn red
I beat my way through the traffic
go to the cafe for a vermouth
devour the band and sway off

Sharply I roar the rain at the Alexanderplatz
the tall block gets wet loses its belt
(I growl: one does what one can)

But it rains the seventh day
and I am cross up to my lashes

I snarl the street empty
and sit down among honest seagulls

They all look left into the Spree
And when I mighty tiger howl
they get what I mean: there must be
other tigers about

(translated from German by Gerda Mayer)

Henriëtte Roland-Holst

(1869–1952)

NETHERLANDS

She was an important socialist, and her stature and influence in the
Netherlands in both poetry and politics are undisputed. Her poetry
made a sharp break with the art-for-art's sake tradition of the 1880s,
shocking readers with its unorthodox rhythms and subject matter.
A student of Marx, she joined the Socialist Party, but in 1915 broke
with the Socialists to found the Revolutionary Socialist Party. Late
in her life she renounced Marxism and violent revolution in favour
of a socialism based on religious ideals. She also wrote biographies
of Rosa Luxemburg, Romain Rolland, and Gandhi, and a verse
drama on Thomas More.

Throughout the day we are able to ban the voices
because the task takes all our strength,

but when day's fruit has ripened into evening
we feel the many questions tightening like bows.

Half content we settle around lamps
and around the sadness-defeating hearth's fire,
relieved that the day which has emptied
has left no dregs of greater pain.

For there is always something that we fear;
we are like the wives of fishermen at sea
who day after day scan water and wind:
all they have heaves on the waves.

Our heart is embarked on world-whirling;
storms and stillnesses move us,
surf breaks against us, and we feel
each shuddering go through our depths.

(translated from Dutch by Manfred Wolf)

MOTHER OF FISHERMEN

Look at me: my mouth unlearned complaining early
my eye is stony as a winter's night
when young, resignation brought me the stick
with which I climb to the end of my days.

I know no hope, no expectation
sons and daughters I bore to bear
what I bear myself: when they lay under my heart
I thought much sadness for their sake.

Something grows in me sometimes on grim nights
when my sons are shuddering on a stormy sea
but when the morning comes I have forgotten;

then it is as if their young heads know something
too joyful for me, as if that habit of expecting nothing
will die with me, and that hopeless peace.

(translated from Dutch by Ria Leigh-Loohuizen)

Katri Vala

(1901–44)

FINLAND

Katri Vala is the pseudonym of Karin Alice Heikel. She was born in Finnish Lapland, the daughter of an official of the Forest Services, and grew up in the country. She held various jobs in remote areas of Finland before settling in Helsinki, where she married and was part of a generally admired group of young writers who practised free verse in the late twenties. In the thirties she wrote for the literary section of a left-wing periodical published by her brother. She suffered from tuberculosis and died in a sanatorium in Sweden during the Second World War. She published six collections of poetry and is regarded as a major Finnish poet.

ON THE MEADOW

O eternal grass,
the green people of your brothers
reaches to the West and to the East
over Europe, Asia, Africa.
The thick black milk of earth
nourishes your smallest brother
on the Cape of Good Hope.

You, the fragrant air of summer,
you touch my eyes
you allow my ears to hear.
Distance and time glide away.
A boundless meadow. Red flowers
are opening in the twilight:
the endless chain of hearts
circles the round globe of earth.
From beyond the centuries – today
a voice, warm like the earth, clear like the day, is sounding:
this is the road of life!

WINTER IS HERE

Winter is here again —

If I were young
perhaps I would sing
about the black bowl of earth
filled with the coolness of snowflowers,
perhaps the dew of the stars
would sparkle on the night-blue meadow of my song.

But the songs of my youth are frozen.
My song is poor and tired
like a woman
with knotty blue hands
gathering sticks
for the fire of her rickety cabin.

I am circling the track of my scanty bread,
cold like the courtyard of a prison.
My senses, my thoughts are rough with work.

Winter is here,
to sharpen misery,
to torture the children of need with the whip of his winds.
But the berries of the rowan-tree
are burning like beacon fires.

(translated from Finnish by Jaakko A. Ahokas)

Eeva-Liisa Manner

(1921–)

FINLAND

The collection *This Journey*, published in 1956, was probably the most influential work in the consolidation of modernism in Finnish poetry during the 1950s. It established Eeva-Liisa Manner's reputation as a major modern poet. She has continued to publish important poems, as well as plays, and in 1972 a novel about contemporary Spain.

from CAMBRIAN
A Suite about the Sea and the Animals

I. To move over shifting borders,
   black waters, imaginary stepping stones,
   to penetrate breaking passes, the slow lines of the mountains,
   the landslides, the snowy clouds, to find the chosen stones
   and to come to a region
   filled with even-numbered footprints, bestial dwellings.

   To see the refracted light from beyond and the earthly worries,
   to eat a bitter fruit under the breadfruit tree
   and to become hungry;
   to stand up and walk, to wear out the plaited shoes,
   to look for the stream and to come to a bank made by men,
   to wash one's hands and hair and to drink the ebbing waters
   and to dream heavy dreams about the last judgement:
   to be allowed to start from the beginning, a muddy puddle
   full of small primitive evil like the Dytiscus or
   late man.

   To move, to move without taking hold of anything
   through the dirt and the snow, the alternating heat
   and the severe past and the glaciation,
   the one which was, and the one to come;
   to sleep in the snow and to melt with one's body a bare spot
   from the great common glacier,
   to learn the skill of the hands, a slow hope,
   to build a house from sticks and to let the rains come,
   to find a worn path and kicked stones,
   the mute density of the stone; and men also,
   and to hate one's neighbour like oneself;
   to eat cones and the food of birds,
   to share one's meal with animals
   and to learn their metaphors and language and quick footsteps.

   To learn the metaphors, and to confuse them with bodily
        matters,

to learn the secrets, and to forget again,
to lose knowledge
during the wandering through time and the stratified chronicles,
the abstruse books of stone and the missing dynasties.
To become empty and to forsake superstition, a faith
which is wisdom, inherited from the animals,
from all the oppressed hearts
and the fettered plants before the making into animals.
To become empty and to forsake —
how heavy is the wandering without a burden,
loneliness without the community of animals,
an unlikeness shunned and feared by the wolves.

To come finally
light, tired,
without words, without a tent and the pity of the animals
to the shore of the sea, to see with one's body all this:
The thickening light and the long severe waves,
the hard space that revolves, squeaks,
and the slowly freezing winds;
to send by habit
an empty boat, a call into the wind
knowing that only shattered bits will reach the goal,
or nothing.

III. The Late Books

Turn the page of stone and there
   are the deeply frozen manifold irises,
   the numbers of the eyes.
A tree with thousand eyes, the germ of the flower and the
      germ of the plant body,
the germ of growth, of rustling, of filling and earth with its
      strength,
which decays or is perhaps carried away
like a prey.
Turn the pages, there is in them the germ of the trembling
      runner,

the germ of the trotting hooves, of the horns, of the cornea in
    the eyes,
the germ of a deer-like flight, fleeing with the wind,
hearing with one's whole body the rustling threat,
smelling it in the wind and tasting it in the inhabited ponds.
To see the thick stones and the danger, throbbing in them,
which is ready to spring, and hits its mark,

for further back come the sly animals, which
have freed the hands and stood up on two legs,
they are the five-toed animals, they
have big and heavy skulls and heavy brains,
and drawn-out legs like a gorilla,
they are industrious animals, and thrifty,
they collect small heads for their belts,
they rattle merrily in the wind
and bring luck, not misfortune
as long as they rattle, the bony jewels,

they are the busy animals, they have clever fingers,
which can count to five and stretch a string,
not for music but for killing,
they adorn themselves with the figures of slaughter and good
    hope
and sharpen the stones into unerring arrowheads,
which have in them the throbbing germ of destruction,
pulled out of the stone,
sinking again to sleep in the stone.

V. Oh Darkness

If they wanted freedom,
the creators of the land, of the sea, the slow givers of life,
why did not they then draw birds,
but fishes, bladders, sponges, soles,
rats, musk rats for whom the traps are set,
and pedestrians with choking lungs
and brains, which branch out like corals
and do not know of anything more.

Oh darkness that swallows everything; the cries for help of
    the animals
that drag themselves slowly through the creation;
what God created this unmercy? Was it God?
what God created these inhumans? was it Satan?
men, greedy of mercy, cruel towards animals,
great in reason, small in mind.

Pray for the animals, you that pray,
you that beg for mercy, for success and for peace,
the immanent spirit has also been poured unto them,
they are also souls, more complete than you,
and clear, brave, beautiful;

and if we begin from the beginning, who knows,
we shall have to share also these sufferings,
simpler, more severe, more unlimited than ours.

                    (translated from Finnish by Jaakko A. Ahokas)

Aila Meriluoto

(1924–)

FINLAND

She was born in Pieksämäki and attended Helsinki University. Her
first collection of poems, *Lasimaalaus* (*The Stained Glass Picture*), was a
literary sensation. She has published eight volumes of poetry, a novel,
fairy tales, children's books and translations of Rilke. In 1948 she
married the well-known Finnish writer Lauri Viita. She is now
divorced and lives in Sweden.

STILL

In the fall, I believe again in poetry
if nothing else it is
a movement of the mind.
Summers ball together

into sticky lumps,
spring evenings are glass beads from one mould
for standard-size youth,
winter a smooth heaviness, not even cold.
But the mind trembles
here, on the brink
the mind trembles
there is life, after all,
there is life, still
unbelief is left.

(translated from Finnish by Jaakko A. Ahokas) ¦

Edith Södergran

(1892–1923)

FINLAND (SWEDISH)

She was born in St Petersburg (Leningrad), where her parents belonged to the Swedish-speaking population of Finns who formed a sizable ethnic group in that city. She was sent to a German school, and it is said that her very free manner of treating the Swedish language was due to her unfamiliarity with its literary traditions. After the Russian revolution, she and her mother took refuge in Finland, near the Russian border, where they lived in extreme poverty. Her poems, published in Helsinki, were bitterly attacked by all but a very few critics, and she was entirely isolated except for her attachment to Hagar Ollsen, a young radical woman writer who introduced her poems to other young Finnish poets. She died of tuberculosis and the effects of hunger. After her death she was hailed as a reformer of Swedish poetry in both Finland and Sweden, and her fame has increased with time.

I saw a tree that was greater than all the others
with cones hanging beyond reach from it,
I saw a great church with open doors
and all those who came out were pale and strong
and ready to die;

I saw a woman, smiling and painted,
who played her luck at dice
and I saw that she lost.

A circle was drawn around all this,
that nobody shall overstep.

PAIN

Luck has no songs, luck has no thoughts, luck has nothing.
Push your luck so that she breaks, for luck is evil.
Luck comes softly in the whisper of morning among the sleeping
  bushes,
luck glides away in the light images of clouds over deep blue
  depths,
luck is the field that sleeps in the burning heat of noon,
or the endless expanse of the sea under the piercing vertical rays,
luck is powerless, she sleeps and breathes and does not know
  anything . . .
Do you know pain? She is strong and big with secretly clenched
  fists.
Do you know pain? She is a hopeful smile with eyes red with tears.
Pain gives us all what we need —
she gives us the keys to the realm of death,
she pushes us through the gate when we still hesitate.
Pain baptizes the children and remains awake with the mothers
and forges all the golden wedding-rings.
Pain rules over everything, she smooths the brow of the thinker,
she clasps the jewel round the neck of the desired woman,
she stands by the door when a man is leaving his love . . .
What else does pain still give to the ones she loves?
I do not know of more,
She gives pearls and flowers, she gives songs and dreams,
she gives us a thousand kisses which are all empty,
she gives us the only kiss that is true.
She gives us our strange souls and curious desires,
she gives to all the highest gain in life:
love, loneliness and the face of death.

HOPE

I want to forget my manners —
I couldn't care less about noble styles,
I roll up my sleeves.
The dough of poetry is rising . . .
Oh, what a sorrow —
I can't bake cathedrals . . .
The soaring high forms —
The goal of persistent yearning.
Child of our time —
doesn't your soul have its right shell?
Before I die
I'll bake a cathedral.

A DECISION

I am a very mature person
but nobody knows me.
My friends have a wrong idea of me.
I am not tame.
With the talons of an eagle I have weighed tameness.
O eagle, how sweet is the flight of your wings.
Shall you be silent like everything else?
Do you perhaps want to write poetry? You shall never write
    poetry any more.
Each poem shall be the ripping apart of a poem,
not a poem, but the marks of talons.

(translated from Swedish by Jaakko A. Ahokas)

Karin Boye

(1900–41)

SWEDEN

She studied in Uppsala and Stockholm and worked for some time
as a schoolteacher. Her first volume of poems appeared in 1922. She

published both poetry and fiction, and her work was very popular, especially during the 1930s, when she was widely regarded as 'the voice of the generation'. In 1941 she committed suicide.

from A DEDICATION

I feel your steps in the hall
I feel in every nerve your hurried steps
that go unnoticed otherwise.
A wind of fire sweeps around me.
I feel your steps, your beloved steps,
and my heart aches.

Though you pace far down the hall
the air surges with your steps
and sings like the sea.
I listen, prisoned in gnawing restraint.
My hungry pulse beats to the rhythm of your rhythm,
to the tempo of your gait.

(translated from Swedish by Nadia Christensen)

Maria Wine

(1912–)

SWEDEN

Her first book of poems appeared in 1943. That book, with three subsequent volumes published during the forties, established her as an important woman writer. Since 1950 she has published at least twelve more volumes, including some prose. She is married to Artur Lundkvist, one of Sweden's foremost literary critics.

Woman, you are afraid of the forest
I see it in your eyes
when you stare into the darkness:
the terrified look of a defenceless creature.

Woman, *you* are a forest
strange and deep: I see
you are afraid of yourself.

LOVE ME

Love me
but do not come too near
leave room for love
to laugh at its happiness
always let some of my blond hair
be free

(translated from Swedish by Nadia Christensen)

Tove Ditlevsen

(1918–76)

DENMARK

She was born in Copenhagen, where her father worked as a fireman.
The family was poor, and she was forced to leave school at the age
of fourteen to seek work. She was married and divorced three
times. She was the author of many volumes of poetry, several novels,
numerous short stories, essays, and a three-volume autobiography.

MORNING

I wake despondent
at three o'clock in the morning
in my narrow
winterbed —
dull hair
covered with withered
leaves
and blood-red, peeling
nailpolish on my toes
from summer's sandaltime.

Ashtaste in my mouth
tired loins
malicious throbbing
in a tooth.

Hostile
furniture from the past
will have nothing to do with
the random hands
of new inhabitants.

Old sentences
in the curtains
words the fugitive
forgot
when he made his hasty
departure —
fragments without
meaning or connection.

Out of step with
the season
entangled as a
ball of yarn the cat
has played with
I stroke its
delicate shoulderblades
that are trembling lightly
in sleep.

No more birds to stalk
no mice to scare.
No way out of memory's
labyrinth.
Slowly life is running out
like drops along a drainpipe.

THE OLD FOLK

The old folk do not lay
plans far into the future
do not postpone anything until
the day after tomorrow.

In the evening they burn
letters in the fireplace.
Each newborn morning
they thank God for life
which is no longer
a matter of course.

If they mention Death
everyone cheerfully protests
which makes them
more alone.
With no one can they talk about
this great
at-birth-ordained
event.

(translated from Danish by Nadia Christensen)

Cecil Bødker
(1927–)
DENMARK

Born in Fredericia, Denmark, she trained and worked for some time
as a silversmith. In 1953 she married and now has four daughters,
including two Ethiopian girls adopted as a result of her five-month
stay in that country. She has published four volumes of poetry, one
novel, one play, and numerous short stories, children's books, and
radio dramas. Her work has received many literary awards.

FURY'S FIELD

Where do you go with your fury,
child,
when the roads are blocked with words
you don't understand
and your fear is worse
than the punishment.

Where do you go with your hate
when your mother
thoughtlessly
misconstrues your sincerity
and strangers laugh
at your games.

Do you then beat flat a field
in a box's amenable sand
and sow
the first seed of your fury.
Do you play a game
of dead dolls.

Say to the upright men
in the world
that they must harvest
your ripened hate
and plough the field of your fury
before they will see your face.

(translated from Danish by Nadia Christensen)

Astrid Tollefsen

(1897–1973)

NORWAY

She was born in Porsgrunn, Norway, and for many years worked
in an office. Her first volume of poems was not accepted for publi-

cation until she was fifty years old, but with her second volume she
came to stand in the forefront of Norwegian modernism; at the cost
of great economic hardship she left her job and devoted all her time
to writing, publishing a total of fourteen volumes, including her
selected works which appeared in 1973.

TOULOUSE LAUTREC

There is red
on the clown-lady's lips
the wine is red
the music loves itself its echo
the ice cubes' clink against glass
intensifies the thirst
the thirst for red
word-waves laughter-shriek song
rises and falls
worst is the silence
in abrupt seconds

The dance was red as long as it lasted
Avril's dance
beautiful rhythmic inciting
hot cool
victorious
not of this world
this lascivious cafe world

There they sit at the tables
and think that they are alive
that their hearts are red
like blood and wine and shame

the night is late
don't let it be morning
before the thirst for red
has found a track to follow!

WORKDAY MORNING

Things
do not know their collective name
the books have no idea
what they contain
the cigarettes are unaware
of their potential
the typewriter
is not longing for hands
the pictures
have never looked in a mirror
the violin is content to keep silent
it has no mind
that can be a conduit
be re-created

The day's first cigarette
is fragrance and glow
fanfare!
the ignorant
silent ones
those with no inklings
longings or searching eyes
the unfeeling
immovable ones
draw imperceptibly closer

(translated from Norwegian by
Nadia Christensen)

Angela Figuera Aymerich

(1902–)

SPAIN

Born in Bilboa, she has worked as a professor of Spanish literature
and language in various institutes in Spain.

WOMEN AT THE MARKET

Old women all their lives, they're a mixture of whitelime and brine,
rubble packed into rusted iron frames.
Their eyes are hard, icy, like sleet,
and their hair droops like trampled weeds.
Soured blood flows through their veins.

They shop early, poking around in the vendors' stands.
Digging almost. They pick out tomatoes that are bruised.
Rotting oranges. Wilted vegetables that smell
like dung. They buy inch-high cylinders
of cooked blood, as dark as mud pies,
and lungs that blush timidly,
obscene-looking things.

Sighs part their lips, when they get ready to pay,
rummaging slowly down into the dirty paunch
of an enormous beat-up handbag with its handles gone;
scowling, scared stiff that they'll touch bottom
and fish out their last filthy cent.

They always take a child along, with a mop of hair and snot
      running from his nose,
who hangs on, trailing from their greasy skirts,
sucking on apple or banana skins.
They manoeuvre him with yells and shoves. They ill-treat
the ropesoles of their grimy espadrilles, on the way back

to a courtyard filled with flies, kids, dogs
and squabbling neighbours. Back to a reeking woodstove,
a tub of dirty wash, a man
who stinks of liquor, sweat and butts.
Who chews in silence, swears something, and spits.
Who maybe that night, in the foul-smelling bedroom,
without petting or any gentle words, brutal,
impatient as an animal, will punish their belly,
loading it down with the weight of one more wretched fruit.
Another long drawn-out spell of weariness.

Oh, no. I'm not trying to find out why it's like this,
but there are skies that look so pure. And beautiful things.

(translated from Spanish by Hardie St Martin)

Gloria Fuertes

(1920–)

SPAIN

She was born and has lived most of her life in Madrid, where she
attended university, worked as a secretary, and from 1939 to 1950 as a
writer of poems, stories, and plays for children's magazines. She has
also edited a review and founded a series of readings by women poets.
She reads her own work widely on the radio, in cultural centres, and
in recent years in the bars and coffee houses of Madrid.

AUTOBIOGRAPHY

At the foot of the Cathedral of Burgos
my mother was born.
At the foot of the Cathedral of Madrid
my father was born.
At the foot of my mother I was born
one afternoon in the middle of Spain.
My father was a worker,
my mother a seamstress.
I wanted to take off with the circus
but I'm only what I am.
When I was little
I went to a reformatory and a free school
As a kid I was sickly
and summered in a sanatorium,
but now I get around.
I've had at least seven love affairs,
some bad daddies,
and a marvellous appetite.
Now I've got two minor convictions
and a kiss from time to time.

CLIMBING

Death was there, sitting by the roadside
– the Death I saw wasn't skinny,
or all bones, or freezing,
and she didn't shroud her thick hair in a rag.

As usual Death was alone
sitting on a rock of the crag
knitting herself a sweater.
She was so busy she didn't see me,
right off she shouted, 'It's not your turn!'
and started knitting like mad.

– OK, you can take these poems away,
this wanting love, this wanting a cigarette,
you can take this body that's killing me,
but be careful not to finger my soul.

I've got Death really thinking
because she couldn't make me mad.

(translated from Spanish by Philip Levine)

Sophia de Mello Breyner Andresen
(1919–)
PORTUGAL

Her first book was published in 1944. In 1961 her collection *Livro
Sexto* won the Grand Poetry Prize of the Portuguese Society of
Writers. She has translated Dante's *Purgatorio* into Portuguese and
major Portuguese writers including Camoes and Fernando Pessoa in-
to French. In 1969 she was an opposition candidate for the Chamber
of Deputies in Oporto.

DIONYSUS

Between the dark silent trees
The scarlet sky burns,
And born in the secret heart of afternoon
Dionysus passes through the dust of the roads.

The abundance of September's fruits
Inhabits his face and each member
Has that scarlet full perfection,
That serene ardent glory
Which distinguishes the gods from mortals.

THE DEAD MEN

Quietly at our side the dead
Drink the exaltation of our life.
Only the shadow following the wake of our gestures
feels them pass
when lightly
they come in the night
to seek our remains.

They pass through rooms where we abandon ourselves,
Wrap themselves in the movements we trace
Repeat the words we have said,
And bending over our sleep
they drink our dreams
like milk.

Intangible, without weight or contour
They warm themselves with the heat of our blood.
Smile at the images we live
And weep for us out of sight,
For they already know to where we are going.

THE MIRRORS

All day the mirrors kindle their brilliance
Never are they empty
And even under the eyelid of darkness
Their smooth pupil blinks and stares
like a cat's.

In the half shadow of the late hour
when stillness installs itself in the centre of silence
Only then
Does the mirrors' own inhabiting light
Surface and quench us:
Light torn from
Within a cold glassy fire.

(translated from Portuguese by Allan Francovich)

Maria Teresa Horta

(1937-)

PORTUGAL

Born in Lisbon, Maria Teresa Horta is the editor of the literary supplement of a leading Lisbon newspaper. In 1970 she published a novel which shocked official public morality with its sexual frankness, and in 1973 she was arrested, along with the two other 'Marias', for their collection of poetry and prose entitled *New Portuguese Letters*, recently published in the U.S.

SWIMMING POOL

Next to will
I value reason

the glass of things
the air as womb

the negation of thirst
and of seduction
the breathing of a body
that hurts to touch

The deep pool
where the wind swims

a secret vagina
with its corridors

I am lost to time
I am lost to time

enclosed in my
fruit
with breath inside

SAVED

From the wind I get
the predicate of plants

And feel the wider cleavage
of your lips
grazing and razing
what is torn from the climate
at the apex of a road

Of the pools I only have the thought
where once I swam and drowned

a memory I quench and cannot grasp
now that I am yours

yours and saved

(translated from Portuguese by Suzette Macedo)

Ada Negri
(1870–1945)
ITALY

Ada Negri was born in Lodi to a poor family and became a school teacher. Her first works were strongly influenced by her commitment to socialism, but she later turned to religious themes. She died in Milan in 1945.

MAKE WAY!

Make way! From the noisy ceilings of workshops,
from shiny ploughs and hellish fires
    of horrid forges,
from caverns where a people weaves, hammers, creates,
from mines I rise and – free plebeian woman —
    raise a hymn to work.

Make way! From woods filled with nests and whispers,
from myrtle bushes and fresh hiding-places,
    from fertile soil,
from blue waters where the gentle halcyon circles,
I rise girdled with flowers and – bold peasant woman —
    raise a paean to the earth.

Who blocks the unleashed course of the stream?
Who halts the flight of the lark through rose skies?
    Who stops the shot arrow?
I am the crashing stream, the sparkling arrow,
the melodious bird; now a wandering swallow,
    now a funereal owl.

Art, it is for you I fight! Future, I await you!
This full-blooming emotion, a waxing flame
    kindling my mind and heart,
I toss to the earth and sky in the bejewelled garb
of a flying strophe, a splendid sheath
    of thunderbolts and flowers!

(translated from Italian by Lynne Lawner)

Antonia Pozzi
(1912–38)
ITALY

Antonia Pozzi was born in Milan on 13 February 1912 and committed suicide at the age of twenty-six. A notebook of poems was found among her papers and has subsequently been published in four different editions. The first edition was issued in Milan in 1939 with an introduction by Eugenio Montale.

TO TRUST

I have so much faith in you. I believe
I could wait for your voice
silently, through centuries
of darkness.

Like the sun
you know all the secrets:
you could make the geraniums
and the wild zagara bloom
deep in the marble
quarries and legendary
prisons.

I have so much faith in you. I'm as calm
as an Arab wrapped
in his white barracan
listening to God
make the barley grow around his house.

(translated from Italian by Lynne Lawner)

Maria Luisa Spaziani
(1924–)
ITALY

Maria Luisa Spaziani was born in Turin and has lived in Milan, Rome, and Paris. She has written essays and lectured on French literature in Italy and abroad. Her second book, *Utilità della memoria,* won the Carducci Prize in 1966.

WINTER MOON

Winter moon filtering slowly down
from the pomegranate through the windowpanes
onto my rapid dreams – dreams of a thief
constantly chased, constantly about to run,
you cloud up, a membrane of tears,
and soon the hour will ring out.
                              Far off
beyond our shores, beyond the bare seasons
mortally tiring us by exalting
and then humbling us, with tide-like rhythms,
you will shine happily, a golden sign,
at the last tavern, a lamp
above the incorruptible table;
and I shall see, one by one
in a circle, the faces
that an empty, cruel burst of wind rubs out.

(translated from Italian by Lynne Lawner)

Margherita Guidacci
(1921–)
ITALY

Born in Florence, Margherita Guidacci took a degree at the University of Florence and now teaches at a secondary school in Rome.

One of the first poets after the Second World War to depart from
the hermetic tradition, she has published four books of poetry, the
first, *La Sabbia e l'angelo*, in 1946. She has also translated Blake,
Emily Dickinson and T. S. Eliot. She is married to the writer Luca
Pinna and has three sons.

from ALL SAINTS' DAY

I

All Saints' Day; November sky
Reflected in the streets' rain-soaked
Asphalt, two parallel greys
To oppress the glance
Wherever it seeks escape. The city
Seems lead and ash, and the raw
Flash of headlights turns pedestrians'
Faces still more ghostly. The hours
Glide by slowly in this roar
Of water, between short splashes
Of mud and the whirling
Of rotten leaves from gardens. It's hard
Today to think of Paradise; everything
Brings us back and drags us down to earth.
There's too much faith needed to leap
Sadness's high barrier. It will,
Instead, be easy tomorrow, in the wake
Of a disintegrating season
To remember the end of all flesh.

II

And still, saints, you come back
Every year, through the heart that can pick you out
Against the background of lives that fall
Like this pouring rain, spilling
On the earth that drinks them greedily,
Deluge from the world's beginning to its end
Crossing the sky – oblique – colourless
Line of tears

As far as the grass of their resting-place.
On this day which for the living is just
The eve of the day to come
(The mercy of flesh, the mercy of dust
And chrysanthemums waiting
To be arranged on graves)
You return with your sure step
Luminous with planets
To light the rain of our
Existences that fall
Inside mercy but outside glory.

III

I have often thought: this is
The year's real end and Apocalypse
With its brown and grey, two empty bezels,
All the coloured gems that stared at us
Before, extinguished. The world is
Dissolved in these rotten ferments
Of death. The water carries the earth
Away from the mountains, leaving
The stones naked, the wind carries the leaves
Away until the final dryness
Of the trees. Nothing remains but to hope
For the time when there will no longer
Be anything to lose. Already under
The anguish of flesh the skeleton
Shows and reaffirms the harsh
And patient wait.
                    This is
The end, not December with crystal
Skies, the Star of the East
And men kneeling to adore
The Child. In silence – though
Hidden from the world – hope will revive
With the seed under the snow. But twice
In these days when earth itself
Resembles a scene from the Last Judgement

Hc who will return is recalled
To us from the altar: no longer a child
To save us, but an adult to judge
The quick and the dead, to exclude any new
Redemption. Then time's hinges
Will turn, huge and bleak,
And eternity shall be. You alone,
Saints, will dare to fix it with your gaze.

(translated from Italian by Ruth Feldman and Brian Swann)

Elena Clementelli

(contemporary)

ITALY

She has published four volumes of poetry, also anthologies of
flamenco songs, Negro spirituals, and Blues. She has also translated
many Spanish poets into Italian.

from ETRUSCAN NOTEBOOK

I

Cerveteri road:
over the drowsy voice of the pines
the long death contains stone words.
The secret language
slips on weapons,
tools,
symbols,
and is gathered up by the sea
which alone can speak to the dead.
In the city of the dead
they tell tales about the living,
with discretion:
about us
and those to come,

heroes of a tradition always in the future
timeless gods.
The man who has bested time
has a different grammar,
therefore we do not comprehend
what the sea, only the sea understands.
To distract
restless curious boys,
a dagger, a rope, a fan,
carved in the tufa.

5

The net rests on the water's surface,
the fisherman of Marina Velca
fishes up sea-flickerings in the sun.
He will make a torch of them for your night,
when sated earth
sweats out the day that has possessed it.
Again you will descend in silence
along the track that repels the footstep of the living,
to the meeting with time.
And you will bring torches
to dream ghosts
where life lights the lamp of its faiths.
Thus tomorrow, every tomorrow
a spark will burn in the eyes
of young Tyrrhenian boys,
transparent memory, or presage,
of eternity.

8

From gorge to gorge
under the mute forest of tufa
the wind's voice moans its appeal.
The wall of the sea replies
with the host of names written on water.

(translated from Italian by Ruth Feldman and Brian Swann)

Anna de Noailles

(1876–1933)

FRANCE

Greatly admired at the turn of the century, Anna de Noailles embodied in her life and her poetry the melancholy, the exoticism and cult of the self which characterized French romanticism decades earlier. The daughter of a Romanian prince and grand-daughter of a Turkish diplomat, Anna was married at 15 to Comte Mathieu de Noailles. She published the first of her nine books of poetry in 1901, and numbered among her friends Proust, Valéry and other writers of her day who regularly visited her salon.

IMAGE

Poor fawn about to die
Mirror me in your pupils' depths
And make my memory fly
Among the changeless shades.

Those thoughtful dead who would delight
In all my games, say that
I dream of them beneath the trees
Where I pass by, small and bright.

You will tell them of my grace
My shadow dance
In orchards full of swaying leaves
Myriad and alive.

You'll say that often I have
Eyelids slow and sad
And dance the evening in my trailing gown
Swept softly by the wind.

You will tell them that I fall asleep,
My naked arms folded beneath my head
That my skin is like new gold
Spun around with violet veins.

Tell them how sweet it is to see
My hair, grape blue,
My feet like mirrors,
And my eyes the colour of the moon.

And tell them, in idle evenings
Lying at the fountain's edge
I have languished for their love
And sought their empty shadows with desire.

(translated from French by Carol Cosman)

Joyce Mansour
(1928–)
FRANCE

Joyce Mansour was born in England of Egyptian parents and is a leading member of the post-war Surrealist movement.

EMBRACE THE BLADE

Hot night of the ramparts
Walls of Heraklaia
The thankless fretwork of the serpent on the smooth back
of the amphora
A woman's shell abandoned on the beach
Hot she too and drab
I remember that shape at the end of the path
Armed with desire and yet unborn
What oil full wine or sacrilegious draught
Filled this belly not so long ago
With its scented weight
A wave of blood hollows my bed
Empty empty empty
As death

AUDITORY HALLUCINATIONS

I would sleep until the mottled jaguar dawn
Surrenders to the deep blue-blackness
Charred forever
Rip my pain on the spiny bush
Of your tawny desire
I would sleep
A thousand deserts between us
Sodom and Gomorrah matchless pleasures
Obscene imaginings
In the air the bracelet of my lips
Forms the O of an unspeakable measure
Then the guards hidden
Under my tongue
Will shatter the millstone and its widow's vibrations
The whining wind rises
Love flows
The round muzzle of the afternoon quivers under bridges
Big white poodles follow the footprints of the fog
Capricorn
Your canines promise horror
The earth is shimmering with December
The rash bird buried
Let's repeat the song of the rain

THE SUN IN CAPRICORN

Three days of rest
Why not the grave
I suffocate without your mouth
Waiting drains the stillborn sunrise
And the long hours on the stairway
Smell of gas
Flat on my face I wait for tomorrow
I see your skin glisten
In the black breach of the night
The slow surge of moonlight

On the inner sea of my sex
Dust on dust
Hammer on mattress
Sun on leaden drum
Still smiling your hand beats indifference
Cruelly clothed bent towards emptiness
You say no and the smallest object a woman's body can shelter
Bows down
Artificial Nice
Synthetic perfume one hour on the couch
For what pale giraffes
Have I left Byzantium
Solitude stinks
A moonstone in an oval frame
Yet another stiff-jointed bout of insomnia
Once more a dagger throbs in rain
Diamonds and delirium tomorrow's desiderata
Sweat of taffeta beaches without shelter
Lunacy of my lost flesh

(translated from French by Carol Cosman)

Anne-Marie Albiach

(1937–)

FRANCE

Anne-Marie Albiach is a member of the editorial board of *Siècle à Mains* and has published two books of poetry. *État*, from which the following extract has been taken, is a single poem which does not progress by images or plot. It makes the general argument that, although everyday language is dependent upon logic, in poetry or fiction it is possible to imagine a free syntax.

from ÉTAT

of the unended in the speed of
the unpointed, unfixed
pose   is the touch-point
                              of which
going on is but the again of the
first   brutal
enigma   of all

knowledge other than movement

A GEOMETRIC UNFOLDING
      THE POSING OF AN UNKNOWN

Grasped in the going-on

After MYTH
                    it is the chorus

CORRESPONDING ORDER:

inverting of adjectives

see it, the one being the other   their
all at once given adjectives
          but no doubt mind glimpse
              the grasping

but by the shuffled
given   of adjectives the voice flees
what twins it

from the centre

but said
where the name is uttered
the place where   is ruled

                              its overwhelming —

white

                    (translated from French by Paul Auster)

Zoé Karélli

(1901–)

GREECE

Zoé Karélli was born in Thessaloníki and received an education befitting the daughter of a good family. She was tutored in languages, singing, recitation and drawing. She has published translations of William Carlos Williams, Djuna Barnes and T. S. Eliot. The author of ten books of poetry, one of which won the State Prize in 1955, she published her collected poems in 1973. In 1959 she was awarded the Palmes Académique by France's Ministry of Education.

PRESENCES

You must remain very much alone,
– quietness of the fragile movement,
anxiety of perception —
that the presences may come.

Do not be afraid,
the dead never die;
even the most humble and forgotten
exist, and when you are very much alone
they come near you
invested with the mystic silence
of the ineradicable,
the incomparable presence of man.

(translated from Greek by Kimon Friar)

Rita Boumí-Pappás

(1906–)

GREECE

Born on the island of Syros, she went to live in Syracuse, Sicily, with her older brother when she was fifteen. As he became involved with the fascist cause, she made a commitment to socialism which was strengthened by the German-Italian occupation. Like Yannis Ritsos, she believes that poetry should have a social purpose. From 1956 to 1958 Boumí-Pappás edited a poetry magazine, and for seventeen years she has written on international politics for progressive Greek newspapers. She and her husband have compiled an anthology of world poetry. She has published over fifteen books of her own verse.

THE CROW
to Stalin

You cannot from the open window invade
the country of my reveries
or my inviolate asylum,
trying to make me believe you are the white dove
for whom I wait and sing.
You cannot take my creations by surprise
to scatter them terrified in the night
to tear our sleep to tatters, our only good,
to spread your black wings and cover my house
to enter my still wet words as in a net
to control their arrangement
to measure their weight grimly
to examine their substratum with suspicion
the aroma I succeeded in finding after so many blendings
to approve
to disapprove
to laugh sneeringly when you catch me weeping
to dictate to me your stupid croakings
to direct me
to perch on my shoulders with your grasping claws
for fear I might escape you
to nest in my conscience
to force your way into my clothing
into my bed
under my skin
seeking to persuade me that you are sage
that your loathsome eyes drip with paternal kindness

that your savage beak cannot possibly commit an injustice
that it has never plunged into human flesh.
Do not touch me!
You cannot count on my own blood also,
it is an undrinkable wine.
You cannot choke me
or steal my soul like a bandit.
I shall resist,
I shall shout for help!

(translated from Greek by Kimon Friar)

Eléni Vakaló

(1921)

GREECE

Born in Athens, she took her degree in archaeology at the University
of Athens in 1946 and studied art history at the Sorbonne in 1948–9.
In collaboration with her husband and a group of painters and art
editors, she founded the Vakaló School of Decorative Arts in 1958.
She is one of the foremost art critics in Greece and the author of ten
books of poetry.

GENEALOGY

my grandmother was a wrinkled little girl
My grandmother's hat

I asked her how she had fallen in love the very
    first time,

I wore a hat
With flowers around it
And on its crown a bird
From the bird hung another branch
And on the branch flowers
At the end a nest

Rested on my neck
And there were birds there too

The birds flew

moral

Our life is harder sometimes than death,
    whatever you make of it,
And beautiful as well
Death has not changed my opinion.

(translated from Greek by Paul Merchant)

SONG OF THE HANGED

And then the knife
Entered more deeply
Men hanging in the moonlight
What will be the end?
The waves came
And covered silence
Men hanging in the moonlight
How did the mourning start?

All the children dear God,
Wanted to be sailors
Men hanging in the moonlight
Speak to it about the dead loneliness
In the masts
And we who opened our hands
To birds
Tell us, tell us
How did the mourning start?

All knives
Have points too hard
For our soft yielding flesh
All ships and all the trees
Have ropes
Dark blue rings
Around our necks.

(translated from Greek by James Damaskos)

Katerina Anghelaki-Rooke
(1939–)
GREECE

Katerina Anghelaki-Rooke was born in Athens and is the god-daughter of Nikos Kazantzakis. Her first volume of poetry, *Wolves and Clouds*, was published in 1963. A later collection appeared in 1971. In 1972 she received a Ford Foundation grant for travel in the U.S.

from NOTES ON MY FATHER

The old man moved into his night
a boat all lights in the evening harbour.
The island was in small spring,
the sun came out suddenly
struck the tiles
and disappeared again.
What could the old man know now of spring?
He spelled it out like a child the ABC's
comprehending the flower slowly.
Already something like soil
he had become only surface.

This mortal moved into
the crack in coal
the old sack
loaded with the four seasons
the four ages
with deep aging.
Brown spotted hands
and desperate blue veins.

The dawn of his birth
the village was in snow
the melon patch purple with cold.
His father came from the woods
with a dead boar

slung over his shoulder;
he dropped it in front of the fireplace.
Snow and game
small magic signs
around a wintry belly
Silence . . .
someone is swaying in the garden
someone is fondling the soil
the white soil of night.
I'm waiting for the moon to grow
for all to ease in me
to remember
to remember all miracles
the unmet
most of all.
I want to be in what's being born
and in what's ending,
I cast spells on my departing father
spells of love.
At the end of night
at the end of the gully
at the setting of the moon
it was me leaving in love
spellbound
exempt in death
all my forces unmouldered
for eternity.

In a green pasture
in a shady pasture
in a barbarous pasture of oleanders,
from under comes all this vegetation
I praise
from under begins
the ascent of fate.

(translated from Greek by the author)

Jenny Mastoráki
(1949–)
GREECE

She was born in Athens and studied there at the University, where
she took a first in Byzantine Studies. She published her first book of
poems, *Rights of Way*, in 1972, and is considered one of the out-
standing new voices in contemporary Greek poetry.

> The bridal bed. Above it
> an icon of Saint Inhumanity, sheep,
> and a deafmute poet covering his eyes.
> On the first Sunday of Lent
> monks from Mount Athos appeared
> with lambs' innards hidden
> in their pouches. Two of them
> cornered a stray cow on the quay
> and cut her up neatly. Then a caïque
> took the monks and meat
> and sailed eastwards. The City*
> was taken exactly forty-eight hours later
> when we were washing away the blood.

THREE POEMS

> Then they paraded Pompey's urn
> simply and soberly
> on the backs of royal elephants.
> They lifted it aboard with pulleys
> in the port of Haifa,
> and the stevedores still brag
> how they debauched with him
> down by the wharfs.

* *Translator's note:* 'The City' is Constantinople, taken by the Ottoman
Turks on 29 May 1453.

The Wooden Horse then said
no I refuse to see the press
and they said why not and he said
he knew nothing about the killing
and anyway he himself always ate
lightly in the evenings and once
in his younger days he'd worked
as a pony on a merry-go-round.

The Crusaders knew the Holy Places
only from post-cards and tourist guides.
So they set off with banners, tents,
tools and sandwiches, just like a school
excursion. One day, Baldwin's mistress
received a polaroid snapshot of
some monument or other. Her beau
was marked with an arrow, one among
a dozen heads. They brought it off —
though it was a fluke, to tell the truth.

The papers of the period
spoke of bloodless operations.

(translated from Greek by Nick Germanacos)

Nigâr Hanim
(1862–1918)
TURKEY

The daughter of an Ottoman pasha, she went to a French school at
age seven. She married at fourteen and after a few years of great un-
happiness was divorced. She was well versed in the cultures of the
East and the West and knew many languages, including French,
Persian, Greek, Arabic, and German. She published three collections
of poetry, a book of literary love letters, a collection of prose pieces,
and a three-act play. Her autobiography was published in 1959.

TELL ME AGAIN

Am I your only love – in the whole world – now?
Am I really the only object of your love?
If passions rage in your mind,
If love springs eternal in your heart —
Is it all meant for me? Tell me again.

Tell me right now, am I the one who inspires
All your dark thoughts, all your sadness?
Share with me what you feel, what you think.
Come, my love, pour into my heart
Whatever gives you so much pain.
Tell me again.

(translated from Turkish by Tâlat S. Halman)

Gülten Akin

(contemporary)

TURKEY

She has won many awards including her country's top poetry prize, given by the Turkish Language Association. She has published five books of poems and several short plays. A graduate of the Faculty of Law, she has practised law and worked as a teacher in several places where her husband served as chief administrative officer.

ELLAS AND THE STATUES

Feeling a pain in his breast, when he speaks
Feeling guilty. As though forced to swallow
Unpalatable things. Nauseated
He casts taut threads into the world with his voice
Facing him one . . . two . . . three statues of mud
Upright, shout at every movement
With every movement crumble a little
Yet

Somewhere there have always been warm rooms
And old men in the warm rooms
Silent men, whose forefathers
Made miracles, always sacred tombs, saints
And candles burning on the gravestones
And birds circling at shoulder height
White birds.
Men have said their morning prayers in open country
Then returned with the birds to the ancient rooms
These two hundred years, the road has been travelled
Captain Dursun's ship has been boarded
Sails have been unfurled. In the middle of the Black Sea
A storm. The passengers pray.
Suddenly someone with a hoary beard —
Hey, captain, who is it, who, who?
He is gone as he has come
The storm has fallen asleep
The sails are full, the ship on course
Someone tells the tale back in Unye
And as he tells it

The birds disappear, the candles go out
The ancestors are dead in their cupboards
But the ordeal goes on, and on
By every hearth
Everyone will die someday, will die
God will remain, the fire will be lighted
There will be people in the rooms

Smiling, bowing their heads, sighing
The wicked as they hide
The good as they grumble
Tall and thin, and wearing soft white garments.
His hand is an ungainly stone upon the table
To hide, but why? One of the statues laughs:
'You have been crushed.'
'Look again . . . me or you?'

Taking breath from the people, breathing incantations on them
O dirty mud of the city, me or you?

The hand on the table has grown more shapely
It will be lifted slowly
The table will shake. This much is clear   ·
The table will be upturned in the end
The hand will grow soft, more delicate
A cluster of yellow narcissus

A gust of wind across the corn
Sudden festivity upon the earth
Girls and machines hand in hand.
Some education from Paris, says one of the statues
To enlighten the towns. The villages . . . how coarse!
Thou knowest, God! Where are you, grandfather, saint
Who with birds upon your shoulders
Gathered the scattered soldiers together
Steered the ship safe upon its course
Destroyed the statues grown too smug

The tangled skein is unwound
Potatoes are buried in ashes, the coffeepot boils
On the path facing the window
The sick on their stretchers, the dead on theirs
Anger is not the broken shoulder, the motionless leg
Anger is the corpse rolling off the stretcher
The secret in the books. The crossways are abandoned
Untangled the skein of wool
The end of the tangled skein in sight

Living with people, as they live
Inhaling the air they breathe
Breathing knowledge into them

(translated from Turkish by Nermin Menemencioğlu)

Rahel

(1890–1931)

ISRAEL (HEBREW)

Rahel Blaustein, who signed her poems simply 'Rahel', was born in Russia and in 1909 emigrated to Palestine, where she became an agricultural worker, participating in one of the early experimental communal settlements. During the First World War she studied painting and agronomy in Europe and taught Jewish refugee children in Russia. After the war she returned to Palestine, where she died of tuberculosis.

TO MY COUNTRY

I haven't sung your praise,
nor glorified your name
in tales of bravery
and the spoils of war.
I only plant a tree
on Jordan's quiet banks.
I only wear a path
over the fields.
Surely very meagre,
Mother, I know.
Surely very meagre,
your daughter's offering:
Only a joyous shout
on a radiant day,
only secret weeping
over your barrenness.

(translated from Hebrew by Diane Mintz)

Leah Goldberg
(1911–70)

ISRAEL (HEBREW)

Leah Goldberg was born in Lithuania and educated at a Hebrew *gymnasium*. She earned a Ph.D. in Semitic languages from the University of Bonn in 1933, and in 1935 emigrated to Palestine where she worked first as a journalist and translator and later as a teacher of comparative literature at the Hebrew University, Jerusalem. As a poet and a scholar she played an important role in transmitting certain aesthetic values from the literary culture of Europe to the new Hebrew culture. Her poetry and her imaginative children's books have enjoyed continuing popularity.

from THE SYMPOSIUM

Outside the cats are wailing.
Yes, that's how it is, Aristophanes my friend,
As always you make fun of me.
You put on your comic performance —
All the cypresses, the olive trees in the square
Answer with laughter to my love.

And it, offspring of a god and a beggar-woman,
Homeless bastard-creature,
Lies pillowless under the star
Hearing the nightingale's voice in the wailing of cats.

And the close sky spreads out.

from MY MOTHER'S HOUSE

My mother's mother died
in the spring of her days. Her daughter
Would not remember her face. Her portrait inscribed
In my grandfather's heart
Was expunged from the world of images
After his death.

Only her mirror was left in the house.
Through the passage of time it had sunk in its silver frame.
And I, her pale grand-daughter, I who do not resemble her,
Today look into it as into
A lake hiding treasures
Under the water.

Deep down, behind my face,
I see a young woman
With ruddy cheeks, smiling.
A wig on her head.
She fixes
A long earring to her earlobe, threading it
Through the tiny hole in the delicate flesh
Of the ear.

Deep down, behind my face, shines
The bright golden fleck in her eyes.
And the mirror maintains
The family tradition:
That she was very beautiful.

(translated from Hebrew by Robert Alter)

Dahlia Ravikovich
(1936–)
ISRAEL (HEBREW)

Born in Ramat-Gan, a suburb of Tel Aviv, Dahlia Ravikovich was
raised on a collective farm. She served for a short time in the Israeli
army before attending the Hebrew University in Jerusalem, where
she studied English literature. *The Love of an Orange* (1959), her first
volume of poems, immediately established her as one of the im-
portant new voices in Israeli poetry. The wryness and frequent
obliquity of her poems and the ironic use of colloquial language are
characteristic of the younger generation of Hebrew poets.

THE BLUE WEST

If there was only a road there
the ruins of workshops
one fallen minaret
and some carcasses of machines,
why couldn't I
come to the heart of the field?
There is nothing more painful
than a field
with a stone on its heart.

I want to reach the other side of the hill,
want to reach
want to be there.
I want to break out of the mass of the earth,
from my head to my footsoles
the mass of the earth.

I want to reach the ends of thought
whose beginnings
slice like a knife.
I want to climb up to the borders of the sun
and not be eaten by fire.

If only one could walk about
with locust feet on the water,
If only one could climb up
on a high arch of the sun's rays,

If only one could reach
all the cities beyond the sea —
And here is another sorrow:
a seashore where there are no ships.

On one of the days to come
the eye of the sea will darken
from the multitude of ships.
In that hour all the mass of the earth
will be stretched out like a sail.

And a sun will shine for us blue as the sea,
a sun will shine for us hot as an eye,
will wait for us till we can climb up
as it heads for the blue west.

(translated from Hebrew by Chana Bloch)

Samar Attar

(contemporary)
SYRIA (ARABIC)

Samar Attar is a Syrian writer who has published her poetry, short
stories and essays in Syrian, Lebanese and English periodicals. She
has a doctorate in comparative literature from the State University of
New York, Binghamton, and is currently teaching at the University
of Algiers.

from THE RETURN OF THE DEAD

And you came back
One summer morning
Like a dreadful dream
Your shroud was loose
Your eyes were glassy
We stood and watched
Our marbles fell and broke
On the cobble road
You waved, then you strolled.

No sparrows, no crows
In the city of shining brass
'Where did they go?'
You asked
'Did they all die?'
  die
  die

And we heard your
            echo
Old man
And we saw your
  rotten teeth
Your gouged eyes
And we ran.

I was a little girl
When I watched you go
From our home.
Big, sturdy men
Carried your coffin
On their heads.
Ah, how the procession went on
                 and on
And I saw the shop-keepers
Close their shops
On a cold winter day
And walk
Behind the weeping crowd
And I heard a man
Singing of the Lord
Women wailed like demons
And we children stood and watched.

The sun was cold
And the long train of chocolate heads
Trotted along the narrow lanes
And when it passed that distant curb
I saw you swaying right and left.
Bare headed men
Do spare the dead
Do hold his shroud
I said, we said
And all the children wept.

Ah city of the dead
We launched our sails
We stored our food

We sang our hymns
But is it true
That over there
No grass will bloom
No tree will bear?

From garden to garden
From bay to bay
We journeyed
Up and down
Night and day
Searching for a spectre
And all the sailors that we met
Talked of nothing
But hooded heads.
Father, where should we go?
Is there a city for the dead?

In a tent we were huddled
            and told
            Mother was dead
            or rather killed
            nobody knew
And we were captives
            in the city
            of our father
            where the wind incessantly blew.

We silently prayed
For your return
Father
We were young and weak.
Our home became a prison
Our streets had different names
Why didn't you deliver us
            spare us a grave
            just a little
            obscure grave?

Today and by the river mouth
We saw your ugly face
Or did you have a face?
You scurried like a rain storm
                        and waved.

Do not say
I am an old man
What can an old man say?

Theories of history
And argumentation
And we little fools
How we prayed
And blessed
This human habitation.
But now you can go
Back to the grave
Your Peace is Hell
Your presence humiliation.

'Who will deliver me?' I said
'I, you, we,' they said
'And the Lord?'
'Let Him be stoned
Your damn Lord'
'Aye, let Him be stoned,' they said.

Our Mother
Take off your veil
For we have come
To cleanse
Your copper plates
Your weedy lawns
Don't you see
Your sons are
Almost men?

(translated from Arabic by the author)

Fadwa Tuquan
(1917–)
JORDAN

The Palestinian poet Fadwa Tuquan is considered one of the best avant-garde writers in the Arab world. She was born of a family of poets and intellectuals and raised in Nablus (formerly Jordan, now part of the territories held by Israel). Her late brother, Ibrahim, was one of the major Palestinian poets of the thirties and forties.

AFTER TWENTY YEARS

Here the foot prints stop;
Here the moon
Lies with the wolves, the dogs, and the stones,
Behind the rocks and the tents, behind the trees.
Here the moon
Sells its face every night,
For a dagger, a candle, a braid of rain.
Don't throw a stone in their fire;
Don't steal the glass rings
From the gypsies' fingers.
They slept, and so did the fish and the stones and the trees.

Here the foot prints stop;
Here the moon was in labour.
Gypsies!
Give her then the glass rings
And the blue bracelets.

(translated from Arabic, translator unknown)

Nadia Tuéni

(1935–)

LEBANON (FRENCH)

Nadia Tuéni is Lebanese and works for a Beirut newspaper, *An-Nahar*. She was educated in both Arabic and French and has published four books of poetry in France, the first *Textes Blonds* (1963), the most recent *Poèmes pour une histoire* (1972).

More distant than the dead sea
of Asia and of flesh
all words are like you
but the grass in your eyes has the blue feel of life.
Are you the patient fear of the morning?
More distant than the man freed
of blood and space, who are you?
Are you the flower open to the love of fire
or the smile sipped?
Between you and the earth there was a common solitude.
There was the torrent of sun
a bird.
Closer than silence
like a hand on the sky, who are you?
There were snows always the same.
There was
a woman like a departure in a fragment of
landscape.

(translated from French by Carol Cosman)

Forūgh Farrokhzād
(1934–67)
IRAN

Born in Teheran, she married at 17, had one son, and separated from her husband three years later. The subject matter of her poetry and the unconventional nature of her private life scandalized conservative Moslem society. She published four volumes of poetry during her lifetime and co-directed one film, a documentary on a leper colony where she lived for some time and adopted one of the children. She died in a car accident at the age of thirty-two.

BORN AGAIN

One dark word is all I am
uttering you again and again
until you wake where you blossom forever

In this word I breathed you, breathed
and in this word bound you
to trees, water, flame

Life may be
a street she walks down every long day, a basket in her hand
Life may be
the rope over the limb he hangs himself with
Life may be a child home from school

Life may be lighting a cigarette in the languid pause of lovemaking

Or the pedestrian's void gaze
as he tips his hat to another's
void smile, saying, Good morning

Life may be that sealed moment
when my gaze disintegrates in the lens of your eyes
and I know myself
sensing the moon in me, and joined to darkness

In a room measured by solitude
my heart
measured by love
finds ordinary excuses for its happiness
the lovely lapse of flowers vased
the sapling you set in our yard
the canaries' cantilena
their singing fills the window

Ah . . .
This has fallen to me
This has fallen to me
This to me
A sky a curtain shrouds
The descent of a broken stair
Marriage to exile and rot
My lot pacing the sad gardens of memory
Dying sorrowing, a voice saying to me:
I love
your hands

In the garden I plant my hands
I know I shall grow, I know, I know
swallows will lay their eggs
in the nest of my inkstained fingers
twin pairs of bright cherries
will be my earrings
and dahlia petals dress my fingernails

There's a certain lane where
boys with the same tousled hair, thin necks and scrawny legs
who loved me once still
recall the simple smile of a girl
swept away one night by the wind

A certain lane my heart stole
from my childhood's quarter

A body wanders time's arid trajectory
If only that body could make that barren path conceive it

A body conscious of an image
Emerging from the festal mirror

And that's how
one dies
how one lingers on

No diver will ever fetch a pearl from the well a brooklet drowns in

I
know a sad little nymph
who lives in the sea
and plays the wooden flute of her heart
tenderly, tenderly
sad little nymph
dying at night of a kiss
and by a kiss reborn each day

> (translated from Persian by Jascha Kessler with Amin Banani)

Ch'iu Chin
(1879–1907)
CHINA

Ch'iu Chin is remembered for her political courage as well as for her
poetry. A lawyer's daughter, she married at 18, but after the birth of
her children left her family to study in Japan. There she joined Sun
Yat-sen's revolutionary party and attained a position of leadership.
In 1906 she returned to teach in a school and founded a newspaper
for women in Shanghai. She joined the staff of the school, which was
the secret headquarters and arsenal for the revolutionary army, and
in June 1907 she was arrested by the Manchu government. Her
poems were used as evidence of treason and she was beheaded on
15 July, fewer than five years before the overthrow of the Manchu
Dynasty.

A CALL TO ACTION

Without warning their nest
Has become dangerous to the swallows.
Our homeland, grown old, suffers
Under heavy burdens —
From the East the constant threat of invasion,
From the West, threats of devious plotting.
Scholars, throw away your brushes!
Secluded women, take up arms!
Only heroes can save us this time.
Together we can hold back
The flooding waves.

TO THE TUNE 'THE RIVER IS RED'

How many wise men and heroes
Have survived the dust and dirt of the world?
How many beautiful women have been heroines?
There were the novel and famous women generals
Ch'in Liang-yü and Shen Yün-yin.
Though tears stained their dresses
Their hearts were full of blood.
The wild strokes of their swords
Whistled like dragons and sobbed with pain.

The perfume of freedom burns my mind
With grief for my country.
When will we ever be cleansed?
Comrades, I say to you,
Spare no effort, struggle unceasingly,
That at last peace may come to our people.
And jewelled dresses and deformed feet
Will be abandoned.
And one day, all under heaven
Will see beautiful free women,
Blooming like fields of flowers,
And bearing brilliant and noble human beings.

(translated from Chinese by Kenneth Rexroth
and Ling Chung)

Ping Hsin
(1900–)
CHINA

Hsieh Wong-ying (whose pseudonym, Ping Hsin, means 'ice heart')
was born in Fukien and educated in missionary schools in Peking.
She attended Yenching University and took an M.A. from Wellesley.
In 1951, after living in Japan for some years, Ping Hsin and her
husband returned to the People's Republic where she was active in
many literary organizations until the Cultural Revolution in 1964.
Considered the finest modern Chinese woman poet, Ping Hsin was
one of the pioneers of the 'new poetry' written in China during the
twenties. She was one of the creators of the *hsiao-shih*, a very com-
pressed, short poem which became popular with the new interest in
Japanese *tanka* and haiku and the short lyrics of Tagore.

from SPRING WATERS

The falling star —
Shines only when crossing the sky of man;
It darts out from darkness,
And flees into darkness again.
Is life also so unaccountable?

In this hazy world,
I have forgotten the first word,
Nor will I ever know the last.

Tiny blossoms on the battlefield,
I adore you for your love most profound
That, braving the rain of bullets,
Comforts the fresh bones.

(translated from Chinese by Kai Yu Hsu)

from MULTITUDINOUS STARS

Void only —
Take away your veil of stars
Let me worship
The splendour of your face.

These fragmented verses
Are only drops of spray
On the sea of knowledge.
Yet they are bright shining
Multitudinous stars, inlaid
On the skies of the heart.

Bright moon —
All grief, sorrow, loneliness completed —
Fields of silver light —
Who, on the other side of the brook
Blows a surging flute?

(translated from Chinese by Kenneth Rexroth
and Ling Chung)

THREE POEMS

The fishing boats have returned!
  Behold the specks of red light above the river!

The evening rain,
Strand by strand is woven into the thought of the poet.

This ancient courtyard,
  This twilight,
    This silken thread of verse
      Closely binds the departing sun and me.

(translated from Chinese by Julia C. Lin)

Pai Wei

(1902–)

CHINA

Pai Wei, 'white fern', is the pseudonym of Huang Su-ju, who was born in Hunan and as a young girl ran away to avoid an arranged marriage. In the twenties she went to Japan to study and took the poet Yang Sao as her lover. She became a Communist and now lives in the People's Republic.

MADRID

Madrid —
Blood drops, drip, drop, from the child in your arms.
And Spain is kept awake all night
By this novel apparition
That frightens the old-time militants.
You are the splendid future,
The ruthless clean sweep,
That pulls the puppet,
Dragging his black shadow,
Marching towards you from Morocco.

You are a woman in childbirth,
Threatened with puerperal disasters,
Who struggles to protect your newborn baby.
I am afraid that your labour
Will have bled you past saving —
Your labour which has exceeded that of St Mary.

(translated from Chinese by Kenneth Rexroth
and Ling Chung)

Lin Ling
(1935–)
TAIWAN

Lin Ling is also known as Li Chi. Both are pseudonyms used by Hu Yun-shang, a native Taiwanese poet. After she left Taiwan for the United States to do graduate work she stopped writing poetry, but her verse is considered important for its imagery and rhythm.

FOOTPATHS CROSS IN THE RICE FIELD

You are horizontal.
I am vertical.
We divide the heavenly bodies
And the four directions between us.
We come from the place of becoming,
Pass by here,
And encounter each other
In this final meeting
In a flooded rice field.
An egret descends on still wings.
We quietly chat about the weather,
And say, 'I'll see you again.'
Quietly make an appointment,
Climb two far apart hillsides,
And look back from the summits.
A pure white feather floats down.
As the feather floats down,
Oh, at that moment
We both hope that happiness
May also be like a white bird,
Quietly descending
We hope —
Even though birds
Are creatures with wings.

(translated from Chinese by Kenneth Rexroth
and Ling Chung)

Cheng Min
(1924–)
CHINA

She studied philosophy and in the 1950s English literature at Brown
University. She returned to the People's Republic of China in 1959.

STUDENT

I go one step forward,
Then stumble one step back.
I join the march
And then slip away to the sidelines.
I look at the posters on the left wall,
And the people gathered around them.
I look at the posters on the right wall,
And the people gathered around them.
They are like soldiers in two bunkers,
Shooting at one another
With arrows that fly away over my head.
O Socrates of the streets,
Where are you?
I heard that you can bring the young to face the truth
Like a shepherd who herds his sheep
Onto the right path,
Like a kind passerby
Who returns a lost child to its mother.
But why have you forgotten
This country more baffled than any other country,
This time more doubtful
Than any other time?
Here yes and no are indistinguishable
Like East and West at the Poles.
Here truth is a puppet
That doubles in two roles.
One self says, 'Whatever is mine must be truth.'
The other says, 'When your "whatever"

Becomes my "whatever", then it is truth.'
Truth becomes a tasty bait
To lure fish obsessed with books.
In their short-sighted, round eyes
They cannot see the many hooks of fraud.
Socrates, if you cannot reappear
In the network of streets
Of the Twentieth Century,
Why cannot truth become simply a baby
That laughs when it is happy,
And cries when it is hurt,
As if to tell me which is itself?

> (translated from Chinese by Kenneth Rexroth
> and Ling Chung)

Li Chü

(contemporary)

CHINA

She is a member of the farm commune of Ta Yeh District in the
Teng-fung county of Honan Province.

HARVESTING WHEAT FOR THE
PUBLIC SHARE

It is a year of good harvest
The wheat is brought to the threshing yard.
The second sister crushes it.
The elder sister threshes it.
The third sister winnows it
Very carefully and throws away the husks.
The golden grain piles high in the yard.
Round, round wheat, better than pomegranate seeds.
Bite it with your teeth, it goes 'go-pou!'
The first pile of wheat is really lovely.

> After we have dried it in the sun,
> And cleaned it,
> We will turn it in as the public share.

> (translated from Chinese by Kenneth Rexroth
> and Ling Chung)

Ishigaki Rin
(1920–)

JAPAN

Born and raised in Akasaka, Tokyo, she joined the staff of the magazine *Dansō* (*Geological Fault*) before the Second World War. In the post-war period she was active in the realist movement in Japanese poetry. Her work is extremely popular; large crowds attend her Tokyo readings, and each Friday the largest newspaper in the world publishes one of her poems and a coloured photograph. She has published two collections, the first in 1954 and the most recent in 1968 when she was awarded the important H. Prize for poetry. She is at present employed in a bank.

CLAMS

> At midnight I awoke.
> The clams I'd bought that evening
> were alive in a corner of the kitchen,
> their mouths open.

> 'In the morning
> *I'll eat you,*
> *every last one of you.*'

> I laughed
> a witch's laugh.
> After that
> I could only sleep through the night,
> my mouth slightly open.

> (translated from Japanese by Hiroaki Sato)

Yosano Akiko
(1878–1942)
JAPAN

She was very influential in the revival of the *tanka* in modern Japanese
poetry and was closely associated with the literary revue *Myōjō*.

> You never touch
> This soft skin
> Surging with hot blood.
> Are you not bored,
> Expounding the Way?

> Spring is short:
> Why ever should it
> Be thought immortal?
> I grope for
> My full breasts with my hands.

> No camellia
> Nor plum for me,
> No flower that is white.
> Peach blossom has a colour
> That does not ask my sins.

> (translated from Japanese by
> Geoffrey Bownas and Anthony Thwaite)

No Ch'ŏn-myŏng
(1913–57)
KOREA

She started publishing her poetry while in college and was a con-
tributing member of the *Siwŏn* magazine. Five volumes of her verse
were published, the last, *The Song of Deer*, in 1958.

DEER

Because of your long neck
you are a sad animal;
always quiet and gentle.
Your line must have been of high birth,
you have their noble crown.
Looking at your image in the water
brings back long-lost tales
with a nostalgia too sharp to bear.
You look over, stretching your sad neck
toward the far hill.

CRICKET

Because my shelter must not be known,
because my poorness must not show,
in hiding through the night I cry.
For somewhere someone weeps like me
I must soak more in the moonlight,
retain the sorrow of my night again
there behind the stone steps.

(translated from Korean by Ko Won)

Kim Nam-jo

(1927–)

KOREA

Kim Nam-jo studied Korean literature at Seoul University and now
teaches at Sukmyŏng Women's University. She has published four
volumes of poetry, the most recent *The Flag of Mind* (1959). She won
the Korea Free Literature Association Prize in 1958.

MY BABY HAS NO NAME YET

My baby has no name yet;
like a new-born chick or a puppy,
my baby is not named yet.

What numberless texts I examined
at dawn and night and evening over again!
But not one character did I find
which is as lovely as the child.

Starry field of the sky,
or heap of pearls in the depth.
Where can the name be found, how can I?

My baby has no name yet;
like an unnamed bluebird or white flowers
from the farthest land for the first,
I have no name for this baby of ours.

(translated from Korean by Ko Won)

Anonymous: Landeys

(living tradition)
AFGHANISTAN (PASHTO)

Landeys ('short poems') are part of the living oral literature of the nomadic Pashtoons of Afghanistan. The genre is very old, one known *landey* going back a thousand years. While in the written literature of Afghanistan women writers have often adopted the point of view of men towards female beauty, in the *landeys* women speak directly in their own voices.

Saints look at dirt
and it turns to gold.
My lover is different.

He calls me gold,
but his glance
turns me to ashes.

★

My God is just, yes he is,
He ruined me, yes he did.

★

My love is tasting the fragrance
of other flowers.

He knows nothing of this yellow one
blooming near by.

★

You spent all summer in cool Kabul.
You return in the fall
and you want your flower intact?

★

Please let my hair grow, mother.
Don't cut it.

A trimmed tree
is no place for song birds.

(translated from Pashto by Saduddin Shpoon)

Sarojini Naidu

(d. 1949)
INDIA (ENGLISH)

She was a champion of women's rights and, a close friend of Gandhi,
was very active in the nationalist movement for Indian independence.
She served as the first woman governor of an Indian state until her
death in 1949.

THE SNAKE-CHARMER

Whither dost thou hide from the magic of my flute-call?
In what moonlight-tangled meshes of perfume,
Where the clustering *keoras* guard the squirrel's slumber,
Where the deep wood glimmers with the jasmine's bloom?

I'll feed thee, O beloved, on milk and wild red honey,
I'll bear thee in a basket of rushes, green and white,
To a palace-bower where golden-vested maidens
Thread with mellow laughter the petals of delight.

Whither dost thou loiter, by what murmuring hollows,
Where oleanders scatter their ambrosial fire?
Come, thou subtle bride of my mellifluous wooing,
Come, thou silver-breasted moonbeam of desire!

Amrita Pritam

(1919–)

INDIA (PUNJABI)

The author of fourteen collections of poetry, thirteen novels, and six collections of short stories, she is a major figure in contemporary Indian literature and the first woman to receive the coveted Sahitya Akademi Prize for her poems. Her work has been translated into English and a number of Indian languages. She also edits and publishes a monthly literary magazine in Punjabi, *naagmanii* (*The Jewelled Serpent*). She lives with her family in a residential district of Delhi.

DAILY WAGES

In a corner of blue sky
The mill of night whistles,
A white thick smoke
Pours from the moon-chimney.

In dream's many furnaces
Labourer love
Is stoking all the fires

I earn our meeting
Holding you for a while,
My day's wages.

I buy my soul's food
Cook and eat it
And set the empty pot in the corner.

I warm my hands at the dying fire
And lying down to rest
Give God thanks.

The mill of night whistles
And from the moon-chimney
Smoke rises, sign of hope.

I eat what I earn,
Not yesterday's left-overs,
And leave no grain for tomorrow.

(translated from Punjabi by Charles Brasch
with Amrita Pritam)

Kamala Das

(1934–)
INDIA (ENGLISH)

She was born in Malabar in the polyandrous community of Nairs and educated at home by tutors. Married at fifteen, she lives now in Bombay. She has published many books of short stories written in Malayalam. Her poetry is written in English. She received the PEN Poetry Award (Asian Award) in 1963.

THE HOUSE-BUILDERS

The cicadas in brambled foliage
Naturally concave. So also these
Men who crawl up the cogged scaffoldings
Building houses for the alien rich.
On some days the hot sky flings at us scraps
Of Telugu songs and we intently
Listen, but we wait in vain for the harsh

Message of the lowly. In merry tunes
Their voices break, but just a little, as
   Though the hero's happiness is too big
A burden on their breath, too big a lie
      For their throats to swallow, but past sunset
      Their jest sounds ribald, their lust seems robust.
Puny, these toy-men of dust, fathers of light
   Dust-children, but their hands like the withered boughs
   Of some mythic hoodoo tree cast only
Cool shadows and with native grace bestow
   Even on unbelievers vast shelters . . .

Anonymous

(contemporary)

BURMA

In Burma it is very common for a poem to be written anonymously
or under a pen name, and poetry plays an important part in love
relationships.

SHOW ME THE WAY

The rose-apple is in fruit
the waters rise
the toddy fruit falls
and slow rain comes down
incessantly.

I would like to go home
to my mother;
husband, show me the way.

FOR A MOMENT

For a moment, unaware,
weary, I fell asleep.
My handsome young man,

who is determined to win,
riding his brown horse,
visited me. On the
low bed we lay down
and gently slept. This
may have been a dream.

May have been a dream.

GUESSING

I await his coming,
Prince of the High Lotus Chamber.

Does he prolong
his absence with
wiles and lies?

It is hard to guess.

(translated from Burmese by U Win Pe)

Mririda n'Ait Attik
(*fl.* 1940)
MOROCCO (BERBER)

In the early 1940s Mririda was a courtesan in the *souk* of Azilal, where she was famed for the strange and beautiful songs she sang to the men who came to her house. Based in part on a flourishing oral tradition and composed in the Berber dialect of *tachelhait*, her songs portray the traditional life of the valley, especially the life of the women. After the war, when Mririda was probably still under thirty, she could not be found in the *souk* or in Magdaz, her native village in the Tassaout valley of the Atlas Mountains in Morocco. René Euloge, a French soldier who knew her well, published a French translation of her poems in 1959.

GOD HASN'T MADE ROOM

My sister, you are a stranger to this place.
Why be surprised that I know nothing?
My eyes have never seen the rose,
My eyes have never seen the orange.
They say there is plenty down there
In the good country
Where people and animals and plants are never cold.
My sister, stranger from the plains,
Don't laugh at a barefoot girl from the mountains
Who dresses in coarse wool.
In our fields and pastures
God hasn't made room for the rose,
God hasn't made room for the orange.
I have never left my village and its nut trees.
I know only the holly and arbutus bush
And the leaves of green basil
That keep the mosquitoes away
When I fall asleep on the terrace
On a warm summer night.

LIKE SMOKE

Lalla Halima!★ Protect abandoned girls!
Whom can you believe, merciful God?
Me, I will not trust men.
Their promises are smoke and wind.

When I was watching the cows in the field,
the son of the *moquaddem*† made great promises,
but the mule that is no longer thirsty
wants no more to drink.

★ *Lalla Halima:* a Mohammedan hermit, who protects the unwed mothers
who invoke her.
† *moquaddem:* the leader of a group of musicians.

The *maoun*,* on leave with his medals,
took what he wanted, like the others . . .
The mule that is without thirst
does not wish to drink.

Ten young men, ten men without wives, ten old men
all gave me promises of marriage.
Not one kept their word.
I quenched their thirst
and they went elsewhere to drink.

Whom can you believe, merciful God?
Me, I will not put my trust in men.
Their promises are like smoke,
like smoke, like smoke, like smoke.

(translated from the French version by
Daniel Halpern and Paula Paley)

Noémia da Sousa

(1927–)

MOZAMBIQUE (PORTUGUESE)

She was born in Lourenço Marques, where she wrote for various
journals and reviews and was associated with the militant African
literature in Portuguese. Like many of the African writers who
protested against the repressive Portuguese government, she was
forced into exile and went to France where she wrote under the
pseudonym Vera Micaia. For some years before her exile she lived
with her Portuguese husband in Lisbon. She is the first black African
woman to gain wide recognition as a poet.

POEM OF DISTANT CHILDHOOD
for Rui Guerra

When I was born in the great house on the bank of the sea
It was midday and the sun shone on the Indian Ocean.
Sea gulls hovered, white, drunk with blue.

* *maoun:* a non-commissioned officer of the Algerian contingent.

The boats of the Indian fishermen had not yet returned
dragging the overloaded nets.
On the bridge, the cries of the blacks, the blacks of the boats
calling to the married women melting in the heat —
bundles on their heads, street urchins at their sides —
the cries sounded like a long song,
long, suspended in the fog of the silence.
And on the scalding steps
beggar Mufasini slept, in a swarm of flies.

When I was born . . .
I know the air was calm, still (they told me)
and the sun shone on the sea.
In the midst of this calm I was launched in the world,
already with my stigma.
And I cried and screamed I don't know why.
Ah, but for the life outside,
my tears dried in the light of revolt.
And the sun never again shone as in the first days
of my existence
although the brilliant maritime scenery of my childhood,
constantly calm, like a marsh,
always guided my adolescent steps —
my stigma, too.
And even more, the mixed companions of my childhood.

Companions
fishing under the bridge with a pin hook and line of thin wire
my ragged friends with stomachs round as baskets
companions running and jumping in the bush and
beaches of Catembe
together in the marvellous discovery of the nest of the warblers
in the construction of a columned snare
with the sticky sap of the wild fig tree
in the hunt for hummingbirds and blue-headed lizards,
and chasing monkeys under a burning summer sun.
Unforgettable figures as I grew up —
Free, happy children:
black, mulatto, white, Indian,

sons of the baker and black washerwoman,
of the black man of the boats and the carpenter,
come from the misery of Guachene
or the wooden houses of fishermen.
Coddled children from the post,
smart-aleck sons of the customs guards of Esquadrilla
comrades in the always new adventure
of assaults on the cashew tree in the vegetable gardens,
companions in the secret of the sweetest cones of the pine,
and in the eerie chill of the 'Island of Lost Ships'
where every sound makes an echo.

Oh my companions, crouched, amazed in the marvellous
gathering of the 'Karingana wa karingana'*
the stories of the old woman from Portugal
in the terrible storm-black sunsets
(the wind shrieking in the zinc roof,
the sea menacing the wooden steps of the veranda,
the causeway groaning, groaning,
inconsolably
and filling our souls with strange, inexplicable fears,
our souls full of toothless spirits
and Massinga kings turned hunchbacked . . .)
Yes, my companions sowed in me the seed of this dissatisfaction
day by day I grow more dissatisfied.
They filled my childhood with the sun that shone
on the day I was born.
With their luminous unthinking comradeship,
their radiant happiness,
their explosive enthusiasm before any winged kite
in the technicolor blue of the sky,
their immediate, unconditional loyalty —
they filled my childhood
with unforgettable happiness and adventure.

If today the sun does not shine
as on the day I was born

* *Karingana wa karingana:* the formula with which the story-teller begins
his tale.

in the great house by the Indian Ocean,
I will not let myself sleep in darkness.
My companions are sure guides
on my life's path
They prove that 'brotherhood' is not a mere pretty word
written in black in the bookcase dictionary:
They showed me that brotherhood is a beautiful thing and is possible
even when skins and surrounding landscapes
differ so much.

So I BELIEVE that one day
the sun will shine again, calm, on the Indian Ocean.
Sea gulls will hover, white, drunk with blue
and the fishermen will return singing,
sailing on the tenuous afternoon.
And this poison of the moon that suffering has infused in my
veins will cease disturbing me forever.
One day,
life will be flooded with sun.
And it will be like a new childhood shining for everyone ...

> (translated from Portuguese by Allan Francovich
> and Kathleen Weaver)

Glória de Sant' Ana

(contemporary)
MOZAMBIQUE (PORTUGUESE)

AFRICAN DAY

The crows mark
long trajectories in the white day,
over the
heads of the black singers.

There is a scattered wind
scratching in the leaves of the trees,

slow melodies
of old disgraces.

And traces of light
from a sun implied by still clouds
fall from the roofs
and beat on the stones.

Everything today is heavy
like an engraving of rhythmical attitude,
struck in glass panes
cut from the Bible.

(translated from Portuguese by
Allan Francovich and Kathleen Weaver)

Annette M'Baye

(1927–)

SENEGAL (FRENCH)

Born in Sokhone, Senegal, she has worked as a teacher in Senegal
and in Paris. Active for many years in radio and journalism, she is
currently with Radio Senegal and serves as editor-in-chief of *Awa:
Journal of the Black Woman.*

SILHOUETTE
for Henriette Bathily

Behind, sun, before, shadow!
A watergourd on a stately head,
A breast, a strip of loincloth fluttering,
Two feet that erase the pattern on the sand.

(translated from French by Kathleen Weaver)

Alda do Espírito Santo
(1926–)
ST THOMAS (PORTUGUESE)

She was born on the island of St Thomas, the former Portuguese colony located off the coast of West Africa in the Gulf of Guinea. She worked as a teacher and was active in nationalist circles until her identification with the liberation movement of the Portuguese colonies in Africa led to her arrest and imprisonment by the Portuguese authorities.

THE SAME SIDE OF THE CANOE

The words of our day
are simple words
clear as brook waters
spurting from rust-red slopes
in the clear morning of each day.

So it is I speak to you,
my brother contracted to the coffee plantation
my brother leaving your blood on the bridge
or sailing the sea, a part of yourself lost
        battling the shark
My sister, laundering, laundering
for bread to feed your sons,
my sister selling pits of fruit
to the nearest shop
for the mourning of your dead,
my adjusted sister
selling yourself for a life of greater ease,
in the end only suffering more . . .

It is for you, my brothers, companions of the road
my cry of hope
with you I feel I am dancing
on idle nights

on some plantation where people gather
together, brothers, in the harvest of cacao
together again on market day
where roasted breadfruit and chicken will bring money.
Together, impelling the canoe along the shore,
joining myself with you,
around the brimming bowl,
joining in the feast
flying through
the ten toasts.

Yet our age-old hands part
on the immense sands
of the São João beach,
because I know, my brother, blackened like you
    by life,
you think, brother of the canoe,
that we two, flesh of one flesh,
battered by hurricane tempests,
are not on the same side of the canoe.

It is suddenly dark.
There on the far side of the beach
on the Point of São Marçal
there are lights, many lights
in the dark palm-thatched sheds . . .
the sweet whistle thrills —
strange beckonings —
invitation to this ritual night . . .

Here, only the initiated
in the frenetic rhythm of the dance of propitiation
here, the brothers of the *Santu*
madly wrenching their hips
releasing wild cries,
words, gestures
in the madness of the age-old rite.
In this side of the canoe, I also am, my brother,
in your agonizing voice uttering prayers, oaths, and maledictions.

Yes, I am here, my brother,
in the endless wakes for the dead
where the people play
with the life of their sons,
I am here, yes, my brother,
in the same side of the canoe.

But we want something still more beautiful.
We want to join our millenary hands,
hands of the cranes on the docks,
hands of the plantations and beaches,
in a great league encompassing
the earth from pole to pole
for our children's dreams
so we may be all of us on the same side of the canoe.

    Afternoon descends . . .
The canoe slips away, serene,
on course to the marvellous beach
where our arms join
and we sit side by side
together in the canoe of our beaches.

> (translated from Portuguese by Allan Francovich
> and Kathleen Weaver)

Anoma Kanié

(contemporary)

IVORY COAST (FRENCH)

She has been ambassador to Israel from the Ivory Coast.

ALL THAT YOU HAVE GIVEN ME, AFRICA

All that you have given me, Africa
Lakes, forests, misted lagoons
All that you have given me,

Music, dances, all night stories around a fire
All that you have etched in my skin
Pigments of my ancestors
Indelible in my blood
All that you have given me Africa
Makes me walk
With a step that is like no other
Hip broken under the weight of time,
Feet large with journeys,
All that you have left to me
Even this lassitude bound to my heels,
I bear it with pride on my forehead
My health is no more to be lost
And I go forward
Praising my race which is no better
Or worse than any other.
All that you have given me Africa,
Savannahs gold in the noonday sun
Your beasts that men call wicked,
Your mines, inexplicable treasures
Obsession of a hostile world
Your suffering for lost paradises,
All that, I protect with an unforgiving hand
As far as the clear horizons
So that your heaven-given task
May be safe forever.

(translated from French by Kathleen Weaver)

Citèkù Ndaaya

(1929?–)

LUBA TRIBE, ZAIRE

This *kàsàlà* was sung on 16 September 1965 at Katende-Kabooke village, Eastern Kasai, Zaire, by Citèkù Ndaaya, professional poet, about thirty-six years old at the time of her recital. The *kàsàlà* is a very ancient song form that probably originated in songs of lamentation for important members of the tribe.

from NDAAYA'S KÀSÀLÀ

Ndaaya, I, am so poor
    you can hear my pestle pounding after sundown.
Already I stand at the crossing of the roads,
    why then have I come to these lamentations . . . ?
This death of yours is men's affair, O Ntumba,
    were it women's affair I'd brandish my pestle.
Why I am what I am remains impenetrable:
    born a man – they would have handed me a sword —
    would I not have become a hero?
Am I not as things are vagabond with a strong gullet?
Could I not then fight as they fight . . .
Dear brothers,
    death came to me like a thief in the night,
    as I went to bed with a divided heart.
The drums of a famous musician, the intrepid one,
    today they are sounding my rhythm.
Ah, daughter of the Ngandu,
    were voice strong as drum
    it would already have reached my mother . . .
But tears will never awaken the dead,
    sooner vase will fill up . . .
War has ravaged me today, sister of Cibangu,
    but who remains to protect Ndaaya?
I must call my comrades, but who will respond?
    who dares summon the strong?
At the crossroads
    I have trapped bitter crickets
    I have grubbed for ashen cicadas
And I go to bed with a divided heart
    restless, I have counted beams
    vagabond, have counted roofs
Daughter of those who bathe till their bodies gleam as with oil,
    ah, my brothers, misfortunes weigh me down:

one part orphan
one part sterile
But what can I say that men might give me credence?
Ah, sister of Cibangu, human things alter:
    a young woman becomes old
    she-goat turns billy-goat
    another, having given birth,
    look – suddenly she's sterile,
    like Ndaaya.
Did I not give birth to a child with gums strong as cut-teeth?
O daughter, quickened in me by ritual,
    since you left, I've been inconsolable
    at the crossroads
Child planted in me by ritual
    see how women of my age prosper:
    third wives moved up to first place
    others demoted
At dangerous crossroads I call
    daughter, returned to my womb by ritual
    Mbombo
    Silence

(translated after the combined French-Luba texts by
Judith Gleason)

Christine Ama Ata Aidoo

(1942–)

GHANA (ENGLISH)

She was born in Ghana and received a degree from the University of
Ghana, Legon, in 1963. She also writes short stories. At present she is
a member of the faculty of the Department of African Studies of the
University of Ghana.

PRELUDE

I am the Bird of the Wayside —
The sudden scampering in the undergrowth,
Or the trunkless head
Of the shadow in the corner.
I am an asthmatic old hag
Eternally breaking the nuts
Whose soup, alas,
Nourished a bundle of whitened bones —
Or a pair of women, your neighbours
Chattering their lives away.
I can furnish you with reasons why
This and that and other things
Happened. But stranger,
What would you have me say
About the Odumna Clan? . . .
Look around you,
For the mouth must not tell everything.
Sometimes the eye can see
And the ear should hear.
Yonder house is larger than
Any in the town —
Old as the names
Oburumankuma, Odapadjan, Osun.
They multiply faster than fowls
And they acquire gold
As if it were corn grains —
But if in the making of
One Scholar
Much is gone
You stranger do not know.

Oumar Ba

(contemporary)

SENEGAL (FRENCH)

DROUGHT

The frail scorched grasses are stripped now
Of their green hues and compared to the
Hot sun. The evil dryness poisons the heart
Of the unconquerable branching rivers and
The harsh shrivelling winds burrow under ground,
Muddied with filth – the forest next,
Now birds give up their songs, and the dug-out
Canoes are lodged in the banks of sand,
Now the sombre salvation from dryness,
A time of gaiety, celebration, but
Stripped of its leaves and useful shrubs,
Nature, after the moist sorrow of the
Fatal loss, weeps like a mother
Bereft of her children, the adornments.
Parched with thirst, the whole tribe of birds,
Song ravaged by unending drought,
Strength pillaged by pain – the tumult dies
Now the sombre salvation from dryness,
The natural fatality of existence.

(translated from French by Kathleen Weaver)

Ingrid Jonker

(1933–65)

SOUTH AFRICA (AFRIKAANS)

Her childhood was an unhappy one, marked by estrangement from
her father, and was to overshadow her life with tragic consequences.
She wrote in Afrikaans and her poetry was well received by young
poets and critics in her own country. Her book of poems, *Escape*,

appeared in 1956, and a second prize-winning volume, *Smoke and Ochre*, in 1963. After she took her own life in 1965 a third volume called *Setting Sun* was put together from manuscripts she had left. She had made English versions of some of her poems and these were used as a basis for translations which appear in *Selected Poems* (1968).

DOG

I lie under your hand – a cur
in the snarling silence
in the whimpering moon
trellised among the stars, she
in her terrifying
white coming and going.

(I too longed to go hunting hares
over my own karoo
over my burning plain
from ochre to ochre, oh
white plains of your hands!)

Tonight with my teeth bared I shall
jerk to the sly rhythm of the moon
listen to my sweetness and distance
my long-echoing bark
from my kennel white moon, white master
in the night.

WHEN YOU WRITE AGAIN

When you write again in your diary
Remember
To see the golden leaf in the summer sun
Or perhaps the blue rock-orchid
On one of our absent wanderings
On Table Mountain
I who have mingled my blood with the blood of
The sun at evening in Lisbon
Have carried you with me like a mirror

And I have written you
On the open page
Of my desolation
Your nameless word
When you write again in your diary
Remember
To see in my eyes
The sun that I now cover for always
With black butterflies

JOURNEY ROUND THE WORLD

Olive journeys
trees water
you with your body of ferns
dreaming in my arms close by the Seine
with your body
of white gables
of bitter sun
in Barcelona
(back of the bullfights
the siestas of your hands)
Journeys of silence
journeys of walls
journeys of marble
couplets of short
hard
words
fade out but you
dreaming in water and ferns and sun
in my arms close by the Seine
go out
make fruitful the earth

(translated from Afrikaans by Jack Cope
and William Plomer)

Delmira Agustini
(1886–1914)

URUGUAY

At the age of ten she was already writing poetry. Her brilliant literary career ended tragically with her marriage. She could not accept the ties of family at the expense of her writing and sought a divorce. Her husband murdered her and himself committed suicide.

FROM FAR AWAY

In slow procession, one by one, silently
I hear the hours pass, rhythmical and cold . . .
Ah! I always weep when you are far away,
Smiling, even in sleep, when your footsteps sound.

I know you will return; another dawn
Darkly will frown over my dim horizon.
Your ringing laughter in this wilderness
Will echo like distant crystal waters.

The day we sadly met along the road,
I placed my fate into your pale white hands.
Nothing greater had they to offer you!

My soul and yours facing each other are
Like sea and sky, between them, like the shadow
Of a flight, pass Storms and Time, Life and Death.

BLINDNESS

I sink into a rare luminous blindness,
A star, almost a soul, shadows my life,
Clinging to me as a gilded butterfly;
Or am I absorbed in its disk of light?

I do not know . . .
                    Rare blindness darkening my world,
Starry soul with which I rise and fall;
Give me your light and hide the world from me!

(translated from Spanish by D. M. Pettinella)

Juana de Ibarbourou
(1895–)
URUGUAY

Born Juana Fernández, she married an army officer, Captain D. Lucas Ibarbourou, and they had one son. After a tour of provincial cities, they settled permanently in Montevideo where, in 1919, the publication of her first collection, *Las lenguas de diamante* (*Diamond Tongues*), caused a literary sensation that spread throughout the continent. In 1929 she was given the name 'Juana de América' in recognition of her great prestige and influence in both Spain and Latin America.

THE STRONG BOND

I grew
for you.
Lay waste to me. My acacia
implores its finishing touch from your hands.

I flowered
for you.
Cut me. When born
my lily doubted being flower or candle.

I flowed
for you.
Drink me. Crystal
envies the clarity of my spring.

I gave wings
for you.
Hunt me. Butterfly of night
I encircle your impatient flame.

For you I will suffer.
Blessed the pain that your love gives me!
Blessed the axe, the net
and praised the scissors and thirst!

My side will ooze blood,
my love.
What lovelier brooch, what handsomer jewel
than a scarlet thorn for you?

Instead of glass beads for my hair
seven long thorns,
and instead of earrings
two hot coals for two rubies.

You will see me laugh
watching me suffer.

And you will cry
and then ... you will be mine as never before!

(translated from Spanish by Linda Scheer)

THE ASSIGNATION

I have fastened everything within a black cloak.
I am very pale, my look ecstatic.
And in my eyes I hold a split star.
Two red triangles in my hieratic face!

Notice I don't even wear one jewel,
nor a pink bow, nor a spray of dahlias.
And I have even removed the rich buckles
from the straps of my two sandals.

But I am this night, without golds or silks,
slender and dark like a vivid iris.
And I am anointed all over with oils of nard,
and I am smooth all over beneath the gruff cloak.

And in my pale mouth the trembling carnation
of my kiss already in flower awaits your mouth.
And desire twists in my long hands
like a crazy invisible streamer.

Undress me, lover! Undress me!
Under your glance I will rise like a
vibrant statue on a black plinth
toward which the moon drags itself like a dog.

(translated from Spanish by Brian Swann)

Alfonsina Storni

(1892–1938)

ARGENTINA

Born at sea to Argentine parents who registered her birth in Switzer-
land, she grew up in the provinces of San Juan and Santa Fé. In her
early twenties she went to Buenos Aires where she lived the rest of
her life. Self-supporting from the age of thirteen, she travelled with a
theatre company, wrote plays for children, worked as a teacher, a
milliner, and a journalist. She had one son. The publication of her
first book in 1916 brought immediate recognition, and she was soon
accorded the stature of a major poet throughout Latin America. In
1938, incurably ill, she drowned herself in the waters of Mar del
Plata.

MEN IN THE CITY

The woods of the horizon
are on fire;
eluding flames,
the swift blue bucks
of twilight
cross.

Little golden goats
migrate toward
the vault
and recline
on the blue moss.

Below,
the city
rises up,
a cement rose,
motionless on its stem
of dark cellars.

Its black pistils —
towers, cupolas —
emerge,
waiting for lunar
pollen.

Suffocated
by the flames of the fire
and lost
among the petals of the rose,
almost invisible,
crossing back and forth
the men . . .

SIERRA

An invisible hand
silently caresses
the sad pulp
of the rolling worlds.

Someone, I don't know who,
has steeped my heart
in sweetness.

In the August snow
the blossom of the peach tree —
early flowering —
opens to the sun.

Stretched out on the sierra's
ochre ridge,
a frozen
woman of granite;
the wind howls
the grief of her lonely bosom.

Butterflies
of moon
sip
her frozen
breasts
by night.

And on my eyelids,
a tear swells
older than my body.

(translated from Spanish by Rachel Benson)

Gabriela Mistral
(1889–1957)
CHILE

'Gabriela Mistral' was the pseudonym of Lucila Godoy Alcayaga
who was born in Vicuna, Chile. She first received literary acclaim in
1915 with her 'Sonetos de Muerte' and was awarded the Nobel
Prize for Literature in 1945. She is considered one of the great lyrical
geniuses of Spanish letters.

SLOW RAIN

This water, sad and fearful,
like a child who suffers,
before touching the earth,
     fades away.

Calm the wind, calm the tree —
but in the tremendous silence,
this lean, bitter song
    is falling.

The sky is like a heart,
immense, opening up, bitter.
It is not rain: it is a bleeding,
    long, and slow.

Men in houses
do not feel this bitterness,
this sad flow of water
    out of the heavens.

This long and tiring
descent of conquered water,
towards Earth, recumbent,
    and paralysed!

It is raining . . . and like a tragic jackal
the night watches over the land.
What is going to spring up, in the shadow,
    out of Mother Earth?

Will you sleep, while outside
falls suffering, this slow water,
this lethal water, sister
    of death?

(translated from Spanish by Gunda Kaiser
and James Tipton)

EVERYTHING IS ROUND

Stars are circles of children
Looking at the earth as they play . . .
Wheat stalks are bodies of children
swaying and swaying as they play . . .

Rivers are circles of children
running off to the sea as they play
Waves are circlets of little girls
embracing this world . . . as they play . . .

(translated from Spanish by D. M. Pettinella)

SLEEP CLOSE TO ME

Fold of my flesh
I carried in my womb,
tender trembling flesh
sleep close to me!

The partridge sleeps in the wheat
listening to its heartbeat.
Let not my breath disturb you
sleep close to me!

Little tender grass
afraid to live,
don't move from my arms;
sleep close to me!

I have lost everything,
and tremble until I sleep.
Don't move from my breast;
sleep close to me!

(translated from Spanish by D. M. Pettinella)

Cecília Meireles

(1901–64)

BRAZIL

She was born and spent most of her life in Rio de Janeiro, where she
lived with her husband and three children and worked as a school
teacher, a librarian, and a Professor of Comparative Literature and

Oriental Languages. She was also a specialist in children's literature and, like her friend Gabriela Mistral, a student of folklore. Twice nominated for the Nobel Prize, she is generally regarded as one of the finest poets in the Portuguese language. Her complete works appeared in 1958.

THE DEAD HORSE

I saw the early morning mist
make silver passes, shift
densities of opal
within sleep's portico.

On the frontier, a dead horse.

Crystal grains were rolling down
his lustrous flank, and the breeze
twisted his mane in a littlest,
lightest arabesque, sorry adornment

– and his tail stirred, the dead horse.

Still the stars were shining,
and that day's flowers, sad to say,
had not yet come to light
– but his body was a plot,

garden of lilies, the dead horse.

Many a traveller took note
of fluid music, the dewfall
of big emerald flies
arriving in a noisy gush.

He was listing sorely, the dead horse.

And some live horses could be seen
slender and tall as ships,
galloping through the keen air
in profile, joyously dreaming.

White and green the dead horse

in the enormous field without recourse
– and slowly the world between
his eyelashes revolved, all blurred
as in red mirror moons.

Sun shone on the teeth of the dead horse.

But everybody was in a frantic rush
and could not feel how earth
kept searching league upon league
for the nimble, the immense, the ethereal breath
which had escaped that skeleton.

O heavy breast of the dead horse!

(translated from Portuguese by James Merrill)

PYRARGYRITE METAL, 9

The piano tuner spoke to me, that tenderest
attender to each note
who looking over sharp and flat
hears and glimpses something more remote.
And his ears make no mistake
nor do his hands that in each chord awake
those sounds delighted to keep house together.

'Disinterested is my interest:
I don't confuse music and instrument, mere
piano tuner that I am,
calligrapher of that superhuman speech
which lifts me as a guest to its high sphere.
Oh! what new Physics waits up there to teach
other matters to another ear . . .'

(translated from Portuguese by James Merrill)

THE ROOSTERS WILL CROW

The roosters will crow when we die,
And a soft breeze, with delicate hands,
Will touch the fringes, the silken
Shrouds.

And the sleep of night will cloud
The clear windows.

And the crickets, far off, will saw silences:
Stalks of crystal, cold long solitudes,
And the enormous perfume of trees.

Ah, what sweet moon will look upon our calm face,
Even yet more calm than her great mirror
Of silver.

What thick freshness upon our hair,
As free as the fields at sunrise.

From the mist of dawn,
One last star
Will ascend: pale.

What immense peace, without human voice,
Without the lip of wolfish faces,
Without hatred, without love, without anything!

Like dark lost prophets,
Only the dogs will talk through the valleys.
Strong questions. Vast pauses.

We shall lie in death
In that soft contour
Of a shell in the water.

(translated from Portuguese by John Nist
with Yolanda Leite)

Magda Portal

(1901–)

PERU

She has published three collections of poetry, one novel, many short
stories, and several volumes of essays, including writings on feminism.

Very active in the Peruvian left, in 1951 after participating in an unsuccessful uprising, she was exiled to Buenos Aires. Her unedited manuscripts, the work of twenty-five years, disappeared with her luggage and were never recovered. José Carlos Mariátegui, the founder of Marxism in Latin America, named Magda Portal and César Vallejo as the first poets to give voice to a truly Peruvian experience.

shores of anguish
there, all the brackish roads
like the sea

under the intimidated night
litany of regret
your hands scratch in the roots of the brain
and all the furrows question
the blank eyes of the night
its paralytic indifference

the sea hunches its black shoulder
like a mountain
                    to look from on high
and emotion races its motors of
anguish and happiness
before the n e w

2,000 kilometres from
REALITY

the telepathic antennas
bring melancholy messages

the odometers signal distances
on the parallel sides of the present
death watches

*

FILM VERMOUTH:
SIX O'CLOCK SHOW

sad lagoons
to bathe the icy stars

I was sick
with my own uncertainty —

Doubt softens with slow hammerblows
and your doubt of me
makes me doubt myself —

With eyes slashed by tiny blades of fear
in the last dusk of dark-circled eyes
– half hour for the promenade of Night —
shivering
asking for help
against myself

and YOU are all
illusionist of my puppet theatre
the taut cord of the ultimate test —
I would walk it calmly
if your terrible eyes
did not announce my fall

Oh equilibrist of life
I want to scream
'Fall, fall!'
spatter the paving stones with blood

under your sentinel eyes
under your hands that own the
powerhouse of my nerves

illusionist of my anguish

I KISS YOUR HANDS

(translated from Spanish by Allan Francovich
and Kathleen Weaver)

Rosario Castellanos

(1925–)

MEXICO

Born in Chiapas, she graduated in philosophy from the University of Mexico and was awarded a scholarship for post-graduate work in Madrid. She began writing poetry in 1940, at the age of 15, and has published seven collections, the first in 1948. She is also highly regarded as a prose writer and critic.

SILENCE CONCERNING AN ANCIENT STONE

Here I am, seated, with all my words,
like a basket of green fruit, intact.
The fragments
of a thousand destroyed ancient gods
seek and draw near each other in my blood. They long
to rebuild their statue.
From their shattered mouths
a song strives to rise to my mouth,
a scent of burned resins, some gesture
of mysterious wrought stone.
But I am oblivion, treason,
the shell that did not keep from the sea
even the echo of the smallest wave.
I look not at the submerged temples,
but only at the trees that above the ruins
move their vast shadow, with acid teeth bite
the wind as it passes.
And the seals close under my eyes like
the flower under the searching fingers of a blind man.
But I know: behind
my body another body crouches,
and round about me many breaths
furtively cross
like nocturnal beasts in the jungle.

I know: somewhere,
like the cactus in the desert,
a constellated heart of spines,
it is waiting for a name, as the cactus the rain.

But I know only a few words
in the lapidary language
under which they buried my ancestor alive.

(translated from Spanish by George D. Schade)

Julia de Burgos
(1914–53)
PUERTO RICO

She was born and raised in rural Puerto Rico, participated on and
off in labour struggles, and wrote for a labour periodical. She suffered
greatly from alcoholism and was in and out of hospitals all her life.
She died anonymously on a street in New York City. She received
little recognition during her lifetime but is now considered a major
figure in Puerto Rican poetry.

TO JULIA DE BURGOS

The people are saying that I am your enemy,
 That in poetry I give you to the world.

 They lie, Julia de Burgos. They lie, Julia de Burgos.
The voice that rises in my verses is not your voice: it is my voice;
For you are the clothing and I am the essence;
Between us lies the deepest abyss.

 You are the bloodless doll of social lies
And I the virile spark of human truth;

 You are the honey of courtly hypocrisy; not I —
I bare my heart in all my poems.

You, like your world, are selfish; not I —
I gamble everything to be what I am.

You are only the serious lady. Señora. Doña Julia.
Not I. I am life. I am strength. I am woman.

You belong to your husband, your master. Not I:
I belong to nobody or to all, for to all, to all
I give myself in my pure feelings and thoughts.

You curl your hair and paint your face. Not I:
I am curled by the wind, painted by the sun.

You are the lady of the house, resigned, submissive,
Tied to the bigotry of men. Not I:
I am Rocinante, bolting free, wildly
Snuffling the horizons of the justice of God.

(translated from Spanish by Grace Schulman)

Nancy Morejón
(1944–)
CUBA

She was born in Havana and graduated with a B.A. in French language and literature from the University of Havana. She has published several volumes of poems and is a member of the editorial staff of the literary magazine *La Gaceta de Cuba*.

CENTRAL PARK *SOME PEOPLE* (*3 P.M.*)

he who crosses a park in great and flourishing Havana
amidst a flood of blinding white light
a white and blinding light
which would have driven that Van Gogh's sunflower mad
that blinding white light
which fills the Chinese eyes of the Chinese street photographers

he who crosses a park and doesn't understand
that blinding white light that almost repeats itself
he who is at a loss at that time of day
takes all kinds of roundabout and unnecessary
sojourns around Havana's Central Park
he who crosses a park strewn with sacred trees
who walks through it with open yet closed eyes
loving the Revolution's impact on the eyes
the impact he felt in his eyes and waist
he who is sustained by that light might know about the night and
 the wine

because in parks and in this one so central the one in Havana
old men sit on benches
light cigars look at each other
and talk about the Revolution and Fidel
the old men who now remain on the benches
and are forever basking in the sun
it is a secret to no one
there go two men and an old worn-out briefcase
a fat bloated hand a shout wearing a grey hat
the old men meet next to the statue
of the Apostle Martí in 1966 in December of 1966
the year nearly over and waiting for
'the anniversary of freedom and paying tribute to the martyrs'
yes for all the men of the people who died and their blood
to bask in the afternoon sun in Havana Cuba free territory of
 America
he who crosses the park this world the womb of the Revolution
 in this manner

must sigh and walk slowly and breathe
and step lightly and sigh and breathe and walk slowly
and forfeit his whole life
rabidly
  compañeros

     (translated from Spanish by Sylvia Carranza)

Amy Lowell
(1874–1925)
UNITED STATES

Born in Brookline, Massachusetts, into the illustrious New England
family of Lowells, she did not decide until she was twenty-eight to
become a poet. One of the major figures in the Imagist movement –
contemptuously dubbed 'Amygism' when her influence supplanted
that of Ezra Pound – she fought for a hard-edged, unsentimental
American verse. Besides poetry and 'polyphonic prose' she wrote
critical essays, collaborated on translations from the Chinese, and
wrote a biography of Keats. Her first important collection, *Sword
Blades and Poppy Seeds*, appeared in 1914. The posthumous edition,
What's O'Clock, was awarded the Pulitzer Prize in 1925.

KATYDIDS
Shore of Lake Michigan

Katydids scraped in the dim trees,
And I thought they were little white skeletons
Playing the fiddle with a pair of finger-bones.

How long is it since Indians walked here,
Stealing along the sands with smooth feet?
How long is it since Indians died here
And the creeping sands scraped them bone from bone?
Dead Indians under the sands, playing their bones
        against strings of wampum.
The roots of new, young trees have torn their graves
        asunder,
But in the branches sit little white skeletons
Rasping a bitter death-dirge through the August
        night.

THE TAXI

When I go away from you
The world beats dead
Like a slackened drum.
I call out for you against the jutted stars
And shout into the ridges of the wind.
Streets coming fast,
One after the other,
Wedge you away from me,
And the lamps of the city prick my eyes
So that I can no longer see your face.
Why should I leave you,
To wound myself upon the sharp edges of the night?

Gertrude Stein

(1874–1946)

UNITED STATES

She studied psychology under William James at Radcliffe and medicine at Johns Hopkins. She settled in Paris in 1903 and never returned to live in the United States. She and her brother began their famous collection of paintings with the work of Cézanne and Matisse. Her association with the Cubist school headed by Picasso and Juan Gris became one of the prime influences in her life and work, and she attempted in her writing to put into practice the ideas of the painters. She herself has written: 'Gertrude Stein, in her work, has always been possessed by the intellectual passion for exactitude in the description of inner and outer reality.' Becoming a legendary figure in her own time, she still realized with regret that her experiments in poetry were little understood or appreciated.

from TENDER BUTTONS, 'Objects'

Nothing Elegant

A charm a single charm is doubtful. If the red is rose and there is a gate surrounding it, if inside is let in and there places change then certainly something is upright. It is earnest.

A Blue Coat

A blue coat is guided guided away, guided and guided away, that is the particular color that is used for that length and not any width not even more than a shadow.

A Piano

If the speed is open, if the color is careless, if the selection of a strong scent is not awkward, if the button holder is held by all the waving color and there is no color, not any color. If there is no dirt in the pin and there can be none scarcely, if there is not then the place is the same as up standing.

This is no dark custom and it even is not acted in any such a way that a restraint is not spread. That is spread, it shuts and it lifts and awkwardly the centre is in standing.

More

An elegant use of foliage and grace and a little piece of white cloth and oil.

Wondering so winningly in several kinds of oceans is the reason that makes red so regular and enthusiastic. The reason that there is more snips are the same shining very colored rid of no round color.

Water Raining

Water astonishing and difficult altogether makes a meadow and a stroke.

from STANZAS IN MEDITATION

'*Stanza XVII*'

How I wish I were able to say what I think
In the meantime I can not doubt

Round about because I have found out
Just how loudly difficulty they do
They will they care they place
Or they do allow or do not bow now.
For which they claim no claim.
It is however that they find
That I mind
What they do when they do or when they do not do
It.
It is not only not kind not to mind
But I do do it.
This is how they say I share I care
I care for which share.
Any share is my share as any share is my share
Of course not not only not.
Of course I do which I of course do.
Once I said of course often
And now I say not of course often
It is not necessary any more.

Elinor Wylie
(1885–1928)
UNITED STATES

She was born in Somerville, New Jersey, into an old and distinguished New England family and raised in Washington, D.C. She married at eighteen and had one son. After several unhappy years she eloped to England with Horace Wylie, whom she later married. They returned to America during the war, and she lived in Boston, Maine, and Washington, D.C., where she met her third husband, the poet William Rose Benét. They were both prominent in the literary world of New York in the twenties. Her first mature collection, *Nets to Catch the Wind*, appeared in 1921, to be followed by three more volumes of poetry and four novels before her death in 1928.

LET NO CHARITABLE HOPE

Now let no charitable hope
Confuse my mind with images
Of eagle and of antelope:
I am in nature none of these.

I was, being human, born alone;
I am, being woman, hard beset;
I live by squeezing from a stone
The little nourishment I get.

In masks outrageous and austere
The years go by in single file;
But none has merited my fear,
And none has quite escaped my smile.

GOLDEN BOUGH

These lovely groves of fountain-trees that shake
A burning spray against autumnal cool
Descend again in molten drops to make
The rutted path a river and a pool.

They rise in silence, fall in quietude,
Lie still as looking-glass to every sense
Save where their lion-colour in the wood
Roars to miraculous heat and turbulence.

H.D. *(Hilda Doolittle)*

(1886–1961)

UNITED STATES

After graduating from Bryn Mawr in 1911 she settled in England, where in 1912 she was one of the founders of the Imagist movement with Ezra Pound and Richard Aldington. She married Aldington before the war but they separated in 1919. She had one daughter,

whom she brought up with the help of her friend Bryher. Besides
many volumes of poetry she published translations from Greek, a
play, a novel, and a prose tribute to Sigmund Freud, with whom she
underwent analysis in Vienna. *The Walls Do Not Fall*, the first book
of her war trilogy, has as its background the bombing of London
during the Second World War.

from THE WALLS DO NOT FALL

34

We have seen how the most amiable,
under physical stress,

become wolves, jackals,
mongrel curs;

we know further that hunger
may make hyenas of the best of us;

let us, therefore (though we do not forget
Love, the Creator,

her chariot and white doves),
entreat Hest,

Aset, Isis, the great enchantress,
in her attribute of Serqet,

the original great-mother,
who drove

harnessed scorpions
before her.

41

Sirius:
what mystery is this?

you are seed,
corn near the sand,
enclosed in black-lead,
ploughed land.

Sirius:
what mystery is this?

you are drowned
in the river;
the spring freshets
push open the water-gates.

Sirius:
what mystery is this?

where heat breaks and cracks
the sand-waste,
you are a mist
of snow: white, little flowers.

Marianne Moore

(1887–1972)

UNITED STATES

She was born in St Louis, Missouri, graduated from Bryn Mawr in
1909, and for five years taught at the government Indian school in
Carlisle, Pennsylvania. In 1918 she moved to New York, where she
worked part time in the New York Public Library and edited *The
Dial* until it folded in 1929. She began to publish during the First
World War; her work was highly praised by T. S. Eliot and Ezra
Pound in Europe, and in the United States she was closely associated
with William Carlos Williams. Her first collection appeared in 1921,
published without her knowledge by H.D. and Bryher. Besides
poetry she wrote criticism and translated *The Fables of La Fontaine.*
She received in one year three major American poetry awards: the
Pulitzer Prize, the Bollingen Prize, and the National Book Award.

THE STEEPLE-JACK

Dürer would have seen a reason for living
   in a town like this, with eight stranded whales
to look at; with the sweet sea air coming into your house
on a fine day, from water etched
   with waves as formal as the scales
on a fish.

One by one, in two's, in three's, the seagulls keep
   flying back and forth over the town clock,
or sailing around the lighthouse without moving their
   wings —
rising steadily with a slight
   quiver of the body – or flock
mewing where

a sea the purple of the peacock's neck is
   paled to greenish azure as Dürer changed
the pine tree of the Tyrol to peacock blue and guinea
grey. You can see a twenty-five-
   pound lobster and fish-nets arranged
to dry. The

whirlwind fife-and-drum of the storm bends the salt
   marsh grass, disturbs stars in the sky and the
star on the steeple; it is a privilege to see so
much confusion.

      A steeple-jack in red, has let
   a rope down as a spider spins a thread;
he might be part of a novel, but on the sidewalk a
sign says C. J. Poole, Steeple-Jack,
   in black and white; and one in red
and white says

Danger. The church portico has four fluted
   columns, each a single piece of stone, made
modester by white-wash. This would be a fit haven for
waifs, children, animals, prisoners,
   and presidents who have repaid
sin-driven

senators by not thinking about them. One
   sees a school-house, a post-office in a
store, fish-houses, hen-houses, a three-masted schooner on
the stocks. The hero, the student
   the steeple-jack, each in his way,
is at home,

It scarcely could be dangerous to be living
   in a town like this, of simple people
who have a steeple-jack placing danger-signs by the church
when he is gilding the solid —
   pointed star, which on a steeple
stands for hope.

AN EGYPTIAN PULLED GLASS BOTTLE
IN THE SHAPE OF A FISH

Here we have thirst
And patience, from the first,
   And art, as in a wave held up for us to see
   In its essential perpendicularity;

Not brittle but
Intense – the spectrum, that
   Spectacular and humble animal the fish,
   Whose scales turn aside the sun's sword with their polish.

THE PANGOLIN

Another armoured animal – scale
   lapping scale with spruce-cone regularity until they
form the uninterrupted central
   tail-row! This near artichoke with head and legs and
               grit-equipped gizzard,
   the night miniature artist engineer is
        Leonardo's – da Vinci's replica —
            impressive animal and toiler of whom we seldom
               hear.

Armour seems extra. But for him,
　　the closing ear-ridge —
　　　　or bare ear lacking even this small
　　　　eminence and similarly safe

contracting nose and eye apertures
　　impenetrably closable, are not; – a true ant-eater,
not cockroach-eater, who endures
　　exhausting solitary trips through unfamiliar ground at
　　　　　　night,
　　returning before sunrise; stepping in the moonlight,
　　　　on the moonlight peculiarly, that the outside
　　　　　　edges of his hands may bear the weight and save
　　　　　　　　the claws
　　　　for digging. Serpentined about
　　　　　　the tree, he draws
　　　　　　　　away from danger unpugnaciously,
　　　　　　　　with no sound but a harmless hiss; keeping

the fragile grace of the Thomas-
　　of-Leighton Buzzard Westminster Abbey wrought-
　　　　　　iron vine, or
rolls himself into a ball that has
　　power to defy all effort to unroll it; strongly intailed,
　　　　　　neat
　　head for core, on neck not breaking off, with curled-in
　　　　　　feet.
　　　　Nevertheless he has sting-proof scales; and nest
　　　　　　of rocks closed with earth from inside, which he
　　　　　　can thus darken
　　　　Sun and moon and day and night and man and beast
　　　　　　each with a splendour
　　　　　　　　which man in all his vileness cannot
　　　　　　　　set aside; each with an excellence!

'Fearful yet to be feared,' the armoured
　　ant-eater met by the driver-ant does not turn back, but
engulfs what he can, the flattened sword-
　　edged leafpoints on the tail and artichoke set leg- and
　　　　　　body-plates

quivering violently when it retaliates
and swarms on him. Compact like the furled
fringed frill
on the hat-brim of Gargallo's hollow iron head
of a
matador, he will drop and will
then walk away
unhurt, although if unintruded on,
he cautiously works down the tree, helped

by his tail. The giant-pangolin-
tail, graceful tool, as prop or hand or broom or axe,
tipped like
the elephant's trunk with special skin,
is not lost on this ant- and stone-swallowing uninjurable
artichoke which simpletons thought a living fable
whom the stones had nourished, whereas ants had
done
so. Pangolins are not aggressive animals; between
dusk and day they have the not unchain-like machine-
like
form and frictionless creep of a thing
made graceful by adversities, con-

versities. To explain grace requires
a curious hand. If that which is at all were not forever,
why would those who graced the spires
with animals and gathered there to rest, on cold luxurious
low stone seats – a monk and monk and monk – between
the thus
ingenious roof-supports, have slaved to confuse
grace with a kindly manner, time in which to pay
a debt,
the cure for sins, a graceful use
of what are yet
approved stone mullions branching out across
the perpendiculars? A sailboat

was the first machine. Pangolins, made
for moving quietly also, are models of exactness,

on four legs; or hind feet plantigrade,
    with certain postures of a man. Beneath sun and moon,
        man slaving
to make his life more sweet, leaves half the flowers
        worth having,
      needing to choose wisely how to use the strength;
        a paper-maker like the wasp; a tractor of food-
          stuffs,
    like the ant; spidering a length
      of web from bluffs
        above a stream; in fighting, mechanicked
        like the pangolin; capsizing in

disheartenment. Bedizened or stark
  naked, man, the self, the being we call human, writing-
master to this world, griffons a dark
    'Like does not like like that is obnoxious'; and writes
        error with four
    r's. Among animals, one has a sense of humour.
      Humour saves a few steps, it saves years. Un-
        ignorant,
      modest and unemotional, and all emotion,
    he has everlasting vigour,
      power to grow,
        though there are few creatures who can make one
        breathe faster and make one erecter.

Not afraid of anything is he,
    and then goes cowering forth, tread paced to meet an
        obstacle
at every step. Consistent with the
    formula – warm blood, no gills, two pairs of hands and
        a few hairs – that
    is a mammal; there he sits in his own habitat,
      serge-clad, strong-shod. The prey of fear, he, always
      curtailed, extinguished, thwarted by the dusk,
        work partly done,
      says to the alternating blaze,

'Again the sun!
  anew each day; and new and new and new,
  that comes into and steadies my soul.'

Edna St Vincent Millay
(1892–1950)
UNITED STATES

Born and raised in Maine, she graduated from Vassar in 1917 and went to New York, where she supported herself writing short stories, translating songs, and working as an actress and playwright for the Provincetown Players. After her marriage in 1923 she settled on a farm in the Berkshires with her husband. Her first collection, *Renascence*, appeared in 1917, and in 1922 she was awarded the Pulitzer Prize. Her work was very popular during her lifetime.

WILD SWANS

I looked in my heart while the wild swans went over; —
  And what did I see I had not seen before?
  Only a question less or a question more;
Nothing to match the flight of wild birds flying.
Tiresome heart, forever living and dying!
  House without air! I leave you and lock your door!
Wild swans, come over the town, come over
The town again, trailing your legs and crying!

Louise Bogan
(1897–1970)
UNITED STATES

She was born in Maine and attended country schools in New England, the Girls' Latin School in Boston, and the Western College for

Women in Oxford, Ohio. Except for a trip abroad to Vienna and a year in Santa Fé, she lived in New York, where she worked as an editor and critic for *The New Yorker*. Her first collection, *Body of This Death*, was published in 1929. During her lifetime she received a number of poetry awards but was known more as a literary critic than as a poet. It is only in recent years and with the appearance of *The Blue Estuaries: Poems 1923–1968* that the stature of her achievement has begun to be recognized.

MEN LOVED WHOLLY BEYOND WISDOM

Men loved wholly beyond wisdom
Have the staff without the banner.
Like a fire in a dry thicket
Rising within women's eyes
Is the love men must return.
Heart, so subtle now, and trembling,
What a marvel to be wise,
To love never in this manner!
To be quiet in the fern
Like a thing gone dead and still,
Listening to the prisoned cricket
Shake its terrible, dissembling
Music in the granite hill.

CASSANDRA

To me, one silly task is like another.
I bare the shambling tricks of lust and pride.
This flesh will never give a child its mother, —
Song, like a wing, tears through my breast, my side,
And madness chooses out my voice again,
Again. I am the chosen no hand saves:
The shrieking heaven lifted over men,
Not the dumb earth, wherein they set their graves.

LATE

The cormorant still screams
Over cave and promontory
Stony wings and bleak glory
Battle in your dreams.
Now sullen and deranged,
Not simply, as a child,
You look upon the earth
And find it harrowed and wild.
Now, only to mock
At the sterile cliff laid bare,
At the cold pure sky unchanged,
You look upon the rock,
You look upon the air.

Muriel Rukeyser
(1913–)
UNITED STATES

She received the Yale Younger Poets Award in 1935 for her book
Theory of Flight and since then has received many other awards for her
work. She has published many books of poetry and prose and
children's books.

READING TIME: 1 MINUTE 26 SECONDS

The fear of poetry is the
fear : mystery and fury of a midnight street
of windows whose low voluptuous voice
issues, and after that there is no peace.

That round waiting moment in the
theatre : curtain rises, dies into the ceiling
and here is played the scene with the mother
bandaging a revealed son's head. The bandage is torn off.
Curtain goes down. And here is the moment of proof.

That climax when the brain acknowledges the world,
all values extended into the blood awake.
Moment of proof. And as they say Brancusi did,
building his bird to extend through soaring air,
as Kafka planned stories that draw to eternity
through time extended. And the climax strikes.

Love touches so, that months after the look of
blue stare of love, the footbeat on the heart
is translated into the pure cry of birds
following air-cries, or poems, the new scene.
Moment of proof. That strikes long after act.

They fear it. They turn away, hand up palm out
fending off moment of proof, the straight look, poem.
The prolonged wound-consciousness after the bullet's shot.
The prolonged love after the look is dead,
the yellow joy after the song of the sun.

Margaret Walker

(1915–)

UNITED STATES

She was born in Birmingham, Alabama, the daughter of a Methodist
minister, and grew up in the South. After graduating from North-
western University in 1935, she worked in Chicago and was a member
of the Federal Writers Project. Later she received a Master of Arts
degree from the University of Iowa. Her first book of poetry, which
was published by the Yale Series of Younger Poets, and her novel,
Jubilee, established her as an important voice among Black American
writers.

LINEAGE

My grandmothers were strong.
They followed plows and bent to toil.
They moved through fields sowing seed.

They touched earth and grain grew.
They were full of sturdiness and singing.
My grandmothers were strong.

My grandmothers are full of memories.
Smelling of soap and onions and wet clay
With veins rolling roughly over quick hands
They have many clean words to say.
My grandmothers were strong.
Why am I not as they?

CHILDHOOD

When I was a child I knew red miners
dressed raggedly and wearing carbide lamps.
I saw them come down red hills to their camps
dyed with red dust from old Ishkooda mines.
Night after night I met them on the roads,
or on the streets in town I caught their glance;
the swing of dinner buckets in their hands,
and grumbling undermining all their words.

I also lived in low cotton country
where moonlight hovered over ripe haystacks,
or stumps of trees, and croppers' rotting shacks
with famine, terror, flood, and plague near by;
where sentiment and hatred still held sway
and only bitter land was washed away.

Gwendolyn Brooks
(1917–)
UNITED STATES

Though born in Kansas she is considered a native Chicagoan, and
Chicago has provided the background for much of her work. A
major figure in the community of Black American writers, she has

published, since 1945, nine volumes of poetry, one novel, and part of an autobiography. Her poetry has received many national awards, including the Pulitzer Prize in 1950 for *Annie Allen*, two Guggenheim fellowships, and a citation of the American Academy of Arts and Letters. In 1968 she was named Poet Laureate of Illinois. She is married and has two children.

A SUNSET OF THE CITY
Kathleen Eileen

Already I am no longer looked at with lechery or love.
My daughters and sons have put me away with marbles and dolls,
Are gone from the house.
My husband and lovers are pleasant or somewhat polite
And night is night.

It is a real chill out,
The genuine thing.
I am not deceived, I do not think it is still summer
Because sun stays and birds continue to sing.

It is summer-gone that I see, it is summer-gone.
The sweet flowers indrying and dying down,
The grasses forgetting their blaze and consenting to brown.

It is a real chill out. The fall crisp comes.
I am aware there is winter to heed.
There is no warm house
That is fitted with my need.

I am cold in this cold house this house
Whose washed echoes are tremulous down lost halls.
I am a woman, and dusty, standing among new affairs.
I am a woman who hurries through her prayers.

Tin intimations of a quiet core to be my
Desert and my dear relief
Come: there shall be such islanding from grief,
And small communion with the master shore.
Twang they. And I incline this ear to tin,

Consult a dual dilemma. Whether to dry
In humming pallor or to leap and die.

Somebody muffed it? Somebody wanted to joke.

Denise Levertov

(1923–)

UNITED STATES

Denise Levertov was born in England. Her mother was Welsh and
her father a Russian Jew who was converted to the Anglican church.
She published her first book, *The Double Image*, in 1946 in England.
In 1948 she came to the United States with her American husband,
Mitch Goodman, a novelist and editor. She has taught at City
College of New York, University of California, Berkeley, and
M.I.T. She has one son, Nikolai, an artist. Her most recent books of
poetry are *Relearning the Alphabet* and *To Stay Alive*.

O TASTE AND SEE

The world is
not with us enough.
O taste and see

the subway Bible poster said,
meaning *The Lord*, meaning
if anything all that lives
to the imagination's tongue,

grief, mercy, language,
tangerine, weather, to
breathe them, bite,
savor, chew, swallow, transform

into our flesh our
deaths, crossing the street, plum, quince,
living in the orchard and being

hungry, and plucking
the fruit.

A DEFEAT

Wanted
to give away pride,
like donating one oil well when you know
you own a whole delta.

Gave away nothing: no takers.
The derricks are idle.

Punt through the shallows,
pushing fat lilies aside,
my shadow,
in your dark boat.

Anne Sexton

(1928–74)

UNITED STATES

Anne Sexton was born in Newton, Massachusetts. She married in
1948 and had two daughters. She studied at Boston University and
Brandeis University and began writing in 1957. A scholar at Rad-
cliffe Institute for Independent Study from 1961 to 1963, she taught
creative writing at Harvard and Radcliffe in 1961 and received several
travel grants and awards, including the Pulitzer Prize for Poetry in
1967 for *Live or Die*. She published six books of poetry, and her play,
Mercy Street, was produced in New York in 1969.

THE TRUTH THE DEAD KNOW

For my mother, born March 1902, died March 1959
and my father, born February 1900, died June 1959

Gone, I say and walk from church,
refusing the stiff procession to the grave,
letting the dead ride alone in the hearse.
It is June. I am tired of being brave.

We drive to the Cape. I cultivate
myself where the sun gutters from the sky,
where the sea swings in like an iron gate
and we touch. In another country people die.

My darling, the wind falls in like stones
from the whitehearted water and when we touch
we enter touch entirely. No one's alone.
Men kill for this, or for as much.

And what of the dead? They lie without shoes
in their stone boats. They are more like stone
than the sea would be if it stopped. They refuse
to be blessed, throat, eye and knucklebone.

THE SUN

I have heard of fish
coming up for the sun
who stayed forever,
shoulder to shoulder,
avenues of fish that never got back,
all their proud spots and solitudes
sucked out of them.

I think of flies
who come from their foul caves
out into the arena.
They are transparent at first.
Then they are blue with copper wings.
They glitter on the foreheads of men.
Neither bird nor acrobat
they will dry out like small black shoes.

I am an identical being,
Diseased by the cold and the smell of the house
I undress under the burning magnifying glass.
My skin flattens out like sea water.
O yellow eye,
let me be sick with your heat,
let me be feverish and frowning.

Now I am utterly given.
I am your daughter, your sweet-meat,
your priest, your mouth and your bird
and I will tell them all stories of you
until I am laid away forever,
a thin gray banner.

Adrienne Rich

(1929–)

UNITED STATES

She was born in Baltimore, Maryland, and graduated from Radcliffe
College in 1951 when her first book of poems, *A Change of World*,
was published by the Yale Younger Poets Series. She lived in Cam-
bridge, Massachusetts, for thirteen years, later travelling to Holland
to learn Dutch and translate Dutch poetry. In 1966 she moved to
New York City and has taught poetry workshops at Columbia
University and City College of New York. A committed feminist,
she won the 1974 National Book Award for poetry (for her latest
book, *Diving into the Wreck*), which she chose to share with the two
other women poets nominated for the award. She is a lesbian and
has three sons.

SONG

You're wondering if I'm lonely:
OK then, yes, I'm lonely
as a plane rides lonely and level
on its radio beam, aiming
across the Rockies
for the blue-strung aisles
of an airfield on the ocean

You want to ask, am I lonely?
Well, of course, lonely
as a woman driving across country

day after day, leaving behind
mile after mile
little towns she might have stopped
and lived and died in, lonely

If I'm lonely
it must be the loneliness
of waking first, of breathing
dawn's first cold breath on the city
of being the one awake
in a house wrapped in sleep

If I'm lonely
it's with the rowboat ice-fast on the shore
in the last red light of the year
that knows what it is, that knows it's neither
ice nor mud nor winter light
but wood, with a gift for burning

AUGUST

Two horses in yellow light
eating windfall apples under a tree

as summer tears apart milkweeds stagger
and grasses grow more ragged

They say there are ions in the sun
neutralizing magnetic fields on earth

Some way to explain
what this week has been, and the one before it!

If I am flesh sunning on rock
if I am brain burning in fluorescent light

if I am dream like a wire with fire
throbbing along it

if I am death to man
I have to know it

His mind is too simple, I cannot go on
sharing his nightmares

My own are becoming clearer, they open
into prehistory

which looks like a village lit with blood
where all the fathers are crying: *My son is mine!*

Sylvia Plath

(1932–63)

UNITED STATES

Sylvia Plath was born in Boston. She attended Smith College and later studied at Cambridge, England, on a Fulbright scholarship. She married the English poet Ted Hughes and they lived in Devonshire with their two children until she committed suicide in 1963. Her first book, *Colossus*, was highly praised, but it was the second, *Ariel*, published after her death, that established her reputation as a major poet and one of the leading figures in what is sometimes called the 'confessional school'. Four books of her poetry have been published and an autobiographical novel, *The Bell Jar*.

NICK AND THE CANDLESTICK

I am a miner. The light burns blue.
Waxy stalactites
Drip and thicken, tears

The earthen womb
Exudes from its dead boredom.
Black bat airs

Wrap me, raggy shawls,
Cold homicides.
They weld to me like plums.

Old cave of calcium
Icicles, old echoer.
Even the newts are white,

Those holy Joes.
And the fish, the fish —
Christ! They are panes of ice,

A vice of knives,
A piranha
Religion, drinking

Its first communion out of my live toes.
The candle
Gulps and recovers its small altitude,

Its yellows hearten.
O love, how did you get here?
O embryo

Remembering, even in sleep,
Your crossed position.
The blood blooms clean

In you, ruby.
The pain
You wake to is not yours.

Love, love,
I have hung our cave with roses.
With soft rugs —

The last of Victoriana.
Let the stars
Plummet to their dark address,

Let the mercuric
Atoms that cripple drip
Into the terrible well,

You are the one
Solid the spaces lean on, envious.
You are the baby in the barn.

ARIEL

Stasis in darkness.
Then the substanceless blue
Pour of tor and distances.

God's lioness,
How one we grow,
Pivot of heels and knees! – The furrow

Splits and passes, sister to
The brown arc
Of the neck I cannot catch,

Nigger-eye
Berries cast dark
Hooks —

Black sweet blood mouthfuls,
Shadows.
Something else

Hauls me through air —
Thighs, hair;
Flakes from my heels.

White
Godiva, I unpeel —
Dead hands, dead stringencies.

And now I
Foam to wheat, a glitter of seas.
The child's cry

Melts in the wall.
And I
Am the arrow,

The dew that flies
Suicidal, at one with the drive
Into the red

Eye, the cauldron of morning.

CHILD

Your clear eye is the one absolutely beautiful thing.
I want to fill it with colour and ducks,
The zoo of the new

Whose names you meditate —
April snowdrop, Indian pipe,
Little

Stalk without wrinkle,
Pool in which images
Should be grand and classical

Not this troublous
Wringing of hands, this dark
Ceiling without a star.

Anne Hébert

(1916–)

FRENCH CANADA

She was born in Sainte-Catherine, Quebec, and brought up in the
city of Quebec, where her father was an official in the provincial
government and a respected literary critic. She received, at her
father's insistence, a rigorous education in the French tradition. Her
first book of poems, *Les Songes en équilibre*, appeared in 1942, and her
first major collection, *Le Tombeau des rois* (*The Tomb of the Kings*),
in 1953. She is also a distinguished novelist and short-story writer
and has written for theatre, film, and television. Her work has
received the highest literary honours of French Canada. For many
years she has lived in Paris.

THE TOMB OF THE KINGS

I have my heart on my fist
Like a blind falcon.

Taciturn bird gripping my fingers
Lamp swollen with wine and blood,
I descend
Toward the tomb of the kings
Astonished
Barely born.

What thread of Ariadne
Leads me through muted labyrinths
The echoing steps are swallowed as they fall.
(In what dream
Was this child tied by her ankle
Like a fascinated slave?)

The maker of the dream
Draws on the thread
And the naked footfalls come
One by one
Like the first drops of rain
In the hold of the well.

Already the odour stirs in swollen storms
Sweats under door-sills
Of secret, round chambers,
There, where curtained beds are raised.

The still desire of reclining kings
Leads me
I see, astonished,
On the black bones gleam
Blue inlaid stones.

A few tragedies, patiently wrought,
Laid on the breast of kings
Are offered me
In the guise of jewels
With no regrets, no tears.

In a single line arrayed:
Smoke of incense, the cake of dried rice
And my flesh, trembling:
Obedient, ritual offering.

Gold mask on my absent face
Violet flowers for eyes,
Love's shadow paints me with small, sure strokes;
And this bird I have breathes
And cries strangely.

A long shudder
Like wind that lifts from tree to tree
Moves the seven great ebony pharaohs
In their solemn, ornate encasings.

It is only the profundity of death that persists,
Simulating the last torment
Seeking its appeasement
And its eternity
In a light clicking of bracelets
Vain hoops, alien games
Circling the sacrificed flesh.

Avid for the fraternal source of evil in me
They lay me down and drink;
Seven times I know the vise of bones
And the dry hand that seeks my heart to break it.

Livid, gorged with the horrible dream
My limbs unlocked
And the dead, thrust out of me, assassinated,
What faint glint of dawn strays here?
Why then does this bird shiver
And turn toward morning
Its blinded eyes?

(*Translator's note:* I am indebted to the interchange between Anne Hébert and F. R. Scott on the subject of Mr Scott's translation of this poem in *Tamarack Review*, August 1962.)

SPRING OVER THE CITY

The day transports fallen snows, muddied, mildewed, ruined

Ice opens its veins and the heart of earth breaks loose
among churning springs

Winter veers and tears like a flaking scale, the world is naked
under bitter lichens

Under masses of mud, old season, old papers, old cigarette
stubs, old deaths flow in the stream

The day easily touches a thousand open cities, each road a
river, each bed a fountain,

The day has lost its special mark, soft moss, soft green wound
washed downstream

The nightmare is wrenched from the madman's breast, along
with his rootless heart

The man at sea, the password in a bottle the poem will be
tossed throughout eternity

The strange sojourn of fire in dark wet places, sacred urns,
rhythms of the world

The unborn does not return into his sleep, the current drags
him by the hair, will change him into algae

On sea stones the burnt offering smokes in strong breaths.
The blood of the dead mixes with salt, strews the sea like
armfuls of sword-grass

Now the season of waters draws back; the city dries like a
beach, licks its wounds that taste of iodine

Spring burns along grey façades and the leprous stones in
the sun have the splendid shine of naked, victorious gods.

(translated from French by Kathleen Weaver)

Margaret Atwood

(1939-)

CANADA

Margaret Atwood was born in Ottawa, Canada, and received a B.A.
from Victoria College, University of Toronto, and an M.A. from

Radcliffe. Her first book of poems, *The Circle Game*, won the
Canadian Governor General's Award in 1967. She has published five
books of poetry and several novels. She now lives in Toronto.

A NIGHT IN THE
ROYAL ONTARIO MUSEUM

Who locked me

into this crazed man-made
stone brain
                where the weathered
totempole jabs a blunt
finger at the byzantine
mosaic dome

Under that ornate
golden cranium I wander
among fragments of gods, tarnished
coins, embalmed gestures
chronologically arranged,
looking for the EXIT sign

but in spite of the diagrams
at every corner, labelled
in red: YOU ARE HERE
the labyrinth holds me,

turning me around
the cafeteria, the washrooms,
a spiral through marble
Greece and Rome, the bronze
horses of China

then past the carved masks, wood and fur
to where 5 plaster Indians
in a glass case
squat near a dusty fire

and further, confronting me
with a skeleton child, preserved
in the desert air, curled
beside a clay pot and a few beads.

I say I am far
enough,   stop here   please
no more

but the perverse museum, corridor
by corridor, an idiot
voice jogged by a pushed
button, repeats its memories

and I am dragged to the mind's
deadend, the roar of the bone-
yard, I am lost
among the mastodons
and beyond: a fossil
shell, then

samples of rocks
and minerals, even the thundering
tusks dwindling to pin-
points in the stellar
fluorescent-lighted
wastes of geology

Mary Elizabeth Coleridge
(1861–1907)
ENGLAND

On the surface her life was an uneventful one of Victorian dullness.
However, her family was on visiting terms with many of the great
artists of the day, including Browning, Tennyson, Millais and
Bridges. She wrote novels and poetry and published both during her
lifetime. Her verse is mainly religious in tone but some of her poems

have a strangeness which recalls the work of her famous kinsman, Samuel Taylor Coleridge.

GIFTS

I tossed my friend a wreath of roses, wet
  With early dew, the garland of the morn.
He lifted it – and on his brow he set
    A crackling crown of thorn.

Against my foe I hurled a murderous dart.
  He caught it in his hand – I heard him laugh —
I saw the thing that should have pierced his heart
    Turn to a golden staff.

THE WITCHES' WOOD

There was a wood, a witches' wood,
  All the trees therein were pale.
They bore no branches green and good,
  But as it were a grey nun's veil.

They talked and chattered in the wind
  From morning dawn to set of sun,
Like men and women that have sinned,
  Whose thousand evil tongues are one.

Their roots were like the hands of men,
  Grown hard and brown with clutching gold.
Their foliage women's tresses when
  The hair is withered, thin, and old.

There never did a sweet bird sing
  For happy love about his nest.
The clustered bats on evil wing
  Each hollow trunk and bough possessed.

And in the midst a pool there lay
  Of water white, as tho' a scare
Had frightened off the eye of day
  And kept the Moon reflected there.

Charlotte Mew

(1870–1928)

ENGLAND

The laconic obituary statement on her death, 'Charlotte Mew, said to be a writer', would have pleased Charlotte Mew herself, as she had a deprecatory opinion of herself and her writing. Yet she had success in the little she did publish, so much so that she was awarded a Civil List Pension on the recommendation of Thomas Hardy, John Masefield and Walter de la Mare. She lived her life in London greatly beset by family cares. Her *Collected Poems* were published in 1953.

FAME

Sometimes in the over-heated house, but not for long,
   Smirking and speaking rather loud,
   I see myself among the crowd,
Where no one fits the singer to his song,
Or sifts the unpainted from the painted faces
Of the people who are always on my stair;
They were not with me when I walked in heavenly places;
      But could I spare
In the blind Earth's great silences and spaces,
   The din, the scuffle, the long stare
   If I went back and it was not there?
Back to the old known things that are the new,
The folded glory of the gorse, the sweet-briar air,
To the larks that cannot praise us, knowing nothing of what we do,
   And the divine, wise trees that do not care.
Yet, to leave Fame, still with such eyes and that bright hair!
God! If I might! And before I go hence
      Take in her stead
      To our tossed bed
One little dream, no matter how small, how wild.
Just now, I think I found it in a field, under a fence —

A frail, dead, new-born lamb, ghostly and pitiful and white,
        A blot upon the night,
The moon's dropped child!

ROOMS

I remember rooms that have had their part
    In the steady slowing down of the heart.
The room in Paris, the room at Geneva,
The little damp room with the seaweed smell,
And that ceaseless maddening sound of the tide —
    Rooms where for good or for ill – things died.
But there is the room where we (two) lie dead,
Though every morning we seem to wake and might just as
        well seem to sleep again
    As we shall somewhere in the other quieter, dustier bed
    Out there in the sun – in the rain.

DOMUS CAEDET ARBOREM

Ever since the great planes were murdered at the end of the gardens
    The city, to me, at night has the look of a Spirit brooding crime;
As if the dark houses watching the trees from dark windows
        Were simply biding their time.

Edith Sitwell
(1887–1964)
ENGLAND

She was brought up in an aristocratic tradition of wealth and culture.
She rebelled at an early age against the social role expected from a
young English girl of high birth. Together with her two brothers,
Osbert and Sacheverell, she delighted in baiting middle-class ethics
and shocking the literary world with experiment. Her innovative
methods in writing poetry based on musical forms are exemplified
in 'Façade' and 'Gold Coast Customs' (1929). In later years she

assumed the role of sibyl, both in her life and in her writing, prophesying destruction and loss, while still evincing a strong personal Christian faith.

TRIO FOR TWO CATS AND A TROMBONE

Long steel grass —
The white soldiers pass —
The light is braying like an ass.
See
The tall Spanish jade
With hair black as nightshade
Worn as a cockade!
Flee
Her eyes' gasconade
And her gown's parade
(As stiff as a brigade).
Tee-hee!
The hard and braying light
Is zebra'd black and white;
It will take away the slight
And free
Tinge of the mouth-organ sound
(Oyster-stall notes) oozing round
Her flounces as they sweep the ground.
The
Trumpet and the drum
And the martial cornet come
To make the people dumb —
But we
Won't wait for sly-foot night
(Moonlight, watered milk-white, bright)
To make clear the declaration
Of our Paphian vocation,
Beside the castanetted sea,
Where stalks Il Capitaneo
Swaggart braggadocio

Sword and mustachio —
He
Is green as a cassada,
And his hair is an armada.
To the jade 'Come kiss me harder'
He called across the battlements as she
Heard our voices thin and shrill
As the steely grasses' thrill,
Or the sound of the onycha
When the phoca has the pica
In the palace of the Queen Chinee!

SWITCHBACK

By the blue wooden sea,
Curling laboriously,
Coral and amber grots
(Cherries and apricots),
Ribbons of noisy heat,
Binding them head and feet,
Horses as fat as plums
Snort as each bumpkin comes:
Giggles like towers of glass
(Pink and blue spirals) pass;
Oh, how the Vacancy
Laughed at them rushing by!
'Turn again, flesh and brain,
Only yourselves again!
How far above the Ape,
Differing in each shape,
You with your regular,
Meaningless circles are!'

DARK SONG

The fire was furry as a bear
And the flames purr . . .
The brown bear rambles in his chain

Captive to cruel men
Through the dark and hairy wood . . .
The maid sighed, 'All my blood
Is animal. They thought I sat
Like a household cat;
But through the dark woods rambled I . . .
Oh, if my blood would die!'
The fire had a bear's fur;
It heard and knew. . . .
The dark earth, furry as a bear,
Grumbled too!

Elizabeth Daryush
(1887–)
ENGLAND

Elizabeth Daryush, daughter of Robert Bridges, continued in her poetry his experimental practice of syllabic metre, and has published several books of verse. She herself chose those poems she wished preserved in an edition of *Selected Poems* in 1972. She distinguishes poems written in syllabic metres by the absence of line-capitals.

THROW AWAY THE FLOWERS

Throw away the flowers,
  they are no use,
  the faery bowers
of the former truce;
    fancy quickly dies
    under fear's dark skies.

Throw away the flowers,
  fetch stubborn rock;
  build for the hours
of terror and shock;
    go to timeless fact
    for what beauty lacked.

> Throw away the flowers,
>   the tender songs;
>   attune your powers
> to eternal wrongs;
>   have but hopeless, hard
>   rebellion for bard.

NOVEMBER SUN

His face is pale and shrunk, his shining hair
    Is prison-shorn;
Trailing his grey cloak, up the short dark stair
    He creeps each morn,

Looks out to his lost throne, to the noon-height
    Once his, then turns
Back to the alien dungeon, where all night
    Unseen he burns.

Laura Riding

(1901–)

ENGLAND

She first became prominent when she was associated with the
'Fugitives' in Tennessee. Moving to Europe, she became known as
an experimental poet and one of the left-wing group of intellectuals
in Paris. She published, in collaboration with Robert Graves, *A
Survey of Modernist Poetry*. After publishing her *Collected Poems* in
1938, Laura Riding renounced poetry and forbade publication of her
poems until *Selected Poems: In Five Sets* appeared in 1970, in England.

THE FORGIVEN PAST

That once which pained to think of,
Like a promise to oneself not kept
Nor keepable, now is grown mild.

The thistle-patch of memory
Claims our confiding touch;
The naked spurs do not draw blood,
Yielding to stoic pressure
With awkward flexibility.

We are glad it happened so
Which long seemed traitorous to hope,
False to the destined Otherwise;
Since by those failures-of-the-time
We learned the skill of failure, time —
Waiting to hold the seal of truth
With a less eager hand,
Sparing the authentic signature
For the most prudent sanctions,
Lest the wax and ink of faith be used
Before to hope's reverses
Succeed the just realities,
And we be spent of welcome
Save for a withered smile.

The transformation of old grief
Into a present grace of mind
Among the early shadows which
The present light inhabit,
As the portentous universe
Now upon earth descends
Timidly, in nostalgic bands
Of elemental trials and errors:
This is how truth is groved,
With wayside nights where sleeping
We wake to tell what once seemed cruel
As dream-dim – in the dream
As plain and sure as then,
In telling no less dark than doubtful.

This is how pleasure relives history,
Like accusation that at last
Settling unrancorous on lies

Gives kinder names to them —
When truth is so familiar
That the false no more than strange is,
Nor wondrous evil strange
But of a beggar's right to tenderness
Whom once in robes of certainty
We stood upon illusion's stage
And then, to expiate our self-deceit,
Sent forth in honesty's ill rags.

Stevie Smith

(1902–71)

ENGLAND

A prolific poet, she recited and sang her poems in public readings and on radio. She also illustrated her books. She expresses a bleak vision in a deceptively whimsical style which is her best-known poetic characteristic.

THE RIVER GOD
(of the River Mimram in Hertfordshire)

I may be smelly and I may be old,
Rough in my pebbles, reedy in my pools,
But where my fish float by I bless their swimming
And I like the people to bathe in me, especially women.
But I can drown the fools
Who bathe too close to the weir, contrary to rules.
And they take a long time drowning
As I throw them up now and then in a spirit of clowning.
Hi yih, yippity-yap, merrily I flow,
O I may be an old foul river but I have plenty of go.
Once there was a lady who was too bold
She bathed in me by the tall black cliff where the water
    runs cold,

So I brought her down here
To be my beautiful dear.
Oh will she stay with me will she stay
This beautiful lady, or will she go away?
She lies in my beautiful deep river bed with many a weed
To hold her, and many a waving reed.
Oh who would guess what a beautiful white face lies there
Waiting for me to smoothe and wash away the fear
She looks at me with. Hi yih, do not let her
Go. There is no one on earth who does not forget her
Now. They say I am a foolish old smelly river
But they do not know of my wide original bed
Where the lady waits, with her golden sleepy head.
If she wishes to go I will not forgive her.

AWAY, MELANCHOLY

Away, melancholy,
Away with it, let it go.

Are not the trees green,
The earth as green?
Does not the wind blow,
Fire leap and the rivers flow?
Away melancholy.

The ant is busy
He carrieth his meat,
All things hurry
To be eaten or eat.
Away, melancholy.

Man, too, hurries,
Eats, couples, buries,
He is an animal also
With a hey ho melancholy,
Away with it, let it go.

Man of all creatures
Is superlative

(Away melancholy)
He of all creatures alone
Raiseth a stone
(Away melancholy)
Into the stone, the god,
Pours what he knows of good
Calling good, God.
Away melancholy, let it go.

Speak not to me of tears,
Tyranny, pox, wars,
Saying, Can God
Stone of man's thought, be good?

Say rather it is enough
That the stuffed
Stone of man's good, growing,
By man's called God.
Away, melancholy, let it go.

Man aspires
To good,
To love
Sighs;

Beaten, corrupted, dying
In his own blood lying
Yet heaves up an eye above
Cries, Love, love.
It is his virtue needs explaining,
Not his failing.

Away, melancholy,
Away with it, let it go.

MOTHER, AMONG THE DUSTBINS

Mother, among the dustbins and the manure
I feel the measure of my humanity, an allure
As of the presence of God. I am sure

In the dustbins, in the manure, in the cat at play,
Is the presence of God, in a sure way
He moves there. Mother, what do you say?

I too have felt the presence of God in the broom
I hold, in the cobwebs in the room,
But most of all in the silence of the tomb.

Ah! but that thought that informs the hope of our kind
Is but an empty thing, what lies behind? —
Naught but the vanity of a protesting mind

That would not die. This is the thought that bounces
Within a conceited head and trounces
Inquiry. Man is most frivolous when he pronounces.

Well Mother, I shall continue to think as I do,
And I think you would be wise to do so too,
Can you question the folly of man in the creation of God?
    Who are you?

Kathleen Raine

(1908–)

ENGLAND

She has won many literary prizes for her poetry and is well known
for her works of literary scholarship. Her *Collected Poems* appeared in
1956 and since then she has published several further books of
poetry. She has also published translations, including some of the
novels of Balzac.

SPELL AGAINST SORROW

Who will take away
Carry away sorrow,
Bear away grief?

Stream wash away
Float away sorrow,
Flow away, bear away
Wear away sorrow,
Carry away grief.

Mists hide away
Shroud my sorrow,
Cover the mountains,
Overcloud remembrance,
Hide away grief.

Earth take away
Make away sorrow,
Bury the lark's bones
Under the turf.
Bury my grief.

Black crow tear away
Rend away sorrow,
Talon and beak
Pluck out the heart
And the nerves of pain,
Tear away grief.

EUDAIMON

Bound and free,
I to you, you to me,
We parted at the gate
Of childhood's house, I bound,
You free to ebb and flow
In that life-giving sea
In whose dark womb
I drowned.

In a dark night
In flight unbounded
You bore me bound
To my prison-house,

Whose window invisible bars
From mine your world.

Your life my death
Weeps in the night
Your freedom bound
To me, though bound still free
To leave my tomb,

On wings invisible
To span the night and all the stars,
Pure liquid and serene,
I you, you me,
There one; on earth alone
I lie, you free.

Elizabeth Jennings

(1926–)

ENGLAND

She was born in Lincolnshire and educated at Oxford, where she now lives. She received the Somerset Maugham Award in 1956. Her collected poems were published in 1967.

ONE FLESH

Lying apart now, each in a separate bed,
He with a book, keeping the light on late,
She like a girl dreaming of childhood,
All men elsewhere – it is as if they wait
Some new event: the book he holds unread,
Her eyes fixed on the shadows overhead.

Tossed up like flotsam from a former passion,
How cool they lie. They hardly ever touch,
Or if they do it is like a confession

Of having little feeling – or too much.
Chastity faces them, a destination
For which their whole lives were a preparation.

Strangely apart, yet strangely together,
Silence between them like a thread to hold
And not wind in. And time itself's a feather
Touching them gently. Do they know they're old,
These two who are my father and my mother
Whose fire, from which I came, has now grown cold?

THE ANIMALS' ARRIVAL

So they came
Grubbing, rooting, barking, sniffing,
Feeling for cold stars, for stone, for some hiding-place,
Loosed at last from heredity, able to eat
From any tree or from ground, merely mildly themselves,
And every movement was quick, was purposeful, was proposed.
The galaxies gazed on, drawing in their distances.
The beasts breathed out warm on the air.

No one had come to make anything of this,
To move it, name it, shape it a symbol;
The huge creatures were their own depth, the hills
Lived lofty there, wanting no climber.
Murmur of birds came, rumble of underground beasts
And the otter swam deftly over the broad river.

There was silence too.
Plants grew in it, it wove itself, it spread, it enveloped
The evening as day-calls died and the universe hushed, hushed.
A last bird flew, a first beast swam
And prey on prey
Released each other
(Nobody hunted at all):
They slept for the waiting day.

THE UNKNOWN CHILD

That child will never lie in me, and you
Will never be its father. Mirrors must
Replace the real image, make it true
So that the gentle love-making we do
Has powerful passions and a parents' trust.

The child will never lie in me and make
Our loving careful. We must kiss and touch
Quietly, watch our own reflexions break
As in a pool that is disturbed. Oh take
My watchful love; there must not be too much.

A child lies within my mind. I see
the eyes, the hands. I see you also there.
I see you waiting with an honest care,
Within my mind, within me bodily,
And birth and death close to us constantly.

Máire Mhac an tSaoi

(1922–)
IRELAND (GAELIC)

Scholar, poet, and translator, she is one of a small group of artists
who continue to write in Irish (Gaelic). She uses the classical forms
of Irish poetry, adapting them to her individual vision.

HARVEST OF THE SEA

We went off to the wake of the 'whelpish youngster'
And in the door of the room his mother was waiting,
'O little son, age was not your portion,
And it is the nature of youth to be wild and scapegrace —'
And Ochone!

Imprinted on my eyes the unpleasant features of her son
And the eerie stammer of his speech a pain in my ears —
We have drowned the ugly fledgeling a second time —
Once in the tide-race and once submerged in flattery —
                              And Ochone!

Two black cinders light up at me from his countenance,
My swift slap left that mark of five fingers
That time I caught him with his fist in the crock —
It is to you I tell it, hole in the wall.
                              And Ochone!

Hark to the mother! '*How he behaved towards me!*
And after he left prison he returned to Confession —'
The sea-wife has spread her blue-green hair over Conaing —
Has abducted the Whitsuntide child from the shadow of
    the gallows!
                              And Ochone!

An abortion reborn from the burial-place of unbaptised infants
Constantly whimpering after lost humanity!
A changeling in non-being going down the wind
Pitiably castrated by this last insult!
                              And Ochone!

Do not rely on me, poor wretch!
In your own quality at least you existed, however sordidly —
But dead and living do not suit together —
Hook your own ground! I am not the bard to lament you.
                              And Ochone!

Force his grip from the gunwale – let them have it their own way —
Set up the waxen image among the candles,
The Phoenix arrayed after his corpse-washing —
And let the spent clout sink to the sea-bed
                              And Ochone! —

I'll tell you a tale of the wake of the whelpish youngster,
Never was seen before such a splendid funeral,
Clerics and laymen and black was made white there,
And the hare-lip was hidden below the coffin-lid!

And Ochone!

(translated from Irish by the Author)

Judith Wright
(1915-)

AUSTRALIA

Born in New South Wales, she is a fifth-generation descendant of
early settlers. She has published many books of verse, critical essays,
and short stories. Her *Collected Poems* appeared in 1972. Judith Wright
is the recipient of numerous awards and honours, including the
Encyclopaedia Britannica Writer's Award.

WOMAN TO CHILD

You who were darkness warmed my flesh
where out of darkness rose the seed.
Then all a world I made in me;
all the world you hear and see
hung upon my dreaming blood.

There moved the multitudinous stars,
and coloured birds and fishes moved.
There swam the sliding continents.
All time lay rolled in me, and sense,
and love that knew not its beloved.

O node and focus of the world;
I hold you deep within that well
you shall escape and not escape —
that mirrors still your sleeping shape;
that nurtures still your crescent cell.

I wither and you break from me;
yet though you dance in living light
I am the earth, I am the root,
I am the stem that fed the fruit,
the link that joins you to the night.

TRAIN JOURNEY

Glassed with cold sleep and dazzled by the moon,
out of the confused hammering dark of the train
I looked and saw under the moon's cold sheet
your delicate dry breasts, country that built my heart;

and the small trees on their uncoloured slope
like poetry moved, articulate and sharp
and purposeful under the great dry flight of air,
under the crosswise currents of wind and star.

Clench down your strength, box-tree and ironbark.
Break with your violent root the virgin rock.
Draw from the flying dark its breath of dew
till the unliving come to life in you.

Be over the blind rock a skin of sense,
under the barren height a slender dance . . .

I woke and saw the dark small trees that burn
suddenly into flowers more lovely than the white moon.

EXTINCT BIRDS

Charles Harpur in his journals long ago
(written in hope and love, and never printed)
recorded the birds of his time's forest —
birds long vanished with the fallen forest —
described in copperplate on unread pages.

The scarlet satin-bird, swung like a lamp in berries,
he watched in love, and then in hope described it.
There was a bird, blue, small, spangled like dew.
All now are vanished with the fallen forest.
And he, unloved, past hope, was buried,

who helped with proud stained hands to fell the forest,
and set those birds in love on unread pages;
yet thought himself immortal, being a poet.
And is he not immortal, where I found him,
in love and hope along his careful pages? —
the poet vanished, in the vanished forest,
among his brightly tinted extinct birds?

ACKNOWLEDGEMENTS TO AUTHORS, TRANSLATORS, AND PUBLISHERS

Every effort has been made to trace copyright holders of material in this book. The publishers apologize if any material has been included without permission and would be glad to be told of anyone who has not been consulted.

Thanks are due to the following (listed by translator) for permission to include works or extracts from works in copyright:

Jaakko A. Ahokas, for translations of Katri Vala's 'On the Meadow' ('*Nittyllä*'), from *Paluu* (*The Return*), and 'Winter Is Here' ('*Talvi on tullut*'), from *Pesapuu Palaa* (*The Tree with the Nest Is Burning*), 1942: by permission of the publishers, Pelastakka Lapset r. y. (Save the Children Association), Helsinki. For the translation of Aila Meriluoto's 'Still' ('*Viela*'), from *Simanitta* (*An Eye's Length*): by permission of Werner Söderström Osakeyhtiö and Aila Meriluoto. For Edith Södergran's 'I saw a tree...' ('*Jag såg ett träd*'), 'Pain' ('*Smärten*'), 'Hope' ('*Förhoppning*'), and 'A Decision' ('*Beslut*'); Larin Paraske's 'Sad Is the Seagull' ('*Alahall'on allin mieli*'), 'My Little Love Lies on the Ground' ('*Jo oli maattu marjueri*'), and 'A Woman Grows Soon Old' ('*Pian nainen vanhenee*'): English translations by permission of Jaakko A. Ahokas. Selections from Eeva-Liisa Manner's 'Cambrian: A Suite about the Sea and the Animals', Part I, Part III and Part V, from *Tämä Matka*, 5th edition, Tammi Oy, Helsinki: by permission of the translator and Tammi Oy.

Christine Ama Ata Aidoo, for 'Prelude', which appears in the special four-language poetry edition of the review *Présence africaine* entitled *New Sum of Poetry from the Negro World*, Paris, 1966, No. 57. By permission of *Présence africaine*.

Gülten Akin, for 'Ellas and the Statues'. Translated by Nermin Menemencioğlu, by permission of Mrs Nermin Streater.

Aline Allard, for translations of poems by Marie de France and Marguerite de Navarre.

Robert Alter, for translations of Rahel Morpurgo's 'Woe is me ...'; Else Lasker-Schüler's 'Reconciliation', from *Gesammelte Werke in Drei Bänden*, Band 1: Gedichte 1902–1943, Kösel, Munich, 1961; and of Leah Goldberg's poems from 'The Symposium' and 'My Mother's House', reprinted by permission of Mrs Zila Goldberg.

Katerina Anghelaki-Rooke, for 'Notes on My Father'.

Samar Attar, for 'The Return of the Dead'.

Margaret Atwood, for 'A Night in the Royal Ontario Museum', from *The Animals in That Country*. Copyright © 1968 by Oxford University Press (Canadian Branch). This poem originally appeared in *The Atlantic Monthly*. Reprinted by permission of Oxford University Press and Little, Brown and Co. in association with Atlantic Monthly Press.

W. H. Auden, translation of Bella Akhmadulina's 'Volcanoes', reprinted from *About the House* by permission of Random House Inc. Copyright © 1963 by W. H. Auden.

Paul Auster, for his translation from Anne-Marie Albiach's *État*. Original copyright © Mercure de France, 1971.

Mary Barnard, for translations from *Sappho: A New Translation*, originally published by the University of California Press. Copyright © 1958 by The Regents of the University of California; reprinted by permission of the University of California Press.

Samuel Beckett, for the translation of Sor Juana Ines de la Cruz's 'This coloured counterfeit . . .', from *Anthology of Mexican Poetry*, edited by Octavio Paz, reprinted by permission of Indiana University Press.

Rina Benmayor, for her translation of 'The Lowly Peasant'.

Rachel Benson, for her translations of Alfonsina Storni's 'Sierra' and 'Men in the City', from *Nine Latin American Poets*. Copyright 1968 by Las Americas Publishing Co. Inc., and reprinted by their permission.

Nguyen Ngoc Bich: *see* Burton Raffel.

R. H. Blyth, for translations of Kaga no Chiyo's 'Spring rain', 'The dew of the rouge-flower', and 'Autumn's bright moon', from *Haiku*. 'Spring rain' and 'The dew of the rouge-flower' copyright © 1967 by Hallmark Cards Inc. Reprinted by permission of Hallmark Cards Inc. and the Hokuseido Press. 'Autumn's bright moon' copyright © 1970 by Hallmark Cards Inc., Kansas City, Missouri and Hokuseido Press. Used by permission.

Louise Bogan, 'Men Loved Wholly Beyond Wisdom', 'Cassandra', and 'Late', from *The Blue Estuaries* by Louise Bogan. Copyright © 1923, 1929, 1930, 1933, 1934, 1935, 1936, 1937, 1938, 1941, 1949, 1951, 1952, 1954, 1968 by Louise Bogan. Reprinted by permission of Farrar, Straus and Giroux Inc.

Geoffrey Bownas and Anthony Thwaite, for translations of Ono no Komachi's 'When my love becomes' and Yosano Akiko's 'You never touch', 'Spring is short', and 'No camellia', from *The Penguin Book of Japanese Verse*, 1964, translated with an Introduction by

Geoffrey Bownas and Anthony Thwaite. Copyright © 1964 Geoffrey Bownas and Anthony Thwaite.

Anne Bradstreet, poems from *Contemplations*: no. 2, 'I wist not what to wish'; no. 8, 'Silent alone, where none or saw, or heard'; no. 18, 'When I behold the heavens as in their prime'; no. 20, 'Shall I then praise the heavens, the trees, the earth'; no. 35, 'O Time the fatal wrack of mortal things', from *Poems of Anne Bradstreet*, ed. Robert Hutchinson. Copyright © 1969 Dover Publications Inc.

Gwendolyn Brooks, 'A Sunset of the City', from *The World of Gwendolyn Brooks*. Copyright © 1960 by Gwendolyn Brooks. By permission of Harper & Row Publishers Inc.

Nadia Christensen, for translations of poems from Swedish, Danish, and Norwegian. To Arena Publishers for Nadia Christensen's translation of Cecil Bødker's 'Fury's Field', from *Fygende Hester*, 1956. For Nadia Christensen's translation of Karin Boye's stanza 10 from the 15-stanza poem 'A Dedication' ('*Tillägnan*'), by permission of the publishers, Albert Bonniers Förlag, Stockholm; this poem appears in *Hearths* (*Här Darna*), 1927. For Maria Wine's 'Woman, you are afraid of the forest' and 'Love Me', by permission of Albert Bonniers Förlag, Stockholm; English translations by permission of Nadia Christensen; 'Woman . . .' was printed without a title and appeared in *Där skönheten tigger sitt bröd*, 1970. For Tove Ditlevsen's 'Morning' ('*Morgenen*') and 'The Old Folk' ('*De gamle*') from *Det Runde Vaerelse*, published by Gyldendal, Copenhagen, © 1973 by Tove Ditlevsen, and English translations by permission of Nadia Christensen and Gyldendal. For Astrid Tollefsen's 'Workday Morning' ('*Arbeidsmorgen*') and 'Toulouse Lautrec' from *På Nattens Terskel*, © 1966 Gyldendal Norsk Forlag A/S 1966, by permission of Gyldendal Norsk Forlag and Margit Skretteberg, and English translations by permission of Nadia Christensen. Also for Nadia Christensen's translation, with Mariann Tiblin, of 'Other Fabrics, Other Mores!' by Anna Maria Lenngren; also by permission of Mariann Tiblin.

Jack Cope and William Plomer, for their translations of poems by Ingrid Jonker, from her *Selected Poems*. By permission of the translators and the Estate of Ingrid Jonker.

Cid Corman and Susumu Kamaike, for their translation of Empress Jito's 'Spring is passing and', to appear in a forthcoming translation of poems, *The Manyōshū*, translated by Cid Corman and Susumu Kamaike. Also from the same work and by the same translators, Princess Nukada's 'Waiting for the Emperor Tenji'. Also by Princess Nukada, 'When, loosened from the winter's bonds' from *The*

386 Acknowledgements

Manyōshū, the Nippon Gakujutsu Shinkōkai translation of One Thousand Poems, with a new Foreword by Donald Keene, Columbia University Press, New York, 1965, by permission of the publishers.

Carol Cosman, for translations of poems by: Nadia Tuéni ('More distant . . .', from *Poèmes pour une Histoire*, Editions Seghers ©, 1972, reprinted by permission of the publishers); Motets (Anon); Anna de Noailles; Louise Labé; Joyce Mansour ('Auditory Hallucinations', 'Embrace the Blade', and 'The Sun in Capricorn', original copyright © 1965, Editions du Soleil, reprinted by permission of the publishers and Joyce Mansour); with Howard Bloch for the Comtesse de Die's 'I sing a song'.

Edwin A. Cranston, for translations of Izumi Shikibu's 'Leaving us behind' (here entitled 'After the Death of her Daughter'), 'Recklessly', 'Never could I think', 'As the rains of spring', 'From that first night', 'From darkness', from *The Izumi Shikibu Diary: A Romance of the Heian Court*, translated with an Introduction by Edwin A. Cranston. Harvard University Press, Cambridge, Mass., copyright © 1969 by the Harvard-Yenching Institute. Reprinted by permission of the publishers.

Bill Crisman, for translations of poems by Catharina Regina von Greiffenberg and Ingeborg Bachmann.

Allen Curnow and Roger Oppenheim, for their translation of the Maori song 'Reply to a Marriage Proposal'.

Elizabeth Daryush, 'Throw Away the Flowers' and 'November Sun', reprinted by permission of Carcanet Press Ltd.

Kamala Das, for 'The House-Builders'.

Frances Densmore, for translations of songs by Owl Woman, from *Papago Music*, Bulletin 90 of the Bureau of American Ethnology, Frances Densmore, 1929. Published by the Smithsonian Institution.

Emily Dickinson poems reprinted by permission of the publishers and the Trustees of Amherst College, from *The Poems of Emily Dickinson*, edited by Thomas H. Johnson. The Belknap Press of Harvard University Press, Cambridge, Mass., copyright © 1951, 1955 by the President and Fellows of Harvard College. Also by permission of Little, Brown and Co. Copyright 1929 by Martha Dickinson Bianchi. Copyright © 1957 by Mary L. Hampson for Number 721 from the same book.

Patrick Diehl, for translations of Kassia's 'Selected Epigrams'.

Eilís Dillon, for the translation of Eibhlín Dhubh Ní Chonaill's 'The Lament for Arthur O'Leary'.

John Dillon, for translations of poems by Corinna, Praxilla, Sulpicia and Hroswitha.

H.D. (Hilda Doolittle), 'We have seen how the most amiable', no. 34, and 'Sirius', no. 41, from 'The Walls Do Not Fall' in *Trilogy*. Copyright 1944 by Oxford University Press, copyright © 1972 by Norman Holmes Pearson. Reprinted by permission of New Directions Publishing Corporation, New York.

Marcia Falk, for translations of selections from *The Song of Songs: Love Poems from the Bible*. Copyright © 1973, 1977 by Marcia Lee Falk; reprinted by permission of Harcourt Brace Jovanovich, Inc. Also for Marcia Falk's translation of Malka Heifetz Tussman's 'Mount Gilboa'. Reprinted by permission of Malka Heifetz Tussman.

Elaine Feinstein and Angela Livingstone for translations of poems from *Marina Tsvetayeva: Selected Poems*, translated by Elaine Feinstein and Angela Livingstone. Copyright © 1971 Oxford University Press. Reprinted by permission of Oxford University Press.

Ruth Feldman and Brian Swann, for translations of Margherita Guidacci's Part I, Part II, and Part III of the five-part poem 'All Saint's Day' ('*Giorni dei Santi*'), from *Poesie*, Rizzoli Editore, Milan, © 1965. By permission of the publishers and translators. Elena Clementelli's 'Etruscan Notebook', Sections 1, 5, and 8, reprinted from *Granite* No. 7, spring 1974. By permission of *Granite*, Elena Clementelli, and the translators Ruth Feldman and Brian Swann.

Angel Flores, for poems by Annette von Droste-Hülshoff, from *An Anthology of German Poetry, from Hölderlin to Rilke*, edited and translated by Angel Flores, Anchor Books. Reprinted by permission of the editor.

Allan Francovich, for translations of Sophia de Mello Breyner Andresen's 'Dionysus', 'The Mirrors', and 'The Dead Men'. Allan Francovich and Kathleen Weaver for their translations of the following poems: Magda Portal's 'shores of anguish' ('*orillas de angustia*') and 'Film Vermouth: Six O'Clock Show' ('*Film Vermouth*'); by permission of Magda Portal. Alda do Espírito Santo's 'The Same Side of the Canoe' ('*No Mesmo lado da Canoa*') and Noémia da Sousa's 'Poem of Distant Childhood' ('*Poema da infancia Distante*') both appear in the special four-language poetry edition of the review *Présence africaine, New Sum of Poetry from the Negro World*, Paris, 1966, No. 57. By permission of *Présence africaine*. Glória de Sant'Ana's 'African Day '('*Dia Africano*'), from *Antologia da casa des estudantes do império*, Preface by Alfredo Margarido, Lisbon, 1962. All by permission of the translators.

Kimon Friar, for translations of poems by Zoé Karélli and Rita Boumí-Pappás. Copyright © 1978 Kimon Friar.

Nick Germanacos, for translations of Jenny Mastoráki's 'The bridal bed...' and 'Three Poems', © Nick Germanacos. Published in *Boundary*, 2, vol. 1, no. 2, *Suny*, Binghamton, N. Y.

Judith Gleason, for her translation of Citèkù Ndaaya's 'Ndaaya's Kàsàlà'. Used by permission of Classiques Africains. Classiques Africains are distributed by Armand Colin, 103 bd St Michel, Paris 5. Translation by permission of Judith Gleason, copyright © 1978 Judith Gleason.

Tâlat S. Halman, for translations of Mihri Hatun's 'At one glance', Leylâ Hanim's 'Let's get going', and Nigâr Hanim's 'Tell Me Again'.

Daniel Halpern and Paula Paley for translations of Mririda n'Ait Attik's 'God Hasn't Made Room' and 'Like Smoke', from *Songs of Mririda*. Copyright © 1974 by Daniel Halpern and Paula Paley. Reprinted by permission of Unicorn Press, PO Box 3307, Greenboro, N. C. 27402.

Michael Hamburger, for his translation of 'Every Day' (*'Alle Tage'*) from Ingeborg Bachmann's *Die Gestundete Zeit*, © R. Piper & Co. Verlag, Munich, 1957, reprinted by permission of the publishers; translation © 1978 Michael Hamburger. For his translation of Else Lasker-Schüler's 'Homesick', © Michael Hamburger, and of Catharina Regina von Greiffenberg's 'On the Ineffable Inspiration of the Holy Spirit', copyright and translation by Michael Hamburger. 'Homesick' also by permission of Kösel Verlag, from *Else Lasker-Schüler, Gesammelte Werke in Drei Bänden*, Band 1: Gedichte 1902–1943, Kösel, Munich, 1961.

Daniel H. H. Ingalls, for translations of Sanskrit poems, from *Sanskrit Poetry from Vidyakara's 'Treasury'*. Reprinted by permission of the publishers, The Belknap Press of Harvard University Press, Cambridge, Mass., copyright © 1965, 1968 by the President and Fellows of Harvard College.

Elizabeth Jennings, 'The Unknown Child', 'One Flesh' and 'The Animals' Arrival', from *Collected Poems 1967*. Published by Macmillan. Reprinted by permission of David Higham Associates Ltd.

Gunda Kaiser and James Tipton, for their translation of Gabriela Mistral's 'Slow Rain'.

Kai Yu Hsu, for translations of Ping Hsin poems from 'Spring Waters', from *Twentieth-Century Chinese Poetry* by Kai Yu Hsu. Copyright © 1963 by Kai Yu Hsu. Reprinted by permission of Doubleday & Co. Inc.

Joan Keefe, for translations of poems by Gormley; Pernette du Guillet, Louise Labé (translated with Richard Terdiman); and Máiri Mac-

Leod; and for an adaptation of a poem by Christine de Pisan. Also for the translation, with Frederick Sweet, of 'On Leaving' by Gertrudis Gomez de Avellaneda.

Donald Keene, for translations of Ono no Komachi's 'This night of no moon' and 'So lonely am I'. Reprinted by permission of Grove Press Inc., copyright © 1955 by Grove Press Inc.

Jascha Kessler, for the translation of Anna Hajnal's 'That's All?' ('*Csak ennyi?*'), from *The American Pen*, vol. V: 1, spring 1973. Reprinted by permission of P. E. N. American Center. Also by permission of Jascha Kessler and Artisjus, The Hungarian Bureau for the Protection of Authors' Rights, Budapest. Also for his translation, with Amin Banani, of Forūgh Farrokhzād's 'Born Again'. This translation first appeared in *Mundus Artium*, summer 1974. It is scheduled to appear in *Selected Poems of Forūgh Farrokhzād*, translated by Jascha Kessler with Amin Banani.

David Kipp, for his translation of Gertrud Kolmar's 'Paris', from *Selected Poems of Gertrud Kolmar*, Magpie Press, London. © 1970 David Kipp.

Carolyn Kizer, for her translation of Rachel Korn's 'Keep Hidden from Me', from *A Treasury of Yiddish Poetry*, edited by Irving Howe and Eliezer Greenberg. Copyright © 1969 by Irving Howe and Eliezer Greenberg. Reprinted by permission of Holt, Rinehart & Winston, Publishers.

Ko Won, for his translation of Hwang Chin-i's 'The blue hill is my desire', and translations of poems by No Ch'ŏn-myŏng and Kim Nam-jo, from *Contemporary Korean Poetry*, edited and translated by Ko Won. Reprinted by permission of the publisher, University of Iowa Press.

C. H. Kwôck and Vincent McHugh, for translations of poems by Li Ching-chao, from *Anthology of Chinese Literature*, vol. 1, edited by Cyril Birch, Grove Press Inc. © 1965 by Cyril Birch.

Lynne Lawner, for translations of poems by Vittoria Colonna, Gaspara Stampa, Veronica Franco, Ada Negri, Antonia Pozzi, and Maria Luisa Spaziani. Copyright © 1978 Lynne Lawner, and reprinted by permission of the translator, Lynne Lawner, from her forthcoming book.

Peter H. Lee, for translations of poems by Unknown Kisaeng, Hwang Chin-i and Hŏ Nansŏrhŏn. Reprinted from *Poems from Korea*, translated and edited by Peter H. Lee, Copyright © 1964, George Allen and Unwin Ltd, London.

Ria Leigh-Loohuizen, for her translation of Henriëtte Roland-Holst's 'Mother of Fishermen'.

Denise Levertov, 'O Taste and See'. Copyright © 1964 by Denise Levertov Goodman. Reprinted by permission of New Directions Publishing Corporation. 'A Defeat', from *Relearning the Alphabet*. Copyright © 1970 by Denise Levertov Goodman. Reprinted by permission of New Directions Publishing Corporation and Laurence Pollinger Ltd.

Philip Levine, for his translations of Gloria Fuertes's 'Autobiography' and 'Climbing'. 'Autobiography' copyright © 1978 by *Antaeus;* 'Climbing' from *Roots and Wings*, copyright © 1976 by Harper and Row.

Julia C. Lin, for translations of Ping Hsin's 'Three Poems', from *Modern Chinese Poetry* by Julia C. Lin. Reprinted by permission of the publishers, University of Washington Press, Seattle, 1972.

Amy Lowell, 'Katydids', from *The Complete Poetical Works of Amy Lowell*. Copyright 1955 by Houghton Mifflin Company, Publishers. Reprinted by permission of the publishers. 'The Taxi', from *A Shard of Silence: Selected Poems of Amy Lowell*, Twayne Publishers, Inc. By permission of Twayne Publishers.

Richard McKane, for the translation of 'I taught myself to live simply and wisely', from *Akhmatova: Selected Poems*. Translation © Richard McKane 1966 (Penguin Modern European Poets, 1969). Reprinted by permission of the publisher.

Suzette Macedo, for translations of Maria Teresa Horta's 'Swimming Pool' and 'Saved'. Copyright © translations by permission of Suzette Macedo. Copyright © originals: 'Saved' from *Candelabro* and 'Swimming Pool' from *Minha Senhora de Mim*.

Kemp Malone, for translations of 'Eadwacer' and 'Wife's Lament', from *Ten Old English Poems*, by Kemp Malone. Reprinted by permission of The Johns Hopkins University Press, ©.

Gerda Mayer, for her translation of Sarah Kirsch's 'Sad Day in Berlin'. Translation © Gerda Mayer, originally published in *Ambit*. Copyright © original, Aufbau Verlag, Berlin. Reprinted by permission of the publishers from *Landaufenthalt*.

Ruth and Matthew Mead, for translations of Nelly Sachs's 'Awakening' and 'Above the rocking heads of the mothers', from *The Seeker and Other Poems*, by Nelly Sachs. Copyright © 1970 by Farrar, Straus & Giroux and reprinted by permission of the publishers.

Paul Merchant and James Damaskos, for translations of 'Genealogy' and 'Song of the Hanged', both poems by Eléni Vakaló, © translators, and reprinted from *Arion's Dolphin*, vol. 1, 4–5, Cambridge, Mass., 1972.

James Merrill, for translations of Cecília Meireles's 'The Dead Horse' and 'Pyrargyrite Metal 9'. Copyright © 1972 by Wesleyan University. Reprinted from *An Anthology of Twentieth-Century Brazilian Poetry*, by Elizabeth Bishop and Emanuel Brasil, by permission of Wesleyan University Press.

Charlotte Mew's poems reprinted by permission of Duckworth & Co. Ltd, London.

Máire Mhac an tSaoi, for the translation of her poem, 'Harvest of the Sea'.

Czeslaw Milosz, for the translation of Wislawa Szymborska's 'I am too near ...', from *Postwar Polish Poetry* by Czeslaw Milosz. Reprinted by permission of Doubleday and Company Inc.

Diane J. Mintz, for her translation of Rahel's 'To My Country'. Copyright Diane J. Mintz.

John Montague, for his translations of Líadan's 'Lament', and of 'The Hag of Beare'.

Marianne Moore: 'The Steeple-Jack', copyright 1951 by Marianne Moore; 'The Pangolin', copyright 1941 by Marianne Moore, renewed 1969 by Marianne Moore; 'An Egyptian Pulled Glass Bottle in the Shape of a Fish', copyright 1935 by Marianne Moore, renewed 1963 by Marianne Moore and T. S. Eliot. Poems reprinted with the permission of Macmillan Publishing Co. Inc., from *Collected Poems* by Marianne Moore. 'The Steeple-Jack' and 'An Egyptian Pulled Glass Bottle in the Shape of a Fish' reprinted by permission of Faber & Faber Ltd, from *The Complete Poems of Marianne Moore*.

Sarojini Naidu, 'The Snake-Charmer', from *The Sceptered Flute* by Sarojini Naidu, Kitabistan Publishers, Allahabad, India.

Usha Nilsson, for translations of Mira Bai's poems from *Mira Bai*. Reprinted by permission of the publishers, Sahitya Akademi, New Delhi.

John Nist and Yolanda Leite, for the translation of Cecília Meireles's 'The Roosters Will Crow', from *Modern Brazilian Poetry: An Anthology*, translated and edited by John Nist with Yolanda Leite. Copyright © 1962 by Indiana University Press, Bloomington. Reprinted by permission of the publisher.

Temira Pachmuss, for translations of poems by Zinaida Hippius.

Vesna Parun, 'Mother of Man'. Published by permission of Jugoslavenskā Áutorska Ágencijā.

Dora M. Pettinella, for translations of poems by Delmira Agustini and Gabriela Mistral.

Sylvia Plath: 'Nick and the Candlestick' and 'Ariel', from *Ariel*, by Sylvia Plath, copyright © 1965 by Ted Hughes, published by Faber & Faber, London; 'Child' from *Winter Trees* by Sylvia Plath, copyright © 1972 by Ted Hughes, published by Faber & Faber, London. Reprinted by permission of Olwyn Hughes and Harper & Row, Publishers, Inc.

Ezra Pound and Noel Stock, translations from *Love Poems of Ancient Egypt*. Copyright © 1962 by Noel Stock, copyright © 1962 by New Directions Publishing Corporation. Reprinted by permission of New Directions Publishing Corporation.

E. Powys Mathers, for translation of Al-Khansâ's 'For Her Brother'. Reprinted by permission of Houghton Mifflin Company. This translation appeared in Mark van Doren's *Anthology of World Poetry*, 1928.

Amrita Pritam, for 'Daily Wages', translated by Amrita Pritam with Charles Brasch.

Burton Raffel and Nguyen Ngoc Bich, for translations of Ho Xuan Huong's 'A Buddhist Priest', copyright © 1969 by The Asia Society Inc.; 'Carved on an Areca Nut, To Be Presented to a Guest', copyright © 1975 by The Asia Society Inc. 'The Jackfruit', translated by Nguyen Ngoc Bich, copyright © 1975 by The Asia Society Inc. Reprinted from *A Thousand Years of Vietnamese Poetry*, edited by Nguyen Ngoc Bich, by permission of Alfred A. Knopf Inc.

Kathleen Raine, poems from *Collected Poems*, copyright © 1956 Kathleen Raine, and from *The Hollow Hill*, copyright © 1965 Kathleen Raine, Hamish Hamilton, London.

A. K. Ramanujan, for translations of poems by Kaccipēṭṭu Naṉṉā-kaiyār, Okkūr Mācātti, and Veṇmaṇippūṭi from *The Interior Landscape: Love Poems from a Classical Tamil Anthology*. Published by Indiana University Press. British copyright held by Peter Owen Ltd. Poems by Mahādēviyakka, from *Speaking of Siva*, edited and translated by A. K. Ramanujan, Penguin Classics, 1973, copyright © A. K. Ramanujan, 1973. Reprinted by permission of the publishers. All of Ramanujan's translations reprinted by permission of The Asia Society.

Dahlia Ravikovich, for 'The Blue West', translated by Chana Bloch. Copyright © by Dahlia Ravikovich. This translation is included in *A Dress of Fire* by Dahlia Ravikovich, published by The Menard Press, London (distributed in the USA and Canada by Serendipity, Berkeley).

Edwin O. Reischauer, for translations of the Nun Abutsu's 'The shore wind is cold', 'Your subdued voice is low, cuckoo', 'Between the pines', from *Translations from Early Japanese Literature*, by Edwin O. Reischauer and Joseph K. Yamagiwa, 2nd edition, abridged, Harvard-Yenching Institute Studies, XXIX, Harvard University Press,

Cambridge, Mass. Copyright 1951 by the Harvard-Yenching Institute. Reprinted by permission of the publishers.

Kenneth Rexroth and Ling Chung, for translations of Chinese poems from *The Orchid Boat*. English translation copyright © 1972 by Kenneth Rexroth and Ling Chung. Used by permission of McGraw-Hill Book Company.

Adrienne Rich, for poems from *Diving into the Wreck: Poems, 1971–1972*, by Adrienne Rich. By permission of W. W. Norton and Company, Inc. Copyright © 1973 by W. W. Norton and Company, Inc.

Laura Riding, 'The Forgiven Past', from *Selected Poems: In Five Sets*, by Laura Riding. Reprinted by permission of W. W. Norton & Company, Inc. Copyright © 1970 by Laura Riding Jackson.

Michael Roloff, for his translation of Nelly Sachs's 'Oblivion! Skin', from *O the Chimneys* by Nelly Sachs, translated by Michael Roloff. Copyright © 1967 by Farrar, Straus & Giroux, Inc. Reprinted by permission of Farrar, Straus & Giroux, Inc.

Frans van Rosevelt, translations of poems by Hadewijch. Thanks also to Rackham Literary Studies.

Muriel Rukeyser, 'Reading Time: 1 Minute 26 Seconds', from *Waterlily Fire*, published by Macmillan Publishing Co., 1968. Copyright © 1939, 1968 by Muriel Rukeyser. Reprinted by permission of International Creative Management.

Hardie St Martin, for the translation of Angela Figuera Aymerich's 'Women at the Market'. Reprinted by permission of the author and translator.

Edna St Vincent Millay, 'Wild Swans', from *Collected Poems*, Harper & Row. Copyright © 1921, 1958 by Edna St Vincent Millay. By permission of Norma Millay Ellis.

Hiroaki Sato, for his translations of Ishigaki Rin's 'Clams' and Princess Shikishi's 'Autumn', 'Winter', and 'Spring'. Translations copyright © Hiroaki Sato, by permission. Princess Shikishi's poems were first published by Granite Publications, 1973. 'Clams' by Ishigaki Rin first appeared in *Chicago Review*, vol. 25, no. 2, 1973.

Dr George D. Schade, for his translation of Rosario Castellanos's 'Silence Concerning an Ancient Stone', from *The Muse in Mexico*, ed. Thomas Mabry Cranfill, Copyright © 1969, University of Texas Press, Austin. Reprinted by permission of the publisher.

Linda Scheer, for her translation of Juana de Ibarbourou's 'The Strong Bond'.

Laura Schiff, for translations of Margit Kaffka's 'Father' ('*Apam*') and Ágnes Nemes Nagy's 'Storm' ('*Vihar*'). Reprinted by permission of Artisjus, The Hungarian Bureau for the Protection of Authors' Rights, Budapest. Laura Schiff and Dana Beldiman, for the translation of Maria Banus's 'The New Notebook'. By permission of the author, translators, and the Writer's Union of the Socialist Republic of Romania.

Paul Schmidt, for his translation of Karolina Pavlova's 'To Madame A. V. Pletneff'.

Grace Schulman, for her translation of Julia de Burgos's 'To Julia de Burgos', from *The Nation*, 9 October 1972. Reprinted by permission of *The Nation*.

Anne Sexton, 'The Truth the Dead Know', from *All My Pretty Ones*, by Anne Sexton, copyright © 1961, 1962 by Anne Sexton. 'The Sun', from *Live or Die*, by Anne Sexton, copyright © 1966 by Anne Sexton. Reprinted by permission of Houghton Mifflin Company.

Saduddin Shpoon, for translations of the landeys 'Saints look at dirt', 'My God is just, yes he is', 'My love is tasting the fragrance', 'You spent all summer in cool Kabul', 'Please let my hair grow, mother', from *The Malahat Review*, No. 21, January 1972. Reprinted by permission of The Asian Literature Program, New York.

Dame Edith Sitwell, poems from *Collected Poems*, published by Macmillan.

Stevie Smith, poems from *Selected Poems*. Copyright © 1962, 1964 by Stevie Smith. Reprinted by permission of New Directions Publishing Corporation, New York.

Gertrude Stein, poems from 'Tender Buttons', from *Selected Writings of Gertrude Stein*. Copyright 1946 by Random House, Inc. Reprinted by permission of the publisher. *Stanzas in Meditation* (Stanza XVII), reprinted by permission of Yale University Press.

Stephan Stepanchev, for his translation of Bella Akhmadulina's 'The Bride', from *Translations by American Poets*, edited by Jean Garrigue, Ohio University Press, 1971. Stephan Stepanchev holds residual copyright.

Susan C. Strong, for her translations of Ricarda Huch's 'Music stirs me' ('*Musik bewegt mich*'), 'Death Seed' ('*Tod Sämann*'), and 'Arrival in Hell'. By permission of Insel Verlag, Frankfurt am Main.

Brian Swann, for his translation of Juana de Ibarbourou's 'The Assignation'. Also for translations with Michael Impey of Nina Cassian's 'Ordeal' ('*Ispita*') and 'Vegetable Destiny' ('*Destinul Vegetal*'). By permission of Nina Cassian, the translators and the Romanian Writers' League, Bucharest. Translations from *An Anthology of Contemporary Romanian Poetry*, edited by Roy Mac-

Gregor-Hastie, published by Peter Owen Ltd, London.

Arthur Symons, for his translation of Saint Theresa of Avila's 'If, Lord, Thy love for me is strong', from *Poems*, vol. I, by Arthur Symons. Reprinted by permission of William Heinemann Ltd, London.

Judith Thurman, for her translations of Louise Labé's Sonnets X and XX, and of poems by Sor Juana Ines de la Cruz.

J. E. Tobin: *see* Angel Flores.

Robert Tracy, for translations of Anna Akhmatova's 'The Grey-eyed King' and 'Hands clenched . . .'.

Fadwa Tuquan, 'After Twenty Years', reprinted from *The Arab World*.

Jean Valentine, for her translation of Kadia Molodowsky's 'Song of the Sabbath', from *A Treasury of Yiddish Poetry*, edited by Irving Howe and Eliezer Greenberg. Copyright © 1969 by Irving Howe and Eliezer Greenberg. Reprinted by permission of Holt, Rinehart and Winston, Publishers.

Arthur Waley, for translations of Lady Ōtomo of Sakanoé's 'Unknown love' and 'My heart, thinking', and Ono no Komachi's 'A thing which fades', from *Japanese Poetry, The 'Uta'* by Arthur Waley, 1919. Reprinted by permission of The Clarendon Press, Oxford.

Kathleen Weaver, for her translation of Anne Hébert's 'The Tomb of the Kings' ('*Les Tombeaux des Rois*') and 'Spring over the City' ('*Printemps sur la Ville*'), from *Poems* by Anne Hébert. By permission of the publisher, Musson Book Company, Don Mills, Ontario. For Annette M'Baye's 'Silhouette', which appears in the special four-language poetry edition of the review *Présence africaine* entitled *New Sum of Poetry from the Negro World*, Paris, 1966, No. 57. For Oumar Ba's 'Drought' ('*Sécheresse*') from the same issue of *Présence africaine*. Both by permission of *Présence africaine*. For Anoma Kanié's 'All that you have given me, Africa' ('*Tout ce que tu m'a donné, Afrique*') from *Antologie Négro-Africaine*, Lilyan Kesteloot, Marabout University, 1967. © Gérard & Co., Verviers, Belgium. By permission of the translator.

Brenda S. Webster, for translations of poems by Veronica Gambara, Vittoria Aganoor Pompili, and Vittoria Colonna.

Daniel Weissbort, for translations of Natalya Gorbanyevskaya's poems, from *Natalya Gorbanyevskaya: Poems, The Trial, Prison*. © Daniel Weissbort 1972. Carcanet/Dufour.

Richard Wilbur, for his translation of Anna Akhmatova's 'Lot's Wife', from *Walking to Sleep: New Poems and Translations*. © 1969 by Richard Wilbur. Reprinted by permission of Harcourt Brace Jovanovich Inc.

Gwyn Williams, for his translation of 'Eagle of Pengwern'. Copyright © 1973 by Gwyn Williams and U. C. Press.

U Win Pe, for translations of anonymous Burmese poems. By permission of The Asian Literature Program, New York.

Yvor Winters, for translations of Madame Deshoulières's 'Reflections', and of Saint Theresa of Avila's 'Poem'. Reprinted from *Collected Poems* © 1960 by permission of The Swallow Press, Chicago.

Manfred Wolf, for his translation of Henriëtte Roland-Holst's 'Throughout the day we are able to ban the voices . . .'.

Benjamin M. Woodbridge, Jr, for translations of poems by Rosalía de Castro.

Harold P. Wright, for his translation of Lady Kasa's 'To love someone'. By permission of The Asian Literature Program, New York.

Judith Wright, 'Extinct Birds', 'Woman to Child', and 'Train Journey'. © 1962, 1949, 1953 by Judith Wright, from *Collected Poems* published by Angus & Robertson Publishers, © 1971.

Elinor Wylie, 'Let No Charitable Hope' and 'Golden Bough', from *Collected Poems of Elinor Wylie*. Copyright 1932 by Alfred A. Knopf, Inc., and renewed 1960 by Edwina C. Rubenstein. Reprinted by permission of the publisher.

INDEX OF AUTHORS